OXFORD STUDIES IN LANGUAGE CONTACT

Series editors: Suzanne Romaine, Merton College, Oxford and
Peter Mühlhäusler, Bond University

Linguistic Consequences of Language Contact and Restriction

OXFORD STUDIES IN LANGUAGE CONTACT

MOST of the world's speech communities are multilingual, making contact between languages an important force in the everyday lives of most people. Studies of language contact should therefore form an integral part of work in theoretical, social, and historical linguistics. As yet, however, there are insufficient studies to permit typological generalizations.

Oxford Studies in Language Contact aims to fill this gap by making available a collection of research monographs presenting case studies of language contact around the world. The series addresses language contact and its consequences in a broad interdisciplinary context, which includes not only linguistics, but also social, historical, cultural, and psychological perspectives. Topics falling within the scope of the series include: bilingualism, multilingualism, language mixing, code-switching, diglossia, pidgins and creoles, problems of cross-cultural communication, and language shift and death.

Linguistic Consequences of Language Contact and Restriction

The Case of French in Ontario, Canada

RAYMOND MOUGEON
ÉDOUARD BENIAK

CLARENDON PRESS · OXFORD
1991

Oxford University Press, Walton Street, Oxford OX2 6DP
Oxford New York Toronto
Delhi Bombay Calcutta Madras Karachi
Petaling Jaya Singapore Hong Kong Tokyo
Nairobi Dar es Salaam Cape Town
Melbourne Auckland
and associated companies in
Berlin Ibadan

Oxford is a trade mark of Oxford University Press

Published in the United States
by Oxford University Press, New York

© Raymond Mougeon and Édouard Beniak 1991

British Library Cataloguing in Publication Data
Mougeon, Raymond
Linguistic consequences of language contact and
restriction: the case of French in Ontario, Canada.—
(Oxford Studies in Language Contact).
1. Canada. French language. Use. Sociolinguistic aspects
I. Title. II. Beniak, Édouard III. Series
447.971
ISBN 0-19-824827-X

Library of Congress Cataloging in Publication Data
Mougeon, Raymond.
Linguistic consequences of language contact and restriction: the
case of French in Ontario, Canada / Raymond Mougeon, Édouard Beniak.
(Oxford Studies in Language Contact)
Includes bibliographical references (p. 228) and index.
1. French language—Social aspects—Ontario. 2. French language—
Ontario—Foreign elements—English. 3. English language—Ontario—
Influence on French. 4. French language—Dialects—Ontario.
5. Languages in contact—Ontario. I. Beniak, Édouard. II. Title.
III. Series.
PC3645.O6M68   1990   306.4'4'089114—dc20   90-7330
ISBN 0-19-824827-X

Set by Joshua Associates Ltd., Oxford
Printed in Great Britain by
Biddles Ltd.
Guildford and King's Lynn

*In memory of our dear friend and esteemed colleague
Michael Canale, who died tragically on 27 June 1989*

Foreword

WE are not accustomed to thinking of world languages like French as 'minority languages'. Raymond Mougeon's and Édouard Beniak's book gives a unique view of a case of language contact involving two of the world's major languages, English and French, and provides a detailed look at the changes which are affecting French in a context where it is a minority language. This study draws on more than a decade of sociolinguistic research conducted in Ontario. Among the concomitants of contact between French and English dealt with here are lexical borrowing, morphological simplification, and stylistic reduction. Mougeon and Beniak break important ground in their attempt to distinguish internally vs. externally motivated change. They also have evidence to support the developmental origin of some of the processes of simplification, which allows them to make a strong case for imperfect mastery and restricted use as prime determinants of change.

Suzanne Romaine

Merton College, University of Oxford

Acknowledgements

THE research reported on in Chapters 5–11 was funded by grants from the Social Sciences and Humanities Research Council of Canada. We wish to thank this agency for its continued support. We would also like to take this opportunity to express our indebtedness to Suzanne Romaine, whose expert commentary allowed us to improve both the form and the content of this book. Finally, our thanks go to David Sankoff and Pascale Rousseau for kindly making the VARBRUL 2S and 3 programmes available to us and for providing helpful advice concerning their use.

Contents

1

Introduction

THIS book is concerned with an increasingly popular aspect of the broad topic of linguistic change, namely change as it takes place in languages in contact, and more specifically in what are commonly referred to as 'minority languages'. Following Dressler and Wodak-Leodolter (1977) and Giacalone Ramat (1979), we understand the term 'minority language' not only in a prestige or social value sense, i.e. a language whose speakers are socio-economically disadvantaged with respect to those of a 'superordinate' language, but also in a demographic sense, i.e. a language whose speakers are in numerical inferiority in comparison with those of a 'majority' language. It could be argued that 'true' minority languages are those which combine both aspects—and many indeed do—yet it is clear that only subordinate social value is a necessary and sufficient condition for minority-language speakers to shift to the superordinate language, since language shift can take place even in situations where the shifting population forms a majority, e.g. the Irish case, the Welsh case, the Québécois case before the advent of the Quiet Revolution in the 1960s, etc. (for further discussion of the definition of 'minority language', see the papers in Haugen, McClure, and Thomson 1981).

The main part of the book (Chapters 5–11) describes a series of studies which were conducted over the course of a recently completed sociolinguistic research project which investigated linguistic variation in a regional variety of Canadian French spoken in the province of Ontario, located immediately west of Quebec. Ontarian French is a 'true' minority language in the sense defined above. Chapter 2 will provide socio-historical background information on the Franco-Ontarian minority, e.g. its origins, demography, institutions, etc.

Bilingual speech communities provide linguists with a favourable and favourite laboratory to study the effects of language contact on linguistic structure, that is, the influence of one linguistic system on another, or what Weinreich referred to as 'interference'. Since in this book we shall follow his example and use interference as a general label for all types of interlingual influence, and 'language contact' as implying bilingualism, it is appropriate to recall at the outset Weinreich's own definition of these terms (1968: 1):

two or more languages will be said to be *in contact* if they are used alternately by the same persons. The language-using individuals are the locus of the contact.

The practice of alternately using two languages will be called *bilingualism*, and the persons involved, *bilingual*. Those instances of deviation from the norms of either language which occur in the speech of bilinguals as a result of their familiarity with more than one language, i.e. as a result of language contact, will be referred to as *inter-ference* phenomena. It is these phenomena of speech, and their impact on the norms of either language exposed to contact, that invite the interest of the linguist.

Surprisingly enough, it would appear that Weinreich did not envisage any other contact-induced linguistic phenomenon besides interference that could, as he says, 'invite the interest of the linguist'. Martinet, in his preface to Weinreich's book (p. viii), explains that the study of linguistic convergence (i.e. the consequence of interference between languages in contact) had been neglected until then: 'Contact breeds imitation and imitation breeds linguistic convergence. Linguistic divergence results from secession, estrangement, loosening of contact. Linguistic research has so far favored the study of divergence at the expense of convergence. It is time the right balance should be restored.'

Without denying the interest or relevance of the so-called contrastive approach to the problem of bilingualism—indeed this book will explore various types of interference (e.g. 'overt' vs. 'covert' interference, lexical borrowing, etc.)—it has none the less to be admitted, as by Giacalone Ramat (1979: 1), that the 'interference model in the study of bilingual communities has proven to be insufficient'. This is evident in minority-language situations where speakers display a significant amount of restriction in the use of the minority language. The linguistic consequences of such restriction may owe nothing to the influence of the majority language but rather constitute autono-mous developments triggered by system-internal tendencies to restructure—the result most often being structural simplification (see Silva-Corvalán 1986*a* for a similar view).

It is important to point out here that restricted users of a minority language may show a pattern either of compartmentalized language use (as when the minority language continues to be used categorically in those societal domains where it is possible to use it, e.g. at home) or of uncompartmentalized language use (as when the majority language is allowed to penetrate into these domains). Both kinds of speakers display restriction in minority-language use in compar-ison with monolingual speakers of the same language elsewhere, but only the ones showing uncompartmentalized language use can be said to exhibit a shift to the majority language. Although it is an interesting theoretical question whether equal amounts of language restriction are going to be associated with the same types and/or degree of linguistic change depending on whether the speaker or the community as a whole show compartmentalized vs. uncompart-mentalized language use, it will only interest us peripherally in this book. The focus will be on the linguistic consequences of minority-language restriction *per se* (with or without shift to the majority language). This book will *not* be concerned with linguistic interference in the opposite direction, i.e. from the receding language (French) into the displacing one (English), nor with possible structural simplifications of the majority language at the hands of the shifting speakers of the minority language; but this is not to suggest that these are not worthwhile pursuits. (For an in-depth discussion of the different types of interference associated with maintenance vs. shift situations, see Thomason and Kaufman 1988.)

Contact situations involving restriction in minority-language use with or without shift typically include speakers that can be placed on a double continuum according to how restricted their use of the minority language is (as measured, for example, by how frequently they report using it in comparison with the majority language) and how proficient they are in each language (as measured, for instance, by self-reports of bilingual ability). This is precisely the kind of situation which obtains among the French-speaking population of Ontario, a fact which is reflected in our sample of adolescent speakers. This provides quasi-experimental conditions for examining the linguistic effects of bilingualism and language-use restriction, the spoken French of the speakers who (1) show the least amount of restriction in minority-language use, and (2) are French-dominant bilinguals serving as the norm of comparison.

In language-death situations the proficiency continuum apparently exists only with respect to the speakers' abilities in the dying language, since all are said to be perfectly fluent in the other language. For example, Dorian (1981: 115) writes that 'there are no Gaelic speakers in East Sutherland today whose English is anything less than fluent'. We have here an interesting difference with situations of 'mere' language contraction (as opposed to impending death), where the minority-language proficiency continuum is of greater breadth because of the continued existence, at its upper reaches, of speakers who remain near-monolinguals. Another way of putting things would be to say that the 'conservative norm' (Dorian 1981: 116) is still alive in a situation of language contraction as opposed to death.

A total of four Franco-Ontarian communities were surveyed; in one francophones formed a strong majority (85 per cent French-speaking) but in the three others they were in the minority. This majority-within-the-minority aspect proved heuristically valuable by providing another natural yardstick for gauging the linguistic impact of language contact, this time at the community as opposed to the individual level. In more ways than one, then, we were concerned not to take some unrealistic external norm (e.g. Standard French) as the reference variety for establishing the linguistic effects of contact and contraction—although reference to the Standard does remain pertinent when it comes to understanding the social stratification of speech. While it is true that the focus on the language of the adolescent generation precludes the possibility of studying change in apparent time (i.e. in progress),[1] we feel that this is more

---

[1] Even change in apparent time may not be true change if it repeats itself each generation (for a perceptive discussion of what synchronic description can tell us about change in progress or not, see Labov 1981).

than compensated for by the fact that the younger generation, more so than the older one, displays wide variation in levels of bilingualism and restriction. In other words, the restriction and proficiency continua alluded to above are stretched to the limit in the case of the younger generation. Chapter 4 will go over these and other methodological aspects of our research.

This book can thus be seen as constituting a response to Andersen's (1982) call for systematic research on the linguistic attributes of language attrition, which, in the minority-language situation under study, is to be taken to involve the dual phenomenon of bilingualism and language-use restriction. We shall now briefly review the different linguistic consequences of bilingualism and restriction as documented by our research.

1.1. Simplification

It appears to be well established now, given the mounting evidence available in the literature on dying/receding languages, that insufficient exposure to and use of a language results in its imperfect learning, as reflected not just in interference of various types but also in internal restructuring of various kinds, most often if not always interpretable as cases of simplification[2] (see, e.g., the studies in Dorian 1989 and Trudgill 1983: Chapters 5 and 6). As such, these findings provide empirical support for Giacalone Ramat's earlier contention that there is more than interference to minority-language change and for G. Sankoff's (1980) more general claim that linguistic structure can be dramatically affected by the social use of language.

In Chapter 5 we examine a case of morpho-syntactic simplification in the area of subject–verb agreement. The adolescents serving as a base-line comparison, i.e. those who show the lowest levels of French-language-use restriction, have no trouble applying the rule of subject–verb concord in the third person plural present and future indicative (the last two tenses of the language to preserve distinctive third person plural forms and only with a limited set of verbs). On the other hand, the more restricted users of French, i.e. those located on the middle or lower portions of the restriction continuum, variably substitute morphologically singular forms for the plural ones, subject to a frequency constraint (as concerns the present), the most frequent verbs being little affected by the levelling process. In contrast, the same speakers level a lot less in the future tense, in spite of the low frequency of this tense. The future third person plural forms, however, are morphologically predictable (i.e.

---

[2] We are aware that simplification is a notion which needs to be handled with care. However, along with Trudgill (1983: Chapters 5 and 6), we believe it aptly applies to internal restructurings which bring about a greater degree of regularity or transparency in the language. A related issue which we wish simply to raise at this stage is whether interference cannot also at times be shown to result in an increase in transparency if not regularity and hence constitute a form of simplification (see section 1.5.1).

stem + inflection -*ont* /ɔ̃/), while the present ones are not (i.e. cases of suppletion) or much less so. These findings bear out exactly Andersen's (1982: 97) prediction that restricted users of a language will at best only variably preserve certain morphological distinctions that are categorically maintained by full-fledged users of that language.

Differences in frequency and regularity (to mention just those that are germane here) entail that linguistic structures are not equal from the point of view of learnability, yet, given sufficient input, any normal human child will in the end learn its mother tongue (for a cross-linguistic perspective on language acquisition, see the papers in Slobin 1985). It is when exposure is insufficient that the learnability differences between linguistic structures may result in imperfect learning. This cause-and-effect phenomenon should be of interest to linguists inasmuch as it is a valuable source of empirical data about linguistic complexity and the ways in which speakers go about resolving it. Dorian (1981: 156) concluded her book with the following comment regarding the significance of 'semi-speakers' (i.e. non-fluent speakers of a minority language): 'they merit special study for the light they may shed on our understanding of the human language facility in general, to the benefit of linguistic description and theory'.

The diffusion of the levelling process along the double dimension of frequency and predictability suggests 'the idea of change sneaking in the back door where it's least noticed' (to use Romaine's metaphor of Naro's 1981 model of syntactic diffusion, p.c.). Interestingly enough, Naro developed his theory on the basis of an examination of a similar phenomenon, namely variable loss of the rule of subject–verb agreement in the third person plural, as it is presently unfolding in popular Brazilian Portuguese. Though he interprets loss of concord as diffusing along a different dimension (i.e. phonetic saliency), we provide arguments in favour of the superiority of frequency and morphological predictability in accounting for the Franco-Ontarian data and propose an integration of these two dimensions in Naro's model of diffusion (see also Kiparsky 1980 for a similar point of view on the multi-dimensionality of saliency).

1.2. Sociolectal reduction

Minority-language restriction, however, is not just a matter of restriction in frequency of use, it is often also a matter of restriction in the social contexts of language use. In a minority-language situation a speaker may not have access to the social contexts which are conducive to use of a particular style of language or sociolect. In such cases it becomes even clearer that the social use of language shapes linguistic structure.

In a very elegant study of style reduction in a language-shift situation, Gal

(1984) showed that young Hungarian–German bilinguals in Oberwart, Austria, because they had been deprived of social contexts for use of Standard Hungarian, had lost or not acquired the ability to shift from local to Standard Hungarian phonological variants when the situation (e.g. a formal interview with an outsider) called for a shift in phonological style. Franco-Ontarian adolescents who experience the 'classical' type of domain restriction and concomitant style reduction investigated by Gal (i.e. restriction of the minority language to informal domains with loss/non-acquisition of skills in the formal style) are relatively scarce, since Franco-Ontarians find themselves in the enviable position (in comparison to other minority-language groups) of being supported by a full-fledged system of French-language schools (see Chapter 3 for an examination of the history and current status of French-language education in Ontario). Since schooling in the minority language is a common denominator of all of our subjects, they all have had access to Standard French. In our own research, the adolescents with the highest levels of French-language-use restriction are quite unlike the young speakers examined by Gal, in that they show the reverse pattern of domain restriction. They have received most of their exposure to French in the *formal* domain of the school. Deprived of significant contact with vernacular French, it is not surprising that they lack familiarity with various non-standard sociolectal features—even when they normally should know them, given the social class to which they belong. To put it differently, the speech of these adolescents shows a decrease or absence of class variation. We find ourselves in complete agreement with Williams (1987: 85) when he writes, speaking of Welsh: 'it is often difficult to determine a bilingual's class location when he/she speaks the minority language, whereas it can be relatively easy when the same person speaks the dominant language'. Reduction of the social stratification of speech is documented in Chapters 6, 7, 9, and 11.

Although sociolectal reduction as we have uncovered it is still perhaps unfamiliar to most investigators because of its rarity, it may become more commonplace as other linguistic minorities come to experiment with education in their own language, a distinct possibility according to Bourhis (1984) now that, for instance, many nation states have signed the European Convention of the Rights of Man, which guarantees among other things the right of linguistic minorities to education in their own language.

1.3. Aborted sociolectal reduction

As has been commonly observed, many features which are found in non-standard speech varieties can be interpreted as the output of natural processes of internal simplification having operated in diachrony. Several authors (e.g. Chaudenson 1979; Kenemer 1982) have been struck by the fact that these same features often show up in the developmental grammars of children whose parents are speakers of the standard variety, as well as in the interlanguage of learners exposed only to the standard variety. In other words, the first- and second-language learners' restructurings of the standard language seem to replicate historical processes of change which the popular (or sometimes simply colloquial) language underwent naturally. These commonalities attest to the universal nature (both through time and across settings) of the solutions to non-optimal structural configurations and to the fact that popular/ colloquial speech can be more 'advanced'[3] than the more conservative standard language (see also Romaine 1988*a*).

Our restricted speakers of French can also be observed to produce developmental solutions to structural imbalances of Standard French. Now, when these solutions coincide with existing non-standard vernacular traits, they may give the impression that sociolectal reduction has not taken place. Such a case of 'aborted' reduction of a non-standard vernacular feature is examined in Chapter 8. The developmental/non-standard form in question is another case of analogical levelling of verb morphology.

Of course, popular/colloquial speech also includes features which have not come about as responses to systemic imbalances. Hence it would be quite unexpected if identical features surfaced as developmental errors in the performance of restricted speakers. Reduction should occur unhampered in such cases, but it does not always, as we were surprised to discover (see Chapter 8). It appears that, independently of their structural status (i.e. greater optimality than their standard counterparts), non-standard vernacular forms that show only *stylistic* variation (i.e. belong to the informal or colloquial speech of all classes) are less likely to get reduced in restricted-speaker performance than non-standard vernacular features which in addition exhibit *social* variation (especially if the social stratification is sharp). In other words, non-standard vernacular features which correspond to informal stylistic variants stand a much better chance than social markers of being internalized by restricted speakers because of their greater availability in the input.

1.4. Absence of child/popular speech features in restricted-speaker performance

This brings us to a third kind of linguistic outcome of restriction, which ensues specifically from the type of domain shrinkage described above, i.e. relegation of minority-language transmission to the school. For the adolescents who have learned the bulk of their French at school, it is perforce the case that they did

---

[3] Translation of the term *avancé* used in French linguistics to refer to the greater degree of structural optimality of popular varieties in comparison to Standard French (see, e.g., Frei 1971).

not begin learning French as early in life as did their less restricted counterparts (see Bickerton 1984*a* on the distinction between primary language
acquisition, that is, acquisition of a language in infancy, and secondary
language acquisition, that is, acquisition of a language—necessarily second—
after age four but before puberty). Dorian (1985), for instance, found that those
among her semi-speakers who had had 'normal' acquisition histories (i.e.
primary acquisition of Gaelic as a mother tongue) were considerably better at
pronouncing difficult sounds of the language than were semi-speakers, who
had had insufficient exposure to Gaelic as children.

In Chapter 6 we examine another kind of effect of such a delayed onstart of
minority-language learning. The feature dealt with in that chapter is a non-
standard vernacular variant of the third person plural imperfect of the copula.
It is present in the speech of the frequent users of French, especially those of
working-class background, but not in the speech of the restricted users of
French. At first sight this would seem to be yet another example of sociolectal
reduction. It is more than just that, however. The interesting problem here has
to do with the fact that the non-standard feature in question is unlike the others
for which we have documented sociolectal reduction: it is a known feature of
child speech. Why, then, would it not also appear in the speech of restricted
speakers, the rationale being that both kinds of learners are known to
restructure their input in similar fashion (see above)? A way out of the apparent
impasse is provided by Kiparsky's (1980: 414) notion of 'false' analogy. It is
argued that the feature arises as a result of the particular way in which the
young child goes about acquiring person, number, and tense distinctions,
which leads it to make a 'false' analogy, that is an analogy resulting in a complication of the grammar but which the child none the less retains (and indeed the
feature which concerns us here has been observed to linger into late childhood). This is probably how it became part of Canadian French as spoken in
popular milieux, where adult filtering of child errors is undoubtedly not as fine
as in higher-class milieux. As restricted users learnt French after infancy, it can
only be surmised that they skipped the above-mentioned developmental stage.
This is supported by research on the learning of French as a second language,
which does not report the false analogy under study.

As Dorian (1981: 155) observes, there is not a complete overlap between
child speech and restricted-user speech, if for no other reasons than that (1) the
child's conceptual powers are not yet fully developed, and (2) restricted
speakers know another language, i.e. the majority language, which may be a
source of both positive and negative transfer. The case of false analogy
examined in Chapter 6 supports Dorian's view. Furthermore, the fact that this
restructuring seems to have an exclusive origin in child language, yet is also
present in adolescent and even adult language, would seem to be a nice
confirmation of the view held by some linguists (e.g. Baron 1977) that children
are sometimes solely responsible for introducing variation and hence potential

changes in a language by not getting rid of their innovations as they grow older.

1.5. Interference

Linguists studying minority languages have sometimes been accused of giving undue emphasis to interlingual explanations for structural developments undergone by such languages (see the beginning of this introduction and, e.g., Poplack 1983 and Muysken 1984 for such accusations). Some of them may have done so because they were operating within a rigid contrastive framework, others because they were members of the majority-speech community and only had superficial knowledge of the minority language, its history, and its dialects, both social and regional (see Chaudenson 1979: 76–7 who makes a similar point regarding research on French-based creoles by non-francophones). In contrast and perhaps even in reaction to contrastivism, other linguists, for whom it is important that minority languages be presented in a favourable light so as to counter exaggerated claims that they are hybrid and that their speakers are inferior, have overemphasized internal explanations of minority-language change, thereby following—knowingly or not—the principle of historical linguistics that change proceeds first and foremost from system-internal causes (Poplack is perhaps the leading figure in this camp, but see also Lass 1980, who says that change without contact is the 'normal' state of affairs, and Trudgill 1983: Chapter 5, who believes that contact-induced change is 'non-natural').

Some would say that sociolinguists have overreacted to the previous practice of contrastivism. Flora Klein-Andreu (p.c.) feels that interference has been seriously neglected in sociolinguistics, but not, she observes, in psycholinguistics. She wrote to us: 'it seems to me that the reason for this neglect is a kind of covert purism: the results of transfer . . . are considered undesirable or "bad"; therefore they are ignored or seriously downplayed, as a kind of courtesy to the population under study'. We are inclined to go along with her assessment of the situation (see also Romaine 1989a: Chapter 8). Talking about interference (more often called 'transfer') in psycholinguistics is acceptable because the integrity of the target language is not at stake (the population under study is composed of second-language learners). In sociolinguistics, however, we are concerned with bilingual speech communities, very often linguistic minorities. Talking about interference here is 'unpalatable' because it operates in the reverse direction, that is from the second (i.e. majority) language into the first (i.e. minority) language. Yet our own feeling is that interference in minority languages might be viewed in a less unfavourable light if it were made more clear (1) what are the sociolinguistic profiles of the speakers most likely to experience interference from the majority language, and (2) that there is a fundamental distinction to be drawn, following Weinreich (1968: 11–12), between interference in speech (or interference proper) and interference in language (or what Mackey 1970 called 'integration').

1.5.1. The problem of 'ambiguous' change

Our own research on variation in Ontarian French, exemplified by the studies in this book, has convinced us that neither of these extreme theoretical positions is valid, since it is not hard to find both types of change, intra- and interlingual. Another reason for rejecting these all-or-none positions is that some minority-language changes that linguists would label as internal or external according to their theoretical persuasion are in all probability both—not even considering for the moment yet a third cause, namely linguistic universals—or in any case very hard to disentangle. As a matter of fact, the possibility of dual or multiple origin is gaining recognition in the literature on language contact (see, e.g., Romaine 1988*b*; Thomason and Kaufman 1988; Trudgill 1986). Current research on pidgins and creoles is also making it increasingly clear that theories which attempt to account for the development of these languages by overly appealing to universals, or to substratum influence, or to superstratum influence are too simplistic (Baker and Corne 1987).

In Chapters 9 and 10 we examine two causally ambiguous developments—involving a redistribution of elements of the prepositional subsystem—which are chiefly characteristic of the speech of the adolescents who display moderate to high levels of French-language use restriction. When the ambiguity is between interference vs. internal simplification, it is difficult to determine whether one putative cause is more likely than the other, for the simple reason that the restricted users of French are just as capable of resorting to internal structural simplification (as demonstrated in Chapter 5) as they are to interference, given that most of them are either balanced or English-dominant bilinguals. These developments are the best candidates for multiple causation.

However, when the ambiguity is between interference and complication (a much rarer occurrence according to our research), it becomes possible to favour interlingual influence as an explanation, since internal complication seems at odds with the notion of more or less restricted use of a minority language (see Thomason 1986, who develops this line of reasoning in connection with the explanation of historical changes having taken place in former contact situations). The prepositional development discussed in Chapter 10 represents one such case of causal ambiguity which we were able to resolve successfully—in favour of interference—via an appeal to this mode of reasoning.

1.5.2. 'Covert' interference

A much less easily detectable outcome of language contact which we have examined in our research is a particular kind of interference for which we have yet to come up with a completely adequate label! (We are only too aware of the lack of agreement over terminology which currently plagues the field of language-contact studies, as underscored again just recently by Appel and Muysken 1987: 154.) We are referring here to the phenomenon whereby a minority-language feature may undergo a gradual decline and eventual loss because it lacks an interlingual counterpart in the majority language. This is accompanied by a concomitant rise in the use of the feature taking over the function vacated by the disappearing feature. In other words, we are concerned here with a peculiar form of interference which does not result in the emergence of innovations but rather simply impinges on the frequency of use of minority-language features that are distinctive from a contrastive viewpoint. As such, then, the quantitative method of variationist sociolinguistics is the only one which is suited to the detection of this kind of interference when it is still in progress (only completed cases can be detected in diachrony without the benefit of quantitative methodology).

Since it would be useful to give interference of this kind a name, and since it is not observable except through quantitative investigation, we propose to call it 'covert' interference. Conversely, all other forms of interference are implicitly 'overt', to the extent that they bring about new features (e.g. constructions, words, meanings, sounds, etc.) in the target language. Though Klein-Andreu (1980: 69) does not refer to covert interference by any special name, she too has brought it to the fore and called for its study via the use of quantitative methods:

contact between languages, like other factors, may bring about changes that only quantitative investigation can detect. In the area of syntax and semantics, interference effects of this kind might be expected to occur where the particular languages in contact have constructions that are parallel morphologically, and that are also similar in their conditions of use, but only partly so. In just such cases we would expect interference to occur, owing to the bilinguals' tendency to equate the two systems in function as well as in form ... Yet such interference may well elude impressionistic observation, to the extent that it does not give rise to utterances that, considered individually, are ungrammatical in the recipient language.

We examine a case of covert interference in Chapter 9. It is shown that to prove covert interference it may be necessary to grapple with the same problem of causal ambiguity as was discussed above regarding some examples of overt interference. Indeed, as Silva-Corvalán (1987) has pointed out, there are cases where the demise of a minority-language form with no equivalent in the majority language can also be attributed to system-internal factors.[4] Our study

---

[4] This point was stated more clearly in a prepublication version of her 1987 paper (Silva-Corvalán 1986*b*: 6): 'Transfer leads to, but is not the single cause of, *convergence*, defined as the achievement of structural similarity in a given aspect of the grammar of two or more languages, assumed to be different at the onset of contact. Indeed, convergence may result as well from internally motivated changes in one of the languages, most likely accelerated by contact, rather than as a consequence of direct interlingual influence.'

suggests a way in which the stalemate can be broken, and that is to see whether the social distribution of the declining form (i.e. between localities and between the different categories of minority-language speakers—unrestricted, semi-restricted, restricted—within a community) is in keeping with the hypothesis of interference and/or internal simplification. Of course, if the bilinguals' tendency to equate the structures of their two languages represents, from an internal structural standpoint, a move in the direction of greater complexity, then we would claim, as above, that this clinches outright the case in favour of covert interference.

1.5.3. Lexical borrowing

Like most other minority languages, Ontarian French has not escaped lexical borrowing. According to Thomason's and Kaufman's (1988) analytic frame-work for the study of contact-induced change, lexical borrowing is precisely the main type of interference which is expected in the direction majority → minority language. Poplack and Sankoff (1984) made the observation that lexical borrowing has been the object of numerous linguistically oriented studies but has received little attention from sociolinguists. According to these authors (1984: 105), this has meant, among other things, that basic assumptions about 'the role of bilingual versus monolingual, or older versus younger speakers, in introducing and propagating loanwords has never been empirically investigated or established', nor has the role of social class we might wish to add. In Chapter 11 we present a quantitative sociolinguistic investigation of the social distribution of an English loanword in Ontarian French (the consecutive conjunction *so*), which is all the more interesting as it constitutes a borrowing into the 'core', that is, into the basic lexical stock, of the minority language (see Scotton and Okeju 1973 on the phenomenon of core lexical borrowing). To the extent that one can try to infer diachronic trajectories from synchronic description, it would appear that this particular core lexical borrowing was instigated by speakers who belong to the working class and who are 'true' bilinguals, to the extent that they make regular use of both their languages (i.e. chiefly semi-restricted speakers).

1.6. Wider issues in the study of language contact

Our research in the Franco-Ontarian community bears on a number of broader issues related to language contact, which we would like to address in this final section of the introduction.

1.6.1. The mechanism of change in minority-language communities

One important, but little investigated issue, is whether or not linguistic change in minority languages proceeds in the way described by Labov for monolingual communities, that is, via the introduction of an innovation by an individual speaker or by a small group of speakers belonging to a particular social class, and its subsequent propagation to other speakers of the same class and eventual adoption by speakers of other classes.

Our research suggests that, in practically all of the cases examined, the answer is no. The picture it reveals is one of linguistic innovations emerging independently and simultaneously for a large number of speakers as a result of widespread bilingualism and/or minority-language restriction, with usually at best only a loose connection to social class (the case of core lexical borrowing examined in Chapter 11 is exceptional in this regard, as it has a strong working-class connection). The reason for this is clear: bilingualization and restriction are overriding sociological processes that cut across the whole social spectrum and free the structural (intra- and/or intersystemic) forces at play. Furthermore, just as new features may emerge in sweeping fashion, existing features may undergo large-scale decline due to the phenomenon of sociolectal reduction. Although Dorian (1981: 152) also reports that social stratification is 'conspicuously absent' in East Sutherland Gaelic, her case is different from ours in that her community was extremely homogeneous (i.e. all fisherfolk with minimum education). There was no social stratification to begin with, so there was no real basis for the phenomenon of sociolectal reduction to operate.

This would seem to mean that the model of linguistic change proposed by Labov for monolingual communities needs to be relaxed in order to allow for the possibility of innovation by many speakers in bilingual speech communities. In other words, a major difference between the respective mechanisms of change in monolingual communities and bilingual communities characterized by advanced bilingualism and more or less pronounced language restriction may reside in the size of the initial group of innovating speakers— thought to be small or even reduced to one individual in the former case, but potentially quite large in the latter case.[5]

Interestingly enough, Labov (1972: 277–8) himself did not entirely preclude the possibility of autonomous innovations by a number of speakers: 'We do not rule out the possibility of independent simultaneous innovation by a number of speakers; but we do find absurd the notion that an entire community would change simultaneously without reference to each other, without a gradual transfer of the pattern from speaker to speaker.'

---

[5] It may perhaps be mentioned in passing here that the diffusion aspect of Labov's model of language change has also been questioned with respect to its applicability to monolingual speech communities (see, e.g., the interesting new model of transmission of linguistic innovations proposed by J. Milroy and L. Milroy 1985).

While we agree with Labov that a speech community is unlikely to change *en masse*, we believe that, in a minority speech community, whole groups of speakers sharing particular patterns of language use and dominance can indeed innovate 'simultaneously without reference to each other'.

Furthermore, we cannot go along with Labov's view of linguistic change as necessarily involving innovation *plus* propagation, since it would logically follow, for example, that linguistic innovations surfacing in the speech of restricted speakers of a minority language, no matter how numerous these speakers happened to be in their community, would not actually count as genuine instances of linguistic change unless evidence could be provided of their propagation to/adoption by at least some of the other, less-restricted language users of the speech community.[6] Obviously, this view of linguistic change is too restrictive for our purpose.

This is not to say that innovations cannot spread outside the originating speaker group(s) in a minority-language community. In this connection, it is relevant to consider the possible linguistic consequences of the dwindling number of fluent speakers of a minority language on the speech of those who remain fluent speakers of that language. To our knowledge this question has been little investigated or even considered, with the notable exception of Dorian (1981) in her research on grammatical change in the dying Gaelic of East Sutherland, Scotland. She found that, while restricted use of Gaelic could be invoked to explain differences between semi-speaker grammar and fluent-speaker grammar, it could obviously not be invoked as an explanation for the departures from the older fluent-speaker norm that were in evidence among the younger fluent speakers. She offered the tentative hypothesis (p. 154) that fluent-speaker grammatical change might be due to the disappearance, during the final stages of a language, of 'vigilant grammatical purists' or 'self-appointed monitors of grammatical norms', who in earlier stages were known to correct the younger fluent speakers' departures from the norm.

In Chapter 10 we are confronted with a similar paradox, i.e. the presence in unrestricted-speaker performance of an interference-caused feature strongly associated with restricted and semi-restricted speech. We explore instead an alternative hypothesis, namely that some linguistic aspects of restricted- and semi-restricted-speaker performance may 'rub off' on the speech of un-restricted speakers if the latter have become a small group relative to the former, as is typical of language-death and advanced language-shift situations. The evidence is not conclusive, however, as the unrestricted speakers in question happen to share one of the two characteristics that would make them prone to innovate on their own (i.e. good knowledge of English—they all claimed balanced bilingualism).

---

[6] This raises another related issue, i.e. what is a speech community and who belongs to it (see Romaine 1982*a* and Romaine 1989*a*: Chapters 1 and 2)?

1.6.2. Universals vs. language-specific change

We have already alluded to the fact that it may be methodologically advantageous and theoretically interesting to compare restricted speech with popular speech, child speech, and the speech of second-language learners, with a view to characterizing and explaining their common features and their differences. Further meaningful comparisons are possible, such as with other minority varieties of North American French (e.g. those still found in a few French-speaking enclaves in the United States, some of which, like Ontarian French, are offshoots of Québécois French) and with French-based creoles. As pointed out by Chaudenson (1989*a*) and Romaine (1989*b*), French is one of only a few languages that are found in such a diversity of guises and settings and for which there are available data. Our research has profited from this comparative approach to one extent or another.

On the specific topic of the relationship of pidginization and minority-language restriction, our work confirms the views expressed by Dorian (1978) that the two are not equatable in terms of their linguistic outcomes. While it is true that the restricted speakers of Ontarian French are prone to doing away with grammatical complexities, their simplifications are far from being as drastic as those which are postulated to have taken place in the sociolinguistic conditions that gave rise to the formation of French-based creoles (see, e.g., Chaudenson 1974; 1979), or which are documented in the pidginized varieties of French spoken in former French colonies, notably in Africa (Manessy and Wald 1984).

Furthermore, we have not observed in restricted-speaker performance the kinds of structures which Bickerton has documented in certain English-based creoles and attributed to the activation of the language bioprogramme. It is probably not necessary to look for any other explanation than the fact that the input to our restricted speakers is not an 'impoverished pidgin', but a full-blown variety—and chiefly the standard one at that! We believe that the ways in which this input can be restructured are largely predetermined, as it were, by the structure of the linguistic system itself (Silva-Corvalán 1986*a*) and/or by that of the bilingual's other language (especially if it is his or her dominant language). This is not to say that the restricted speakers' restructurings of the minority language are never guided by linguistic universals (e.g. *à la* Bickerton 1981; 1984*a*, *b*). We only wish to imply that it was not necessary for us to invoke universals in the case of the limited number of developments examined in our research. And what if we are faced with the thorny problem of causal ambiguity, i.e. a minority-language development compatible with both a universalist explanation and a language-specific one (in the latter case, either interference or autonomous internal change)? In raising the same question regarding interlanguage developments, Bickerton himself (1984*a*: 155) is prepared to admit that such ambiguous cases are *inconclusive* support for the language-bioprogramme hypothesis.

In our opinion, the appeal to alleged linguistic universals to explain minority-language change makes the most sense in the case of developments which turn out to resist an explanation in terms of majority-language interference and/or in terms of minority-language specific internal restructuring (bearing in mind, as Chaudenson 1982: 94 has cautioned in his review article of Bickerton 1981, that it is risky indeed to claim universal status for linguistic structures based on a comparison of only a limited number of languages—e.g. Bickerton's language-bioprogramme hypothesis is based in very large part on a consideration of strictly English-based creoles; Fournier 1987 has shown that the language-bioprogramme hypothesis is not supported by the evidence provided by French-based creoles).[7]

1.6.3. Thresholds of restriction and associated types of change in minority languages

In the concluding chapter we try to articulate the major findings of our research in terms of French-language-restriction thresholds and their associated linguistic outcomes. Judging by these findings, Ontarian French is behaving as expected of a minority language in that the major linguistic developments that we have been able to uncover—morphosyntactic simplification, interference, and monostylism[8]—are precisely the same three which have most often been reported in the literature on minority languages (Appel and Muysken 1987: 42–5). What our synthesis tentatively suggests—based on the limited number of linguistic variables examined—is that these linguistic processes are ordered implicationally, with a sub-hierarchy within interference. Most pervasive, that is, occurring even in the speech of the speakers with the lowest levels of French-language restriction resident in the majority francophone control community, is lexical borrowing. Next are two other forms of interference, namely covert interference and semantic extension, which are observable everywhere except in the speech of the former speakers. Then comes structural simplification, which requires more or less restricted use of French. Finally, least pervasive are sociolectal reduction and what could be called 'gross' or deviant forms of interference such as calquing (i.e. literal translations), both of which signal out the restricted speakers. This implicational scale strikes us as a natural one; indeed, as Appel and Muysken (1987: 1) put it, 'language contact inevitably leads to bilingualism', to which we would add 'and bilingualism

---

[7] It should be noted, however, that Bickerton's definition of a 'true' creole is very restricted, so that perhaps only a few of the languages known traditionally as 'creoles' actually fit his definition (Bickerton 1981: 2–4).

[8] In the Franco-Ontarian situation, however, it must be remembered that monostylism is a consequence of the reduction of non-standard vernacular features, not standard ones as is usually the case in 'classical' minority settings with no educational support for the minority language.

may—but need not—be accompanied by more or less severe restriction of the original language', so that the linguistic effects of bilingualism are expected to manifest themselves first and separately from those of any ensuing restriction (at least in minority-language settings which involve prolonged contact with and gradual shift to the majority language).

2

Socio-historical Background

THE purpose of this chapter is to provide historical, sociological, and demographic information concerning Ontario's francophone population. This will allow the reader better to situate the four Franco-Ontarian communities in which our adolescent speakers were selected, in terms of geographical location, local demographics, language maintenance and shift, local economic activity, etc. Because of the specific topic of this book, we shall pay special attention to the data on bilingualism and language shift among Franco-Ontarians.

2.1. Origins of Ontario's francophone population

The origins of the francophone minority in Ontario can be traced to explorers and colonizers who came up the St Lawrence River and into the Great Lakes area from the main areas of French colonization in what is now the Province of Quebec, in the late 1600s and early to mid-1700s.[1] When the British conquered Canada in 1760, pockets of francophones were still to be found in these areas, mainly around Detroit. The still existing francophone community of south-western Ontario can, then, trace its origins to this early settlement. Other francophones from nearby settlements, displaced as a result of boundary changes related to the War of 1812 between Canada and the United States, established themselves further north, around Penetanguishene on Lake Huron, in 1828. These two pockets of settlement constitute the kernel of the francophone population in Ontario (see Map 2.1).

The second wave of immigration was directly related to overpopulation in rural areas of Quebec, which, starting around 1830, touched off an exodus which reached its height around 1840. This exodus was initially directed towards the textile mills of New England, but the Catholic Church determined to keep these francophones within its jurisdiction, that is, within Canada, and succeeded in redirecting some of this migration towards Ontario. Most of the new settlers established themselves in the dairy-farming areas of eastern Ontario, in the triangle formed by the Ottawa and St Lawrence Rivers, immediately adjacent to Quebec, where they could continue their traditional rural life-style, to the satisfaction of the Catholic Church. Here, within a few decades, their growing population began to surpass that of the original

[1] Material presented in this section is drawn mainly from Arnopoulos (1982), Choquette (1980), and Vallières (1980).

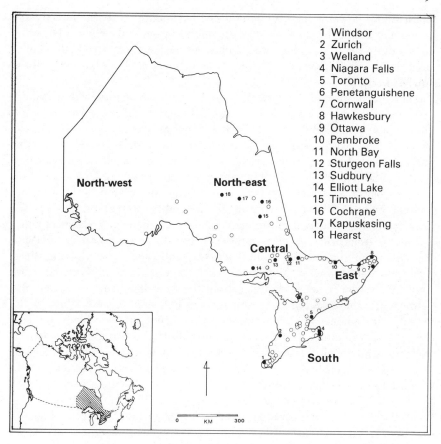

MAP 2.1. *Regions and localities with francophone concentration in Ontario.*

Source: adapted from Mougeon and Heller (1986: 223)

anglophone settlers. Three of the four communities where we gathered our speech corpuses belong to this area. They are the French-speaking communities of Cornwall, Hawkesbury, and Pembroke (see points 7, 8, and 10 on Map 2.1). Other francophone settlers from Quebec established themselves near the existing francophone settlement of Penetanguishene.

The third wave of immigration began around the 1880s, with the opening up and colonization of the central and northern parts of Ontario. While some francophone settlers came from eastern Ontario and New Brunswick (Acadia), most continued to come from Quebec. Also, while settlers included anglophone Canadians and non-francophone Europeans, francophone Canadians formed a large proportion of the population in this area. Colonization continued well into the 1930s. While this population continued to be primarily agricultural, towards the beginning of the twentieth century the forestry and mining industries became the main providers of work in the region. The other community where we interviewed adolescent speakers is located in the central area of Ontario. This is the francophone community of North Bay (see point 11 on Map 2.1).

The fourth wave of immigration is in fact both a migration within Ontario and an influx from outside Ontario. Internal migration took the form of a shift of the population from primarily rural agricultural sectors to urban industrial centres, both within regions and on a province-wide scale. Although this process started as early as the late 1800s, it only reached significant proportions after the Second World War. In northern and eastern Ontario, regional urban centres began to attract population from farms to the growing forestry and mining industries and, in Ottawa, to the public sector and service jobs generated by the federal government established there with Canada's independence from Britain in 1867. At the same time there was a more general shift of population from the north and east to the centre and the south-west, where industry was strongest. Francophones from elsewhere in Canada, again principally from Quebec, but also from the Maritime provinces, were also attracted to these central and south-western industrial regions. Thus, by the 1950s, francophones in Ontario were engaged mainly in the primary (agriculture, forestry, mining) and secondary (industry, construction) economic sectors, while a minority were also engaged in tertiary sector occupations (services, small business, sales, transport, etc.). They were also principally of Canadian origin, that is, descendants of the original settlers of the French colony of New France or of Acadia.

The fifth wave of immigration began in the 1960s and is connected to major changes in francophone social mobility across Canada at that time. Increase in government control over social services, leading, among other things, to increased access to education and growth in the economic importance of the public sector, combined with other factors to permit the development of a new francophone middle class in Canada. This phenomenon, along with the rising importance of Toronto and Ottawa as economic centres in Canada, is tied to the increase in numbers of francophones in tertiary and quaternary occupations (administration, science, arts, etc.) starting in the 1960s. These francophones were drawn not only from a socially upwardly mobile local population but also from the new francophone middle class elsewhere in Canada (again, mainly in Quebec), and from francophone regions and countries outside Canada (Africa, Asia, Europe, the Caribbean). In addition, immigration of foreign francophones of other social classes also increased. It should be noted, however, that the immigration of foreign-born francophones is largely confined to the cities of Ottawa and Toronto.

In sum, the nature of the francophone minority in Ontario has changed significantly over time. A once homogeneous, principally agricultural population, with its demographic weight mainly in the north and east, has become increasingly diversified in terms of its social and economic organization, and its demographic weight has shifted from rural to urban communities and towards the central region. Further, the financial and political centres of Toronto and Ottawa have attracted an even more heterogeneous francophone population, which is varied not only in terms of its economic characteristics, but also in terms of its regional and cultural origins, and of the varieties of French spoken.[2]

2.2. Current demographic status of Ontario's francophones

According to the national census of 1981 (the one which most closely approximates the time period when we gathered our speech corpus—late 1970s; see Chapter 4—and from which all of the data to be presented here are taken, unless otherwise specified), there were 475,605 individuals who claimed French as their mother tongue in Ontario. It is important to consider how Statistics Canada defines mother tongue, i.e. the first language learnt in childhood and still *understood* at the time of the census. A shortcoming of this definition is that, as Castonguay (1981: 7) has indicated, it encompasses individuals who may no longer be able to speak their mother tongue. However, these individuals with only passive knowledge of their mother tongue are identifiable through their answers to the official languages question (see section 2.3). Be that as it may, in this chapter we use the terms francophone, anglophone, etc. as convenient synonyms for French mother tongue, English mother tongue, etc.

Another serious limitation of the 1981 mother-tongue question is that it did not allow respondents the possibility of indicating multiple (i.e. two or more) mother tongues. Thus those who had two or more mother tongues were forced as it were to report but one of them. In spite of this, no fewer than 60,000 Ontarians actually took the initiative of mentioning on their census forms that they had learned French *and* English simultaneously in infancy. Statistics Canada specifies that, in cases where several languages were reported, the multiple responses were distributed (equally?) among the component languages. That being the case, one could probably minimally augment the 1981 French-mother-tongue population by 30,000 (half of 60,000) to 505,605. This drawback has been remedied in the recent 1986 national census, in which responses indicating more than one language were accepted. It reveals that alongside 424,720 individuals who claimed French as their sole mother tongue,

---

[2] Lest we give the reader the wrong impression, we should point out at this stage that we have not attempted in this book to capture this new linguistic heterogeneity. On the contrary, the book's linguistic focus is on the traditional variety of French, i.e. that spoken by individuals of French-Canadian extraction.

there were another 119,105 who in addition to French claimed English and/or another language as a mother tongue! All told, French was the mother tongue of 543,825 Ontarians in 1986. This suggests that the official 1981 figure of 475,605 is an even more serious underestimate of the actual number of French-mother-tongue Ontarians than previously thought. Be that as it may, since there is no accurate way of assessing the real number of multiple-mother-tongue respondents in 1981, we shall have to live with the official census figure for that year of 475,605 French-mother-tongue Ontarians.

Ontario's French-mother-tongue population constitutes the largest francophone community in Canada outside Quebec, the one and only predominantly francophone province of Canada. Despite their numbers, the nearly half million francophones of Ontario (we will stick with the official figure of 475,605) make up only 5.5 per cent of the provincial population. By way of comparison, the next largest francophone minority in the country, the francophones of New Brunswick, although only half as many in absolute numbers, none the less represent a substantially greater proportion of the provincial population (33.6 per cent). Since the remaining population of Ontario is made up of 77.4 per cent anglophones and 17 per cent 'allophones' (i.e. individuals whose mother tongue is neither English nor French), Ontario's francophones are therefore clearly outnumbered by an anglophone majority. Table 2.1 summarizes the mother-tongue population statistics for the three provinces under comparison.

Though the overall ratio of Franco-Ontarians is low compared to the provincial population, at a local or regional (e.g. county) level the concentration of francophones varies considerably, ranging from highs of over 90 per cent to lows of less than 1 per cent. Several counties and many localities where francophones constitute strong majorities (more than 80 per cent of the population) can be found in the rural agricultural region of south-eastern Ontario near the Quebec border. This includes the francophone community of Hawkesbury, which makes up 85 per cent of the town's population (9,880 inhabitants). In the regions of central and northern Ontario, where the bulk of the province's mining and forestry industry is located, there are a few localities

TABLE 2.1. *Population by mother tongue (MT) for Ontario, Quebec, and New Brunswick*

Province	Population	English MT		French MT		Other MT	
		N	%	N	%	N	%
Ontario	8,625,105	6,678,765	77.4	475,605	5.5	1,464,410	17.0
Quebec	6,438,405	706,110	11.0	5,307,015	82.4	421,655	6.5
New Brunswick	696,400	453,310	65.1	234,030	33.6	8,170	1.2

Source: Statistics Canada, 1981 census (100% data)

which are more than 70 per cent francophone (e.g. Hearst, Sturgeon Falls). There are also, in northern Ontario, many localities where Franco-Ontarians make up roughly half of the population (e.g. Cochrane, Kapuskasing, Timmins). Strong francophone minorities (between 20 and 40 per cent) can also be found there, as well as in the central and eastern regions (e.g. Elliott Lake, Sudbury). The francophone community of Cornwall is one such strong minority: it makes up 35 per cent of the total city population of 46,145. Finally, weak francophone minorities (less than 20 per cent) are to be found in all regions of the province, but especially in southern Ontario, the province's industrial heartland (e.g. Niagara Falls, Toronto, Welland, Windsor). The francophone communities of North Bay and Pembroke are two such weak minorities. In North Bay francophones account for 17 per cent of the city's population of 51,260. In Pembroke only 8 per cent of the population of 14,025 is of French mother tongue. It is precisely because they represent different points along the continuum of francophone concentration at the local level that the four Franco-Ontarian communities under study were selected.

2.3. Bilingualism

The Canadian census provides data on the respondents' knowledge of the country's two official languages, French and English, defined as the ability to conduct a conversation in one and/or the other language. As crude as this measure may be (i.e. it does not allow to distinguish between levels of proficiency), the data on official languages enable one to calculate a rate of 'bilingualism' for Ontario's French-mother-tongue population. In 1981 no less than 84 per cent of French-mother-tongue Ontarians reported being able to conduct a conversation in both official languages.[3] Only 12 per cent claimed they were unable to carry out a conversation in English. The remaining 4 per cent were individuals who had actually lost the ability to converse in their mother tongue, French. By way of contrast, in the overwhelmingly francophone province of Quebec, the province from which most of the Franco-Ontarian community stems, the proportion of French-mother-tongue Quebeckers who were bilingual in English was only 29 per cent. Thus bilingualism is a key characteristic which sets off Franco-Ontarians from French Quebeckers. Given what was just said above concerning multiple-mother-tongue responses, we know that this bilingualism is not entirely acquired through socialization, but is often transmitted in the home by already bilingual parents. French–English bilingualism in Ontario is still very much a one-way phenomenon, however, since no more than 7 per cent of

[3] These figures are estimates based on 20 per cent sample data; only one in five households receives the long version of the census questionnaire which includes the questions on knowledge of the official languages and language (most often) spoken at home.

English-mother-tongue Ontarians were bilingual in French in 1981. To continue the contrast with Quebec, 53 per cent of English-mother-tongue Quebeckers were bilingual in French. Extending the comparison to New Brunswick, 61 per cent of the French-mother-tongue population of that province was bilingual in English, but only 9 per cent of the English-mother-tongue population was bilingual in French (see Table 2.2).

TABLE 2.2. *Bilingualism by mother tongue for Ontario, Quebec, and New Brunswick*

Province	English MT (% bilingual in F)	French MT (% bilingual in E)	Other MT (% bi- or trilingual)			
			In E	In F	In E/F	In neither
Ontario	7	84	84	0.2	7	10
Quebec	53	29	26	18.0	45	12
New Brunswick	9	61	79	0.9	15	5

Source: Statistics Canada, 1981 census (based on 20% sample data)

The last set of columns in Table 2.2 provides an interesting insight into the attraction power of the two official language groups, the French and the English, in each province, as indicated by the proportion of the other mother-tongue groups who become bilingual in one or other official language or indeed trilingual. As can be seen, in Ontario and New Brunswick the great majority of allophones choose to learn the English language, as might be expected given the majority status of English in these two provinces. However, if demographic strength were the only conditioning factor, one would have expected a clear-cut advantage of French over English in Quebec, which is certainly not the case. English and French seem there to be engaged in a linguistic tug-of-war, with only a minority of allophones opting exclusively for French. The other conditioning factor, of course, is socio-economic power. By the looks of it, the once socio-economically dominant English minority of the province of Quebec still wields considerable power. French would still seem to have a long way to go before becoming an automatic choice for all newcomers to the province of Quebec.

The general percentage of bilinguals among Franco-Ontarians, while very high, hides a significant amount of variation as a function of the demographic strength of francophones at the local level. To take only our four francophone communities as examples, the rate of bilingualism is considerably lower than the provincial average in the strong majority francophone community of Hawkesbury (66 per cent), higher than the provincial average in the strong minority francophone community of Cornwall (90 per cent), and higher still in the weak francophone communities of North Bay (95 per cent) and Pembroke (97 per cent).[4]

Just as the general rate of bilingualism among Ontario's francophones conceals intercommunity variation, so does it hide intergenerational differences, as shown in Table 2.3.

The dangers inherent in translating synchronic age distributions into diachronic trends are well known. Thus care must be taken not to interpret the much lower ratio of bilingual Franco-Ontarians in the youngest age group (0–4) as an indication of a recent sharp decline in bilingualism. Rather, it merely

TABLE 2.3. *Bilingualism by age group for French-mother-tongue (FMT) Ontarians, Quebeckers, and New Brunswickers*

Age group	FMT Ontarians (% bilingual)	FMT Quebeckers (% bilingual)	FMT New Brunswickers (% bilingual)
0–4	36	2	12
5–14†	76	7	40
15–19	90	26	63
20–4	92	34	72
25–9	93	37	76
30–4	92	41	78
35–9	91	41	76
40–4	90	38	76
45–9	88	38	74
50–4	87	37	70
55–9	86	36	69
60–4	83	34	65
65+	78	28	59
All ages	84	29	61

† Statistics Canada did not break this age group down into two five-year cohorts (5–9 and 10–14).

Source: Statistics Canada, 1981 census (based on 20% sample data)

[4] Statistics Canada does not provide cross-tabulated data (mother tongue by official language) for agglomerations—such as the four localities under study—which are not components of a larger metropolitan area. Thus the rates of bilingualism that we have calculated are maximum estimates based on the difference between the number of French-mother-tongue individuals and the number of individuals who report being able to converse in French only. These rates are trustworthy, though, since they are based on two rather safe assumptions, namely that (1) those who can conduct a conversation only in French are of French mother tongue, and (2) there are very few French-mother-tongue individuals who in the course of their lifetime lose the ability to sustain a conversation in French (only 4 per cent for the total French-mother-tongue population of Ontario—see the beginning of this section).

reflects the fact that many of these infants and young children are still monolingual in French, in all likelihood for want of exposure to English at home. Nevertheless, more than a third of the 0–4 year-olds *are* bilingual, a fact which probably reflects in large part their having been handed down both French and English by their parents (see preceding section). In any case, as these young monolingual Franco-Ontarians grow older and come into contact with English in the wider community, they too quickly become bilingual, a development which is prefigured by the linguistic abilities of the French-mother-tongue individuals belonging to the immediately older age groups (5–14 and 15–19), of whom 76 and 90 per cent respectively are bilingual. In short, an overwhelming majority of Franco-Ontarians are bilingual by the end of adolescence. This pattern of very early and extremely widespread bilingualism stands in sharp contrast to the pattern of later and less widespread bilingualism found among French Quebeckers, with the pattern for French-mother-tongue New Brunswickers falling in between.

Considering now the adult portion of Table 2.3, one would expect age grading in the acquisition of bilingualism to continue right up to the end of a Franco-Ontarian's working life, i.e. until around age 65, since participation in the mainly English-speaking job market should have a cumulative effect on the development of English language skills. In fact what we get is a continuation of age grading until the 25–9 cohort, and then a gradual decline in the proportion of bilinguals as we move on to the oldest adults. If we stick to our assumption that the oldest adults are to be taken as the reference group to establish the peak rate of bilingualism reached by an age cohort, then Table 2.3 suggests that the rate of bilingualism has been steadily increasing over the past decades among Franco-Ontarians, from a low of 78 per cent for the oldest age group (65+) to a high of 93 per cent for the young adults aged 25–9 (a rate which may still climb as this age cohort goes all the way through its occupational life cycle). In any case, practically all young Franco-Ontarians today grow up to be bilingual in English. Similar increases in the rate of bilingualism are noticeable as well for Quebec and New Brunswick francophones.[5]

Ideally, in order to support fully the claim that bilingualism is on the increase among Franco-Ontarians, we would need information on the rate of bilingualism for the same age groups in earlier decennial censuses, i.e. 1971,

---

[5] Despite recent legislative efforts by the provincial government to promote French as the work language in Quebec, English continues to enjoy considerable prominence in the employment domain. That bilingualism also appears to be on the increase among French Quebeckers is therefore not all that surprising. A different interpretation can be found in the work of Lieberson (1972), however. Working with 1961 census data, he argued that the age correlation of bilingualism for Montreal francophones—which showed the same curvilinear distribution as does the general rate for French Quebeckers in 1981 (see Table 2.3)—reflected age grading in the acquisition and subsequent loss of bilingualism in English as francophones enter and then leave the English-dominated work sphere. Thus he concluded that bilingualism was in fact not on the increase among French Montrealers.

1961, etc. Since this information is not available, we can only go by the general rate of bilingualism for Franco-Ontarians as a whole. The latter has indeed increased steadily through the thirty-year period 1951–81: 77 per cent in 1951, 78 per cent in 1961, 82 per cent in 1971, and 84 per cent in 1981.[6]

Unfortunately, for reasons previously mentioned, census data on bilingualism broken down by age group are unavailable for agglomerations such as the four under study. However, if the age correlation of bilingualism discovered by Mougeon and Beniak (1989) for the French minority of the city of Welland (16 per cent of the population of 45,480) is any indication—it basically matches the provincial pattern (see Table 2.4)—one may expect a similar curvilinear distribution to hold for any given minority Franco-Ontarian community.[7] In other words, it is probably the case that, in the three Franco-Ontarian communities under study where francophones are in the minority, the rate of bilingualism increases rapidly through the 0–24 age groups, crests in the 25–34 age group, then decreases slightly through the older age groups, such a decrease actually being indicative, we would claim, of a rise in the rate of bilingualism in real time. Presumably, bilingualism is not acquired with such

TABLE 2.4. *Rate of bilingualism by age group for French-mother-tongue Wellanders*

Age group	FMT (N)	Bilingual FMT	
		N	%
0–4	425	230	54
5–14	810	730	90
15–24	1,355	1,265	93
25–34	1,250	1,195	96
35–44	925	850	92
45–54	930	805	87
55–64	710	545	77
65+	535	430	80
All ages	6,950	6,050	87

Source: Statistics Canada, 1981 census (based on 20% sample data)

[6] The rates of bilingualism that we have calculated for 1951 and 1961 are again maximum estimates based on the difference between the number of French-mother-tongue Ontarians and the number of Ontarians who report being able to converse in French only (see n. 4). These earlier censuses do not provide cross-classifications of mother tongue by official language.

[7] It is because it is a component of the census metropolitan area of St Catharines–Niagara that these cross-tabulated data are available for the city of Welland. Note that Statistics Canada did not break down the age groups into five-year cohorts for this particular set of data.

precocity in the majority francophone community of Hawkesbury, nor to the same degree.[8]

Societal bilingualism is frequently mentioned as a prerequisite for language shift (Fasold 1984: 216–17). Admittedly, it is difficult to imagine a linguistic group adopting a new language without first going through a phase of bilingualism, or, put differently, abandoning a language without first having found a substitute for it. As we have seen, this precondition certainly holds for Franco-Ontarians as a group as well as for the specific Franco-Ontarian communities that concern us, including seemingly even the majority francophone community of Hawkesbury, where as much as 66 per cent of the French-mother-tongue population purports to be bilingual in English. Furthermore, there are proportionately more and more bilingual Franco-Ontarians as each new generation reaches adulthood, to the point where there is hardly any more room for bilingualism to progress.[9] The issue to which we now turn is the extent to which the situation of increasingly advanced societal bilingualism described above is accompanied by a shift to English.

2.4. Shift

Before we analyse the data which will enable us to answer this question, we would like to make explicit our conception of language shift as it relates to exogenous minorities (i.e. groups who have emigrated). Language shift can be documented as concerns both skills in the minority language and its domains of use. We shall say that there is shift when (1) certain members of the minority community lose productive skills in the minority language or when certain members of that community are not or only minimally transmitted the minority language, and (2) the majority language encroaches in the domains which are the primary determinants of intergenerational language transmission and in which the minority community could exclusively use its language if it so decided. We include in these domains first and foremost the home and the community's own institutions (e.g. educational, religious, cultural, etc.).

Canada's 1981 census data allow ready calculation of two measures of language shift as we have just defined it, using the previously defined concepts of mother tongue and official language, and a third concept, home language: (1) loss of the ability to carry out a conversation in French by individuals of French mother tongue, and (2) adoption of English as the language most often spoken at home by individuals of French mother tongue.

[8] The latter part of this prediction will be proven true in Chapter 4, where we shall show that the adolescent subjects from Hawkesbury have developed a French-dominant bilingualism, whereas most of their minority-community counterparts are either balanced or English-dominant bilinguals.

[9] At the risk of sounding repetitious, it needs to be remembered that bilingualism is used here in the Statistics Canada sense to refer only to the ability to sustain a conversation in French and English.

The first measure is the strictest, since it identifies those French-mother-tongue Ontarians who have actually lost the capacity to conduct a conversation in French. These individuals may be likened to the two categories of 'low-proficiency semi-speakers' and 'near-passive bilinguals' which Dorian (1982: 26) identified in the East Sutherland Gaelic speech community. Along with that author, we could say that such individuals constitute the margin of a bilingual minority community. We saw above that Franco-Ontarians who have lost productive competence in French during their lifetime are a marginal lot, accounting for no more than 4 per cent. This finding is significant considering that, as we saw earlier, 84 per cent of the Franco-Ontarian population is bilingual, with approximately one-fifth of this latter population being of dual mother tongue (extrapolating from the most recent 1986 census). Even if we restrict the calculation of the rate of loss of productive competence in French to the bilingual portion of the Franco-Ontarian population, the rate is only fractionally higher. Given the overwhelmingly anglophone context of Ontario, we might have expected bilingual Franco-Ontarians, and especially those who were childhood bilinguals, to be more vulnerable to losing their spoken proficiency in French. That they are not, means that intra-individual loss of productive skills in French is not a major form of shift.

This does not mean, however, that some Franco-Ontarians are not exposed to the risk of experiencing a partial loss of productive competence in their mother tongue, whereby they can no longer speak French as well as they once could—although still well enough to carry out a conversation and thus qualify as bilinguals according to the census definition of bilingualism. The Canadian census statistics simply do not make it possible to assess the size of this group, since, as was previously mentioned, there were no questions on the respondent's degree of bilingualism.

In spite of the small size of the group of Franco-Ontarians who have lost the capacity to speak French in the course of their existence, we may wish to study their distribution as a function of age group, since we saw earlier in Table 2.3 that there is non-negligible variation in the rate of bilingualism by age group. Since loss of the ability to speak French is necessarily dependent on bilingualism in English, one would expect the variation in the proportion of bilingual French-mother-tongue Ontarians across age groups to be matched by a corresponding variation in the proportion of French-mother-tongue Ontarians who have lost spoken proficiency in French.

As can be seen from column one in Table 2.5, the pattern that is observable is actually the reverse of what was found for the rate of bilingualism by age group. The age groups which exhibit the highest rates of loss of ability to speak French (the very youngest and oldest ones) are those which feature the lowest rates of bilingualism (see Table 2.3)! Restricting the calculation of the loss of productive skills in French to the bilingual portion of the Franco-Ontarian community (i.e. the only individuals who are at risk of undergoing such a loss)

TABLE 2.5. *Loss of ability to speak French and use of English as home language (EHL) by age group for French-mother-tongue Ontarians*

Age group	% loss of French		% EHL	
	FMT	Bilingual FMT	FMT	Bilingual FMT
0–4	6	14	13	19
5–14	4	4	19	20
15–19	4	5	24	23
20–4	3	3	34	33
25–9	3	3	40	40
30–4	3	3	42	42
35–9	4	4	43	44
40–4	4	4	45	46
45–9	4	4	41	42
50–4	4	4	41	42
55–9	4	5	40	41
60–4	4	5	38	40
65+	5	6	33	37
All ages	4	4	34	36

Source: Statistics Canada, 1981 census (based on 20% sample data)

does not change anything: the age groups most at risk of losing proficiency in spoken French are again the youngest and oldest ones.[10] In fact, this time the 0–4 age group stands out much more and the oldest bilinguals are twice as prone to losing spoken French competence as the young adults. Is this a sign that loss of ability to speak French is sharply on the increase among the youngest bilingual generation after having shown a steady decrease from the oldest to the youngest adults? We think not and would rather interpret this pattern as reflecting age grading in the loss of productive skills in French. As concerns the 0–4 age group, Castonguay (1984: n. 1) talks of 'profound assimilation' when referring to so precocious a loss of the ability to speak one's mother tongue. The most likely setting for such a loss is the linguistically mixed household where the primary caretaker is French and has attempted to pass the language on to the child, though English is the dominant medium of

---

[10] We need to provide a brief word of explanation concerning the method of calculation which was used to arrive at the percentages in column two of Table 2.5. It is based on the assumption that the French-mother-tongue individuals who have lost the ability to converse in French were necessarily bilingual in French and English earlier in their lives. The number of such French-mother-tongue individuals by age group was then simply divided by the same number plus the number of French-mother-tongue individuals who have remained bilingual.

communication in the home (an extremely common outcome in such house-holds, as has been shown by Castonguay 1979; see also Williams 1987 on Welsh).[11] Since the wider community will provide few opportunities of exposure to French, especially in localities where francophones are in the minority, these youngsters are unlikely to reacquire French later in life, *unless they are sent to a French-language school.* Thus the marked decline in the rate of loss of ability to speak French noticeable between the 0–4 and 5–14 age groups could reflect a reacquisition of conversational skills in French through the school. This would be a nice illustration of the role of the minority-language school as one of the 'primary determinants of intergenerational language transmission', to use the words of Fishman (1987: 7).

As to the decreasing rate of loss of spoken French ability from the oldest to the youngest adults, we suggested above that it reflects age grading, namely gradual intra-individual linguistic erosion or deacquisition of spoken French competence probably affecting mostly those individuals who never reached full spoken French competence and who, when they became adults, did not have or seek opportunities to use or be exposed to the French language. On the other hand, it may also reflect a change in real time, there being proportionally fewer and fewer bilingual Franco-Ontarians who lose productive ability in French as one moves from the past to the present. This alternative explanation is also plausible given that in the past French-medium schooling was less available than today (see Chapter 3) and hence reacquisition of lost productive competence in French (see above) was less likely to occur. Only a study of age cohorts over several census periods could allow one to verify these two scenarios.

Table 2.5 also gives the results concerning the second measure of language shift, i.e. use of English as home language.[12] Note that it is an indirect measure

[11] However, it should be remembered that the 0–4 age group includes linguistically immature individuals (i.e. infants who have not yet learnt to speak their mother tongue). For purposes of classification, the Canadian census instructs parents to report such children as being able to speak the language most often spoken in the home. So it would be possible for the primary caretaker who speaks to the young infant in French but who lives in a home where English is the predominant language to report the young child to be of French mother tongue yet only capable of speaking English! Since we know that Franco-Ontarians frequently outmarry (see next section), this could explain in part why the 0–4 age group features a disproportionately high rate of loss of ability to speak French.

[12] Up until and including the 1981 census, if more than one language was used in the home, the one spoken most often was to be reported. This point is worth bearing in mind when considering the statistics on language shift in the home. Language choice in the home is not necessarily categorical in bilingual speech communities. In fact, the very existence of a sizeable proportion of French-mother-tongue Ontarians who claim also to have English as a mother tongue testifies to the frequency of Franco-Ontarian households in which both French and English must be spoken. In addition to altering the formulation of the mother-tongue question in 1986 so as to allow for the possibility of multiple responses, Statistics Canada did likewise as concerns the home-language question. Results just released reveal, as expected, that, out of a total of 391,320 French-mother-tongue Ontarians who maintained French at home in 1986, a substantial number (111,320 or 28.45 per cent) also used English.

of language shift, since it pertains to language disuse in a particular domain rather than loss of linguistic ability. Its relevance, though, resides in the fact that, if English language shift at home can be documented for the parental generations, it can then be inferred that French-language transmission to the replacement generations is being curtailed.

As the third column of Table 2.5 shows, a substantial proportion (34 per cent) of French-mother-tongue Ontarians reported using English as their (main) language of communication at home in 1981. (There were also an insignificant number—fewer than 0.5 per cent—who reported using a language other than English at home.) In 1971, the first year in which the Canadian census gathered information on home language use, the proportion of French-mother-tongue Ontarians using English at home was 27 per cent. Over the ten-year period 1971–81 the rate of English language shift at home therefore rose by 7 per cent.[13]

The breakdown by age groups reveals that the rates of home-language shift are significantly higher than average for the adults who are of prime child-rearing age (i.e. the 25–44 year-olds), approaching the 50 per cent level for the 40–4 age group, a finding which does not augur well for the prospect of French-language maintenance in Ontario (see further in this section). Furthermore, this pattern is in line with the one found for the rate of bilingualism across age groups (see Table 2.3). So, unlike the phenomenon of loss of productive skills in French, English home-language shift is pegged to the rate of bilingualism. This would seem to give credence to Lieberson's contention (1972) that the rate of bilingualism of a minority group is a sensitive indicator of the risk of a shift (here home-language shift). It would be interesting to see whether other studies confirm the poor predictive value of rate of bilingualism as concerns the other type of shift examined here, i.e. loss of productive skills in the minority language.

One thing needs to be made clear about these rates of English home-language shift. Some individuals have no real choice as to home language, for the simple reason that they are not bilingual. Thus the 12 per cent of French-mother-tongue individuals who do not know English well enough to hold a conversation obviously cannot shift to that language at home. Neither can the 4 per cent of French-mother-tongue individuals who have lost the ability to speak French continue to use this language at home. Thus another calculation

---

[13] Again, on the basis of the 1986 census, an ardent supporter of French in Ontario might think he had cause to rejoice, seeing that the rate of English home-language shift (28 per cent) has in appearance reverted to near-1971 levels. However, since the data from the 1986 census are not strictly comparable with the data from the previous censuses, it is more prudent to abstain from making such comparisons, unless an adjustment is made to the 1986 French home-language maintenance figure. The adjusted figure calculated by Statistics Canada stands at 340,545 (down from 391,320—see n. 12), which translates into an English home-language shift rate of 37 per cent. This is 3 per cent higher than the 1981 rate, and in line with the rising trend noted previously for the period 1971–81.

of the rate of English language shift at home could focus on the bilingual portion of the French-mother-tongue population. The rates obtained by performing this calculation are given in the fourth column of Table 2.5. The only noteworthy differences between the new and old rates lie at the two extremes of the age spectrum. When one singles out the bilinguals, there are appreciably more Franco-Ontarians belonging to the youngest and oldest age groups who switch to English as their home language. Be that as it may, the interesting outcome of the measure of English home-language shift which is restricted to the bilingual portion of the Franco-Ontarian population is that it reveals a pattern which once again closely resembles the pattern of bilingualism by age group (see Table 2.3). Were bilingualism the only factor conditioning home-language shift, then factoring it out should have resulted in a flat pattern. That we do not get such a pattern can only be taken as an indication that there are other factors besides bilingualism contributing to home-language shift. One which leaps to mind and will be examined in detail in the following section is linguistic exogamy, which almost always translates into the adoption of English as home language. Suffice it to say here that French–English mixed marriages have two characteristics which are generally consistent with the curvilinear pattern of the 'corrected' rates of English home-language shift in the last column of Table 2.5: (1) they essentially apply only to the adult portion of the age spectrum (which would explain the lower rates for the children and adolescents), and (2) more and more Franco-Ontarians are entering into such marriages (which would account for the gradual rise in English home-language shift from the oldest adults to the middle-aged ones). Another factor which can be invoked for the lower rates of home-language shift found for the non-adult generations is that they are not at an age yet where they can exercise full freedom of language choice at home (see the next chapter on the language-use patterns of Franco-Ontarian students). There is also an additional explanation for the older francophone adults' lesser proclivity to shift to English at home. Extrapolating on the basis of the findings of Mougeon and Beniak (1989a) concerning Welland francophones, it may be surmised that the older Franco-Ontarian generations are less proficient in English than the younger ones, hence not as likely to abandon French, their stronger language, at home. (Again, one can only regret that the Canadian census question on bilingualism is not more precise.)

The 1981 census returns for the three minority communities under study also indicate substantial rates of English language shift at home among the French-mother-tongue population. The rates fall on either side of the provincial average: Pembroke (65 per cent), North Bay (42 per cent), and Cornwall (29 per cent). In contrast, the rate is only 4 per cent for the Hawkesbury francophones.[14] These rates are inversely proportional to the

[14] Rates which concern only the bilinguals cannot be provided for the four communities under study, nor can rates broken down by age group (for the reasons mentioned in n. 4).

degree of francophone concentration in each of the localities, which, it will be remembered, is respectively 8, 17, 35, and 85 per cent. In 1971 the rates of English language shift at home were lower: Pembroke (44 per cent), North Bay (37 per cent), and Cornwall (18 per cent).[15] The rates of English language shift at home, already important in 1971, have therefore increased to even higher levels in 1981 in the three minority communities, leaping by as much as 21 per cent in Pembroke, where well in excess of half the French-mother-tongue population now speaks English at home!

We said above that the abandonment of French at home by the parental generations boded ill for the long-term survival of this language in Ontario. It remains to examine to what extent English home-language shift does translate into an erosion of the French-mother-tongue population among the replacement generation. The best evidence that there is less than full transmission of French to the younger generations by Franco-Ontarian parents would be information on the mother tongue of their own offspring. Since Statistics Canada does not carry out such detailed cross-tabulations, we have to rely on various other bits of evidence. One is the recent drop in the size of the French-mother-tongue population (see Table 2.6). The decade 1971–81 marks the first time that the Franco-Ontarian population has declined in absolute numbers (by 6,435 or 1.3 per cent).[16] Whatever factors served to buttress and indeed to augment the French-mother-tongue population in the past (e.g. net gains through immigration, high birth-rate, etc.) are either no longer present or are insufficient to counterbalance the effects of English home-language shift.

When we look at what is going on at the local level (i.e. the four communities investigated), we see that the dwindling of the French-mother-tongue minority of Pembroke has reached alarming proportions, since there has been a 29 per cent drop in its size between 1971 and 1981, almost twice the rate of decline of the general population. Somewhat surprisingly, Cornwall is next, with a drop of 12 per cent of the French-mother-tongue group (six times the negative growth rate of the general population). According to the expectation we have come to have, i.e. a linear correlation with local francophone concentration, North Bay francophones should normally have shown the second highest negative growth, but in fact they have held their own. However, as we shall see

[15] These rates were calculated by dividing the French home-language population (unavailable for the town of Hawkesbury in 1971) by the French-mother-tongue population. This method of calculation (the only one feasible in 1971) is not as precise as that used for the 1981 data, the latter only taking into consideration, as should be, the French home-language population with French as its mother tongue. The margin of error is small, however, and amounts to a slight underestimation of the true rates of home-language shift for 1971.

[16] Previous to that, the Franco-Ontarian population was growing at a strong—albeit diminishing—rate. The French-mother-tongue population figure for 1971 (482,040) represented a 13.3 per cent increase over that of 1961 (425,302), which itself amounted to a 24.5 per cent increase over the 1951 figure of 341,502. We refrain from trying to determine the trend between 1981 and 1986 because of the previously mentioned problems of comparability of the French-mother-tongue data from these two censuses.

TABLE 2.6. *Evolution of the French-mother-tongue population of Ontario and the four localities under study between 1971 and 1981*

Province/ locality of residence	Total population				FMT population			
	1971	1981	Growth N	Growth %	1971	1981	Growth N	Growth %
Ontario	7,703,105	8,625,105	+922,000	+12	482,040	475,605	−6,435	−1
Pembroke	16,560	14,025	−2,535	−15	1,680	1,185	−495	−29
North Bay	49,185	51,270	+2,085	+4	8,535	8,545	+10	+0.1
Cornwall	47,225	46,145	−1,080	−2	18,165	15,965	−2,200	−12
Hawkesbury	9,380	9,880	+500	+5	7,955	8,355	+400	+5

Source: Statistics Canada, 1971 and 1981 censuses (100% data)

shortly, this should not be taken to mean that North Bay francophones are not undergoing assimilation. Their stability is only apparent. In this connection, it may be noted that, of the three localities including francophone minorities, North Bay is the only one whose population grew between 1971 and 1981, yet its francophone community did not grow nearly as fast as the general population. As to the Hawkesbury francophones, their numbers reveal a small but significant increase of 5 per cent.

Another indicator of shift is the drop in the proportion of French-mother-tongue individuals by age group (relative to the total population of the province/locality for each age group). Table 2.7 shows that, whereas 6.4 per cent of Ontarians belonging to the 35–9 age group were of French mother tongue in 1981, the same was true of only 4.3 per cent of the 0–4 age group, a drop of no less than one-third![17] Conversely, we can mention that the proportion of English-mother-tongue individuals for the same two age groups went up from 73 per cent to 86 per cent. Of course, this increase has been at the

TABLE 2.7. *French-mother-tongue population by age group for Ontario and the four communities under study, relative to total population for each age group*

| Age group | % FMT relative to total population for each age group | | | | |
	Ontario	Pembroke	North Bay	Cornwall	Hawkesbury
0–4	4.3	1.9	12.2	27.0	87.7
5–9	4.4	4.1	12.2	29.2	87.7
10–14	4.6	5.5	12.4	31.6	87.0
15–19	5.3	4.6	14.1	32.8	86.5
20–4	5.6	7.8	16.7	32.4	85.3
25–9	5.8	9.7	17.0	33.4	86.8
30–4	5.7	9.5	17.6	35.2	83.6
35–9	6.4	10.6	19.2	37.6	79.8
40–4	6.3	10.5	19.7	38.7	83.3
45–9	6.3	10.0	20.0	38.0	84.0
50–4	6.1	13.4	20.8	40.4	79.6
55–9	5.7	13.2	18.0	38.0	83.5
60–4	5.8	10.1	18.6	39.9	84.7
65+	5.1	9.9	20.3	36.5	82.1
All ages	5.5	8.4	16.7	34.6	84.6

Source: Statistics Canada, 1981 census (100% data)

[17] We would like to thank Marielle Tétreault of the Ontario Ministry of Citizenship and Culture for permission to consult the Ministry's Ethnocultural Data Base. Table 2.7 is based on information extracted from this data base, which consists of special cross-tabulations of the 1981 census data.

expense not only of Franco-Ontarians but also of the non-official language groups.

In the three francophone minority communities we have an even better illustration of the impact of home-language shift on the proportion of French-mother-tongue individuals among the younger generations. For instance in Pembroke, over an age range of fifty years, the ratio of French-mother-tongue individuals has plunged from more than one in seven (13.4 per cent for the 50–4 age group) to less than one in fifty (1.9 per cent for the 0–4 age group). Language contraction has now been going on so long in Pembroke that the situation is on the verge of slipping into the next phase, language death, since practically no children are acquiring the language anymore. Similar but less dramatic decreases are observable through the age groups in North Bay and Cornwall. This is in sharp contrast to the majority francophone community of Hawkesbury, where there is even evidence of a slight but steady increase in the proportion of French-mother-tongue individuals from the older to the younger generations, and this despite the fact that, as we saw earlier, 4 per cent of Hawkesbury's French-mother-tongue population has shifted to English at home. It is the town's English-speaking minority that is losing more members than it is gaining![18]

In sum, to answer an earlier question, the advanced societal bilingualism found among Franco-Ontarians is indeed accompanied by language shift. The intergenerational pattern of shift we have uncovered for Franco-Ontarians is quite like that which has been observed with regard to contracting or threatened linguistic groups elsewhere: the replacement generation is not handed down the minority language in the home. Indeed, as Fasold (1984: 216–17) has been able to assert on the basis of his survey of the literature: 'Almost all cases of societal language shift come about through intergenerational switching ... In other words, a substantial proportion of the individuals in a society seldom completely give up the use of one language and substitute another within their own lifetime. In the typical case, one generation is bilingual, but only passes on one of the two languages to the next.'

2.5. Causes of shift

Language shift is not an all-or-nothing phenomenon. There may be conflicting tendencies within a minority speech community, for instance shift in some homes but maintenance in others, loss of skills by certain individuals but not others, etc. We shall say that a minority speech community is shifting only if a *significant* number of its members are; we shall say that it is maintaining itself if the number of shifting speakers is too low to pose a threat to the language (see

---

[18] The proportion of English-mother-tongue individuals drops from a high of 15.8 per cent for the 65+ age group to a low of 10.7 per cent for the 0–4 age group.

Muysken 1984: 54–8 who distinguishes stable bilingualism from language shift on the basis of similar criteria). According to these definitions, and in view of the evidence adduced in the preceding section, a shift towards English is definitely under way in the Franco-Ontarian community as a whole and in the three minority francophone communities of Pembroke, North Bay, and Cornwall, but not in Hawkesbury.

Let us now examine some of the primary causes or conditions—in addition to societal bilingualism—of shift to English in the Franco-Ontarian community, here meaning home-language switch and corresponding failure to transmit French to the future generations.

First, the census data reviewed in the previous section brought out the obvious connection which exists between the local level of francophone concentration and shift. Where Franco-Ontarians are in the minority locally, they are undergoing losses at the hands of the English-speaking majority; where they are in the strong majority, they are, on the contrary, gaining at the expense of the English-speaking minority.[19] One explanation which can be proposed for this correlation is that demographic concentration conditions the extent to which francophones are able to create a French environment for themselves, e.g. develop a separate economic base, use French in the local institutions, interact with other francophones, etc. In other words, in communities where francophones are only a small group, French correspondingly rates low on the status and usefulness scales and may therefore be perceived as not worth transmitting, especially if there has been a partial loss of skills as a result of insufficient opportunities to hear and use French. Having said this, it should be pointed out that local francophone concentration is not a perfect predictor of the *rate* of English language shift. There are several Franco-Ontarian communities which exhibit rates of English language shift which are lower than expected for the local level of francophone concentration. A number of community studies have discussed some factors which may counteract the impact of low francophone concentration. For instance, Lamy (1977) attributed the low rate of English home-language shift found for Ottawa francophones (19 per cent of the city population) to: (1) its status as a national capital, a fact which means that there are proportionally more institutions which function in French in Ottawa than in other cities of similar francophone concentration, thereby providing services and jobs for francophones; (2) its location on the Ontario–Quebec border, so that, for instance, Ottawa francophones have easy access to the Quebec French-language media and contact with Quebec francophones; and (3) the steady inflow of francophones into the community over the last decades. In a similar vein, Mougeon and Hébrard

[19] Just how strong the local francophone population has to be in order to stave off assimilation is an open question. We have not yet had the opportunity to conduct sociological surveys in Ontarian localities where francophones form weaker majorities than in Hawkesbury (or, for that matter, stronger minorities than in Cornwall).

(1975) attributed the unexpectedly high rate of French-language maintenance at home found for Welland francophones (17 per cent of the city population) to: (1) the recency of French settlement, (2) the geographical concentration of francophones in the city, and (3) strong participation in the local French-Canadian socio-cultural organizations. Finally, Maxwell (1977) pointed out that the higher-than-expected level of French-language maintenance at home for Toronto (a city in which francophones make up less than 2 per cent of the population) may be attributed to the fact that francophones have moved steadily into that city over the last decades.

Second, Franco-Ontarians are lagging behind Anglo-Ontarians as concerns levels of income (Allaire and Toulouse 1973; D'Costa 1972; Fédération des francophones hors Québec 1978). With few exceptions, English is the language used in the employment domain. It should not be forgotten that the historical motivation behind the emigration of francophones from Quebec to Ontario was essentially socio-economic. Earning a living was uppermost in the minds of these French-speaking emigrants. Maintenance of the old language and culture in the new setting, if it was perceived at all as a potential problem, was one they would deal with when the time came. Many of these adult emigrants experienced considerable personal frustration at work and in the local public institutions as a result of their poor skills in English. Understandably, they made sure that their children learned and mastered the new language, even if it meant using English in the home. To quote Le Blanc (1988: 24): 'parents who belong to the minority group consider it vital for their children to master the language of the majority. In their opinion, the children absolutely must be bilingual because their survival depends on it. This is especially true for unilingual Francophones who moved to Northern Ontario or the West. Given the difficulties they encountered as a result of their unilingualism, it is hardly surprising that they determined that their children would master English.'

Third, the influence of the Catholic Church on Franco-Ontarians is declining and so is the Church's involvement in the fight for the preservation of the French language (Welch 1988). This factor is by no means negligible, since the Catholic Church has long been rightly regarded as a bastion of the French language in Ontario and elsewhere in Canada. As Welch (1988: 279–80) explains:

The past strength of the Church could be traced to a number of factors. The Catholic faith as seen and practiced until the late 1950s in French Canada gave the Church enormous prestige and legitimacy, since it was the sole definer of faith and morals. Second, the Church remained the main dispenser of social services within French speaking Ontario, reinforcing in a very material way its links with the people as well as their dependency on these same institutions. Congregations of nuns had founded French language hospitals, orphanages, social services as well as schools across the province, fulfilling a role the state was only beginning to take in hand. Third, since the 19th century, the French Canadian Catholic Church outside Québec had been leading the defense of the language and cultural rights of the French Canadian minorities. Finally, all of the above factors together established the Church as the main ideological definer of French Canadian identity in French Canada . . .

Fourth, in recent decades Franco-Ontarians from the north and central regions, and to a smaller extent from the east, have been migrating to the central and south-western industrial urban centres. This did not pose an immediate threat to the maintenance of their language and culture, since, as Welch (1988: 119) writes, they were often able to reconstitute the strong patterns of community life which they had established in their regions of origin: 'The French Canadians not only adapted themselves to urban life but also adapted urban life to their own culture. They tended to emigrate to the city as a family unit and settle in homogeneous neighbourhoods, close to kin and other French Canadians.'

In time, though, the much more intensive contacts with the anglophone population which the urban setting afforded and the residential dispersion which came with social mobility served to weaken progressively these initially homogeneous, French-speaking, working-class, inner-city communities.

Summing up, migration with consequent 'minoritization' and subordination, industrialization, urbanization, secularization, etc. are the very same primary causes which have been identified in most situations of language shift (see Fasold 1984: 217). Yet we are in agreement with Castonguay (1979) that, while together they constitute a favourable climate for shift to English on the part of Franco-Ontarians, they do not afford an insight into the *process* of language shift. In what follows we will try to unravel what may well be the most important mediating factor in shift as it operates in the Franco-Ontarian setting. As Castonguay (1979: 23) explains: 'If the interaction between these primary causes and language shift can be relatively difficult to determine, there is, however, a phenomenon which can be easily quantified and which can be conceived as exercising as it were a mediating role between these primary causes and their result. This is the linguistically heterogeneous or *heterolinguistic* marriage, contracted between persons of different mother tongues.' (Our translation from the French original.)

In order to gain a better understanding of the process of shift to English among Franco-Ontarians, we therefore need to examine above all what goes on in the primary domain of transmission of French, namely the home. We saw earlier in Table 2.5 that a substantial and growing proportion of the adult French-mother-tongue population has shifted to English in the home. What might have led them to make such a switch over and above the general causes enumerated above? An answer emerges from a detailed study of Franco-Ontarians who were married and living with their spouse in 1971 (Castonguay 1979).

Relying on specially requested data derived from the 1971 census, Castonguay was able to calculate rates of English home-language shift separately for

Franco-Ontarians who had outmarried and for those who had not. He found that in nine out of ten French–English mixed marriages in Ontario (90.1 per cent), the French-speaking spouse used English as his/her main language of communication at home. In contrast, only one in six endogamous French couples (16.4 per cent) was found to use English as the main home language. Castonguay inferred from these results that the children of mixed couples who used English as their main home language would not be transmitted French.[20]

It appears clearly, then, that mixed marriages have a stong negative impact on French-language transmission at home. But, in order to prove that they constitute a major threat to the maintenance of French in Ontario, we have to assess whether they are a sociological phenomenon to be reckoned with. Castonguay showed that they are becoming just that, since their proportion has steadily risen over the decades. In 1971, whereas only 17 per cent of francophones who were aged 65+ and married had an anglophone spouse, the proportion was up to 35.5 per cent for the 15–24 age group.[21] Thus it seems that fewer and fewer Franco-Ontarians of nuptial age are seeking one another out on the matrimonial market. To arrive at a true estimate of the impact of mixed marriages, Castonguay actually measured, by age group, what proportion of the total Franco-Ontarian population who had shifted to English at home were accounted for by linguistically exogamous francophones. The results were as follows: 15–24 (34.6 per cent), 25–34 (67.8 per cent), 35–44 (59.6 per cent), 45–54 (55.2 per cent), 55–64 (46.3 per cent), 65+ (27.8 per cent).[22] Here too we note a steady rise in the proportion from the oldest to the youngest adults. The conclusion is inescapable: mixed marriages are playing an increasingly important role in language shift among Franco-Ontarians by drastically curtailing the transmission of French to the replacement generation. Castonguay concluded

[20] While this inference is quite reasonable, it must be remembered that the declaration of home language is based on an overall evaluation of the frequency of use of (in this case) English or French at home by the respondent to the census questionnaire. If the focus were just on the language use of the parents with their children, there would perhaps be a somewhat less gloomy picture of the transmission of French in mixed marriages, i.e. we might find that some francophone parents in mixed marriages make a special effort to speak French to their children (we shall examine this possibility in Chapter 4).

[21] The frequency of French–English mixed marriages can be related to the fact that there are no real barriers—linguistic, racial, religious, or otherwise—to exogamy. Franco-Ontarians who have achieved native-like proficiency in English are virtually indistinguishable from 'true' anglophones. They are not a visible minority. And the waning influence of the Catholic Church has opened the floodgates, so to speak, to mixed marriages, whereas formerly they were frowned upon because of the threat that they posed not only to the French language but also and perhaps more importantly to the Catholic faith (for they were usually mixed in terms of religion as well, i.e. Catholic–Protestant). Even religion is no longer a barrier, as the Catholic population of Ontario has increased considerably over the last decades with the immigration of various peoples from Europe who belong to this faith, so that francophones who outmarry no longer run the same risk of 'losing their faith' as a result.

[22] The dip observable for the 15–24 age group—seemingly paradoxical given that this is the age group which exhibits the highest rate of linguistically exogamous marriages (i.e. 35.5 per cent as indicated above)—is simply due to the fact that the majority had yet to enter into wedlock.

his study on this dire note (1979: 31): 'To the extent that linguistically mixed marriages . . . will continue to initiate or confirm the almost universal preponderance of English as the home language of the francophone spouse and, consequently, as the mother tongue of his/her children, it has to be acknowledged that, with a rate of linguistic exogamy . . . of more than one-third among the youngest generation, Franco-Ontarians seem already . . . to have gone beyond the point of no return.' (Our translation from the French original.)

However important the role of linguistic exogamy is in English language shift, we should not lose sight of the fact that it is one of mediation or catalysis (a fact acknowledged by Castonguay himself), since shift also takes place in homogeneous marriages, as we have seen. In fact, the more one goes back in time, the more English language shift at home was taking place primarily within non-mixed couples. Remember that only 27.8 per cent of the 65+ francophones who had shifted to English at home formed mixed marriages. This would seem to underline the importance of the general conditions favourable to language shift which we reviewed above. We see no reason why they would not also play a part in the process of shift as it operates in mixed marriages. By this we mean that there are no doubt linguistically exogamous francophones who base their decision to switch to English at home partly on an assessment of the instrumental value of French, of their own socio-economic position, of their skills in French, etc., rather than solely on the need to accommodate a unilingual anglophone partner—not to mention those francophones who, for the same reasons, switch to English prior to outmarrying. When the home does not transmit the language, the burden of linguistic reproduction shifts to institutions like the school.

2.6. Conclusion

The Franco-Ontarian community's transition from monolingualism to bilingualism is to be seen as a useful and probably inevitable adaptation to the surrounding English-speaking environment, since it allows better integration into it, a reality which Franco-Ontarians readily acknowledge themselves, as we saw above. Given that they emigrated to their new host environment out of a desire to improve their lot in life, that they relocated in localities where French often does not rank high on prestige, usefulness, and visibility, and that in such conditions it is difficult to maintain high levels of skills in French, it is perhaps not hard to understand why some go one step further and do not transmit French to their children, all the more if they enter into a linguistically mixed marriage.

Yet there are those investigators who, like Fasold (1984: Chapter 8), would claim that, no matter what are the conditions that can be associated with a language shift in a given minority speech community, it is almost always possible to cite the example of some other linguistic minority which, under essentially the same sociolinguistic conditions, has *not* accomplished a shift.[23] These researchers believe that language shift will happen only to the extent that the minority lets it or desires it. Shift will take its course only if and when the minority no longer wishes to be seen as a distinct socio-cultural collectivity. If that is the case, then one of the surest signs of shift would be evidence that the minority is indeed no longer attempting to set itself off from the majority by preserving and cultivating its own identity. And this brings us back to linguistic exogamy, which, in the Franco-Ontarian setting, is not only a major mediating factor in the shift to English, as we have seen, but also a tell-tale 'manifestation of a collective predisposition towards cultural mutation' to use Castonguay's (1979: 31) words (our translation from the French original).

One final point before moving on to the next chapter. Theoretically at least, language shift is not necessarily an inexorable process, especially where it is slow and gradual as opposed to sudden and rapid (a crucial distinction made by Mertz 1989). The particular set of sociolinguistic conditions which lead a minority community to start adopting the majority language at the expense of its own may change over time and possibly trigger a reversal back to a process of maintenance (see Fishman, Gertner, Lowy, and Milan 1985 on 'ethnic' revival). The next chapter will show that French in Ontario is moving into new and important domains and expanding its presence in other domains into which it had already partially spread. This makes the long-range prediction of the fate of French in Ontario rather risky indeed. In fact, there is probably reason for at least guarded optimism. Nancy C. Dorian (p.c.) once reminded us of the fact that French is not at all 'your average minority language'. This is so true that we tend to take it for granted. Indeed, even though French is a minority language in Ontario and in Canada as a whole, none the less it is an international language which comes second only to English in importance and is widely learned as a second language in and outside Canada, it is one of the two official languages of the country—a first-world nation—and may well soon achieve the same status in Ontario (see next chapter), and it is the majority and sole official language of the neighbouring province of Quebec. In other words, there are a number of higher-order factors which confer significant status to the French language in Canada and make it a 'permissible' language for transmission purposes. These broad positive factors have probably been responsible in part for the gradual nature of shift to English among Franco-Ontarians and could be capitalized upon with a view to turning the tide of assimilation.

---

[23] Fasold may have overstated his case, since it is probably hard to identify *true* examples of stable bilingualism in situations where a good many of the conditions for language shift obtain (Muysken 1984: 56). It may be more than coincidental, then, that Fasold, in his chapter, fails repeatedly to mention explicitly even one minority community exhibiting stable bilingualism under adverse sociolinguistic conditions, while he has no problems providing examples of minority communities that are shifting or have shifted under the same conditions.

3

French-language Spread

THE overall tone of the preceding chapter was admittedly pessimistic. It is time now that we took a look at a different and more optimistic side of the situation of French in Ontario. Indeed, a number of primary causes traditionally invoked to explain language shift do not obtain in the case of the Franco-Ontarian minority. Probably foremost among these is the language of education (but there are also the mass media, community organizations, and government services). Most linguistic minorities around the world do not enjoy the privilege of having elementary and secondary schools in their own language, but Franco-Ontarians do. According to Fishman (1987), the elementary school ranks with the other 'primary determinants of intergenerational language transmission' that are the home and neighbourhood. Franco-Ontarians, conscious of the difficulty of maintaining their language and culture in Ontario, have always considered that their schools should play a central role in preventing assimilation. It will be instructive, therefore, to trace the development of French-language education in Ontario during the nineteenth and twentieth centuries, and to discuss the problems and challenges it faces currently in helping to keep alive the French language and culture in this province. In so doing, we shall help to publicize a still relatively poorly known form of French-medium education in Canada and contribute to the dissemination of much-needed information, on the basis of which more realistic and socially responsive programmes of minority-language education may be established.[1]

We shall also take a brief look at the expansion of French into the other above-mentioned institutions or domains. The chapter will end with a discussion of the seemingly paradoxical co-occurrence of English language shift on the one hand and French-language expansion on the other, and go on to give a glimpse of some of the possibilities of further French-language expansion.

3.1. French-language schooling in Ontario

3.1.1. History

As pointed out in the preceding chapter, the arrival of significant numbers of francophones in Ontario dates back to about 1840. From that time to the end of the nineteenth century Franco-Ontarians were allowed to set up their own

---

[1] The section on Ontario's French-language schools is based on Mougeon and Heller (1986).

elementary schools. In such schools the children were taught in French and received instruction in the Catholic faith. These schools were part of the system of 'Separate' schools which was in place in Ontario at the time and which also provided education in English for the benefit of the English-speaking Catholic community. In addition to the system of Separate schools, there was a system of English-language public schools, which served the educational needs of Ontario's non-Catholic population. Both school systems (public and Separate, i.e. Catholic) were financially supported by the provincial government. Education in French at the secondary level was also available, but only in a small number of schools. These were private institutions run by the Catholic Church. From the end of the nineteenth century to 1915 the principle of French-language schooling came increasingly under attack. These attacks were to a large extent a reaction to a sharp increase in the influx of francophone Catholics from Quebec, which took place towards the end of the nineteenth century and which was then viewed by some as a threat to the survival of the 'English Protestant race' in Upper Canada (now Ontario). The offensive against French-language schooling culminated in its almost complete abolishment in 1915 by an act of the provincial legislature. The implementation of this law (the infamous Regulation XVII) triggered a movement of resistance among the francophone population. Resistance to the act took two main forms: (1) a challenge of its legality on the basis of Canada's constitution (the British North America Act[2]), and (2) the establishment of parallel schools supported by parochial funds and by donations from Quebec organizations (including the Quebec government). The resistance movement won a major victory when the act was abrogated in 1927. After 1927 it became possible again to school francophone students in their mother tongue in the elementary Catholic schools of Ontario. Such schools continued to be supported by provincial funds. However, they tended to receive fewer funds than the majority public schools. Schooling in French in the Catholic high schools was allowed and supported by public monies up to grade 10 (again, the amount of financial support received by such schools was less than that received by their public counterparts); from grades 11 to 13 (the end of the secondary cycle), parents had to pay for the education of their children. Because they received comparatively fewer funds, and because they functioned as private institutions in the upper grades,[3] the French-language Catholic high schools failed to attract a significant portion of the francophone students who had been schooled in the French-language Catholic elementary schools. Such failure may also be attributed to

[2] The judiciary committee of the Privy Council in London, which acted as Canada's supreme court, examined the constitutionality of the provincial act. It concluded that the abolishment of French-language schooling by the Ontario legislature was not unconstitutional since the BNA only guaranteed the principle of instruction in the Catholic faith and not in the French language.
[3] It should be noted that the same was true for English Catholic schools, but, since the francophone population was (and is) relatively less well off, this presented more of a problem for francophone than for anglophone Catholics.

the fact that not all Franco-Ontarian parents endorsed the principle of French-language schooling at the secondary level. Those parents were probably sensitive to the fact that post-secondary education and the job market in Ontario were dominated by English, and therefore were convinced of the necessity that their children receive their high-school education in the majority language.[4] In any case, before 1968 (the second major turning-point in the history of French-language schooling in Ontario), there were proportionally fewer Franco-Ontarian students than Anglo-Ontarian students who continued their studies beyond grade 10, and many of the Franco-Ontarian students who did so were sent to English-language high schools, in which they may have experienced the problems and frustrations of educational and linguistic submersion.

The history of French-language post-secondary education can be briefly summarized as follows. Before the 1960s some measure of French-language post-secondary education (up to the BA level) was available in a number of private 'classical colleges' run by the Catholic Church. In the late 1960s, many of these colleges either disappeared or were replaced by public community colleges when provincially funded university education expanded. In the 1960s two of these classical colleges, one in Sudbury and one in Ottawa, were incorporated respectively in the University of Sudbury (Laurentian) and the University of Ottawa. These two institutions are the only post-secondary establishments which provide education through the medium of French beyond the bachelor's degree. The University of Ottawa offers most of its programmes in French (as well as in English). Sudbury's Laurentian University, however, offers only a limited number of courses in French.

The 1960s were a period of major change in Canada as concerns the status of minority-language rights and services. The fundamental social and economic reasons for this change are too complex to go into here, but have to do with a strengthening of francophone power bases in Quebec (see Clift and Arnopoulos 1979; Heller 1982; Wade 1968, for more detailed discussion of this historical development). The most visible effect of this change was the reassessment of francophone rights by the federal government, resulting in a report which recommended increased government support for francophone institutions and services across the country (Government of Canada 1969). The federal funds made available as the government implemented the report's recommendations had the effect of provoking provincial-government reassessment of franco-phone services, since the provinces control the provision of services in many domains, such as education, while profiting from federal-government subsidies for those services. In Ontario, after 1968, significant increases and reforms were

---

[4] These explanations have been extrapolated 'retroactively' on the basis of attitudinal data gathered in a survey of groups of Franco-Ontarian parents from several localities representing the major regions of francophone concentration in the province (Chaperon-Lor 1974; see also Mougeon and Beniak 1989*a*).

implemented in the provision of a variety of French-language services, among others, in the area of education.

The reader will recall that the province did not provide funds for Catholic schools beyond grade 10, and that Franco-Ontarians wishing to study past that level had to switch either to English public high schools or to private Catholic colleges. One way for the provincial government to provide Franco-Ontarians access to subsidized French-medium secondary education would have been to extend public funding of Catholic schools beyond grade 10, a solution which this minority would have liked. At that time, however, the government did not think that the English Protestant population was ready for such a measure and feared that it would translate into the loss of electoral support. Therefore it decided to provide French-language secondary education through the public system. The main consequence of this reform was the widespread transfer of private Catholic French-language high schools to the public system, and an opening up of access to secondary and post-secondary education for francophones. As a result, francophone enrolment in secondary school programmes increased dramatically, although it stabilized in the mid-1970s at a level still somewhat lower than that of anglophones (Churchill, Quazi, and Frenette 1985). While these changes can certainly be looked upon as beneficial for the Franco-Ontarian community, they also entailed the cessation of the French Catholic Church's influence over secondary education, a development which was not welcomed by all community leaders and parents. There remained important restrictions on the provision of French-medium schooling, however, as eventually encoded in the Education Act of 1974. The first has to do with the provision that such schooling was to be made available 'where numbers warrant'. Such a restriction is often imposed on linguistic minorities (see Dorian 1981 for a parallel case in the Scottish Gaelic setting). It has, however, the unfortunate consequence of depriving linguistic-minority members of mother-tongue schooling in those settings where it is most badly needed. The second restriction has to do with the fact that French-language education continued to be provided within the existing school board structure. That is, French-language schools are part of Separate or public boards which, in most cases, are dominated by an English-speaking clientele (this is most true of the public boards). The result was that only a certain number of 'autonomous' (i.e. self-contained, free-standing) French-language high schools were set up, while in areas where the francophone population was small, no such schools were provided or compromises had to be worked out. They took one of three forms: (1) mixed schools, where francophones and anglophones, though administratively separate, are housed in the same building; (2) 'modules', or francophone sections in predominantly English schools; or (3) French 'classes' in English schools.[5] Unfortunately, as Churchill (1976) has pointed out, francophone

---

[5] One noteworthy consequence of the lack of direct control by francophones over French-language schools is that in fundamental ways French- and English-language education are now

students in mixed schools (and undoubtedly, *a fortiori*, in modules and classes; Heller and Swain 1985) tend to enrol in English-language courses, thereby defeating the purpose of the provision of French-language educational services. (The same phenomenon has been noted elsewhere; for example, in Yugoslavia, Hungarian students in Hungarian–Serbo-Croatian mixed schools often choose to enrol in Serbo-Croatian courses; Mikes, p.c.). Reasons for this have to do with the range of courses and services provided in the English section which are not available in the French section, and with the general economic attractiveness of the dominant language. In connection with this last point, it can be mentioned that, in those localities where a homogeneous French-language school and mixed school coexist, the latter type of school functions as an acceptable option for those francophone parents (usually of a working-class background) who fear that schooling in French at the secondary level will handicap their children's chances of obtaining better jobs.[6] For essentially the same reason, in communities where the 'mixed-school option' is not available, certain francophones (many being of working- or lower-middle-class background) have pushed (sometimes successfully, e.g. in the cities of Welland and North Bay) for the teaching of scientific and technical subjects in English at the secondary level. In so doing, they have met the resistance of other francophones (usually members of the local élite) who militate in favour of the maintenance of the French language and culture and who believe that, in a minority context, education in French in *all* subject matters is a minimum requirement for achieving such maintenance. Both homogeneous (i.e. 'autonomous') and mixed secondary schools tended in any case to draw their clientele from Catholic elementary schools, and in certain areas of the province, notably the south, they had to draw from a very large catchment area in order to establish a large enough student body. The decision to attend a French-language high school therefore meant shifting from Catholic to non-denominational education and often travelling long distances. Another limitation is that in most boards the provision of services (e.g. special education, guidance counselling, libraries, etc.) is calculated on the basis of numbers of students. French-language schools, as minority schools, necessarily have a lower enrolment than English-language schools, and therefore find themselves at a chronic disadvantage in terms of competing for the scarce resources allocated at the board level. On the other hand, where francophones are very much in the minority, being part of a larger board can mean access to

quite similar. While there are differences in the sources of teaching material (e.g. French-language schools tend to draw their material from Quebec), and in some course content (e.g. Franco-Ontarian history, French-language arts and literature), other aspects of curricula and of educational objectives, methods, and services are designed centrally.

[6] In those instances where francophone parents fought for the replacement of a mixed school by an autonomous French-language school, other francophone parents at the same time sided with the anglophone school-board members (i.e. those who pushed for the mixed-school approach in the first place) and fought against such replacement.

services and resources which, alone, the francophone schools would not be able to afford. As of 1984, then, French-language education was integrated into the government-funded school systems, and French-language schools formed part of regional boards organized on a Separate vs. non-denominational basis, each type of board containing, usually, both French- and English-language schools. Broadly speaking, most French-language elementary schools were to be found in Separate boards, although some French-language public schools were opened in the 1970s (especially in such urban areas as Ottawa and Toronto), while French-language secondary schools were to be found in public boards.

Very recently, certain changes in the legal framework of French-language minority education in Ontario have occurred which are having far-reaching consequences. In 1985 Franco-Ontarians obtained the right to French-medium instruction at the elementary and secondary levels irrespective of the size of the local francophone population. This means, for example, that, if the request for such instruction is made by only one parent, local school authorities must provide it or pay for transportation (and boarding if necessary) to a neighbouring school board with French-medium schools. In other words, the previous restriction of 'where numbers warrant' has been removed from the Education Act (Government of Ontario 1985). Second, it was also in 1985 that, capitalizing on their growing strength, the Catholic community (close to 36 per cent of the total Ontario population in 1981) finally succeeded in persuading the provincial government to take the historical step of extending the subsidization of Separate schools beyond grade 10. As a result, the last two or three years have witnessed a restructuring of Ontario's school system, characterized among other things by a painful shrinkage of the size and number of public high schools (due to pullouts of Catholic pupils) and a subsequent expansion of the system of Separate schools. As far as the French public high schools are concerned, in theory they could be fully absorbed by the new alternative Catholic high schools which are being established in many Franco-Ontarian communities, since nearly all of the students enrolled in the French public high schools are Catholic. However, in many instances the public schools have resisted absorption by their newly created Catholic counterparts, indeed rivals. The resistance seems to be concentrated among the public-school staff, who have come to appreciate the greater openness and freedom offered by public-school education and are unwilling to give it up, or who cannot be hired by the Catholic school system because of their moral beliefs, life-style, etc. (e.g. agnostic, divorced). This is another sign that the once strong influence of the Catholic Church on the Franco-Ontarian community is waning. In several communities the end result of this tug-of-war between the two education systems is a French public high school which has suffered student losses which are seriously affecting its viability and a French Catholic high school which is unable to reach a threshold of viability. The situation is hardly better at the

elementary level. The public elementary school system is under much pressure
to give up some of its vacant or underused school facilities to the expanding
Catholic school system which badly needs them, but it is showing stiff
resistance to the idea. In short, it is possible that French public schools will be
taken over by Separate boards, or that French public and Separate schools will
compete for clientele until one of them disappears or they reach a new
equilibrium. In some localities, community members are proposing innovative
administrative solutions, such as the sharing of facilities, while in others the
issue of linguistically defined boards with denominational and non-
denominational sectors has resurfaced (see conclusion).

The situation in the area of post-secondary education has not changed much
from what it was before 1968. At the moment there are still only two officially
bilingual universities in Ontario, the one in Ottawa and the one in Sudbury
(only the first one offers a wide range of French-medium courses). There is also
a smattering of French-medium course offerings in several other universities
and community colleges. The impact of this state of affairs on the population is
similar to that of the situation obtaining in secondary-level education before
1968, in that proportionately fewer francophones have access to university
studies (in either language) than do anglophones. Furthermore, there is an
impact on secondary-level education, in that francophones make choices
concerning the language of instruction and the domain of training at the
secondary level as a function of what is realistically available to them at the
post-secondary level. Those who wish to continue to study in French must
stream themselves into those areas of study where French-language university
programmes are available. Otherwise, preparation is better had in English
(with negative consequences such as higher drop-out rates due to the difficulty
of second-language study), or, in many cases, the pursuit of education at the
post-secondary level is forgone altogether. Finally, the subject areas in which
French-language university programmes are available tend to be among the
least economically rewarding (Churchill, Quazi, and Frenette 1985; Government of Ontario 1984).

In sum, the last two decades have seen a considerable consolidation and
expansion of French-medium instruction at the elementary and secondary
levels in Ontario. Although improvements still need to be made at the post-
secondary level, the Franco-Ontarian community can pride itself on having
achieved a level of success in the education sphere that would be the envy of
many a minority linguistic group, both within and without North America.

3.1.2. Student population and teaching objectives

In a survey of parents who send their children to Toronto's French-language
schools, Heller and Swain (1985) identified several groups of parents. In terms
of home language use, they identified parents who spoke French or mostly

French, parents who spoke English or mostly English, and parents who spoke another language. In terms of ethnic origin, they identified parents of French origin (Canadian born and non-Canadian born), parents of English origin (Canadian and non-Canadian born), and parents who were neither of French nor of English origin. As concerns marriage patterns, they found both linguistically homogeneous couples and linguistically heterogeneous ones. Within each of these two major categories, they identified several subgroups, namely marriages between francophones, marriages between anglophones, marriages between speakers of another language, marriages between an anglophone and a francophone, marriages between a francophone and a speaker of another language, and marriages between an anglophone and a speaker of another language. While Toronto represents an extreme example, the processes of language shift, intermarriage, and immigration which produced the heterogeneity described here have also affected the French-language school population of other communities (see Mougeon 1977 for Welland and Chapter 4 for Cornwall, North Bay, and Pembroke). The presence of such a heterogeneous clientele in schools which were originally set up to help Ontario's francophone minority maintain its language and culture is attributable to several factors.

First, although French-language schools were initially established to serve the educational needs of a francophone community which was largely monolingual, we saw that, as time passed, that community became more and more bilingual and exogamous, with the concomitant result that a non-negligible number of francophone parents tended to shift to English in the home. In spite of their having made such a shift, many of these parents decide to enrol their children in the French-language schools (see Cole 1975 for a similar contradiction between home language use and parental support for German-medium schooling in the Alsatian setting). Though no provincial data are available on their numbers as yet, the results of a survey carried out among Welland francophones (Mougeon 1977) provide an interesting glimpse of what the provincial situation might resemble. As expected, a very high proportion (95 per cent) of homogeneous French couples had enrolled their children in a French-medium school, but nearly half (44 per cent) of the heterogeneous French–English couples had done so as well! Obviously, linguistic accommodation between the partners in a French–English mixed marriage is much easier when what is at stake is the language of schooling rather than the language of the home. No research has yet been carried out to determine how mixed couples arrive at the choice of school language. Does the choice of French require arm-twisting on the part of the francophone parent? Or is the anglophone parent already convinced of the growing instrumental value of bilingualism in French in a province (and country) where this language is spreading more and more into what Fishman (1987) would label 'High' domains of society, such as higher education, government services, and the mass media (see section 3.2)? Another relevant question concerning children of mixed marriages who are schooled in French is what proficiency level they ultimately attain. The linguistic studies in this book will provide an answer to this question as concerns specifically grammatical and stylistic competence. In any case, it is clear that French-language schools are now faced with a new challenge, namely that of 'Frenchifying' the offspring of francophone parents who for one reason or another have given up using French in the home. However, not all Franco-Ontarian parents and educators see that as a goal that the French-language schools should pursue (see further in this section).

Second, immigration patterns are bringing to Ontario a wide variety of francophones from other Canadian provinces and from outside Canada, as well as groups whose second language is French and who speak no English. Finally, declining enrolments, or initially insufficient enrolments, in some of the more recently established French-language schools, caused these schools to open their doors to the children of anglophone couples or of couples who speak neither English nor French. Such parents tend to look upon the instruction provided in the French-language schools as a better alternative to the French-immersion programmes offered in the English-language schools.[7] Since bilingualism is becoming more important for social mobility in Canada, it is not surprising that French-language schools should be attractive to non-francophones, while at the same time, as we have seen earlier, some homogeneous Franco-Ontarian couples send their children to English-language schools. Although this may seem a paradox, we are reminded once again by Le Blanc (1988: 25) that, as concerns French-Canadian minorities, 'many parents who consider a knowledge of English essential to social mobility mistakenly believe that their children will be more educated if they study entirely, or at least half the time, in English'.

The presence of children raised in non-French-speaking homes in the French-language schools is viewed by many Franco-Ontarian educators as a major educational problem. It is thought that these English-dominant students have a retarding effect on the learning of French and of other subject matters by the French-dominant or by the balanced bilingual students, the other two major categories of students (in terms of bilingual competence) present in the French-language schools (Desjarlais, Cyr, Brûlé, and Gauthier 1980). This perception explains why in recent years Franco-Ontarian educators have developed two different curricular approaches to cope with this problem. The first one consists of *classes d'accueil*, i.e. special immersion classes (usually set up

---

[7] French-immersion education is a form of bilingual (i.e. French- and English-medium) schooling for the children of the English-speaking majority in Canada (see Swain and Lapkin 1982 for more details on this well-publicized approach to the teaching of French as a second language in Canada). As concerns the involvement of anglophone parents in the establishment of certain French-language schools (notably in Toronto and Ottawa), in all fairness it should be pointed out that in several localities these parents played a key role, since francophone support for such schools was initially low. Motivation on the part of these anglophones is partly instrumental and partly derived from an ideological commitment to minority rights.

in the lower grades) in which the English-dominant students are grouped separately, and whose teacher benefits from the added help of a part-time French-language instructor. As a rule, the English-dominant students are enrolled in the *classes d'accueil* for one or two years (sometimes more), after which they are mainstreamed into the regular classes. The second approach consists of the provision of special remedial French-language instruction (*cours de refrancisation*) to the English-dominant students. The duration and frequency of these remedial classes vary from one school board to another. Not all French-language schools, however, have adopted the approaches described above. In fact, in their provincial survey, Mougeon, Bélanger, Heller, and Canale (1984) discovered that the majority of Ontario's French-language schools did not include any special programme designed to cope with the problem of the English-dominant students. Most of the schools which adopt this 'unstreamed' approach are to be found in areas where francophones represent either a strong majority or a very weak minority of the population. In localities where francophones are a strong majority, the problem is simply not as critical, and so there is less need for an institutional response. In areas where francophones form only a weak minority, the problem is felt to be acute, since the French-language schools include proportionately more English-dominant students than French-dominant ones. In such communities the parents of French-dominant students tend to favour the *classe d'accueil* approach, since it temporarily curtails large-scale peer-group exposure to non-native French or to English on the part of their children. The parents of the English-dominant students, on the other hand, are generally not in favour of *classes d'accueil*, since they deprive their offspring of peer-group exposure to native French. It was this potential for such exposure that led many of them to enrol their children in French-language schools rather than in the French-immersion programmes of the English-language schools in the first place. The fact that these parents are in the majority probably explains why, in weak francophone communities, unstreamed classes prevail.

To summarize this section, changes in the sociological and demographic make-up of Ontario's francophone community which have taken place over the last fifty years or so, in conjunction with changes in the status of French-language education, have had a major impact on the composition of the clientele of Ontario's French-language schools and consequently on various aspects of the educational policy of such schools. In short, schools which were initially designed to serve the need of a primarily monolingual francophone population are now increasingly faced with the problems of a linguistically and culturally heterogeneous student population and of conflicting parental aspirations and priorities. It remains to be seen whether schools are able to achieve their goal of French-language maintenance among this heterogeneous population. In the sections that follow we shall examine students' patterns of language use outside and inside the school, and their proficiency in French and English.

3.1.3. Language-use patterns

We shall focus on the language-use patterns of Franco-Ontarian students in areas of medium-to-low francophone concentration (less than 50 per cent of the local population), that is, areas which are most affected by the heterogeneity described above.

As concerns language use outside the school, Heller and Swain (1985) in their survey of Toronto French schools, and Mougeon (1984) and Mougeon, Brent-Palmer, Bélanger, and Cichocki (1982) in a survey of seven francophone minority communities in Ontario (including Cornwall, North Bay, and Pembroke), found that the student population of the French-language schools was made up of three main categories according to their language-use patterns with various interlocutors (i.e. parents, siblings, and friends) in the two important domains of the home and neighbourhood. The three main groups were: (1) students who are frequent users of French, and consequently infrequent users of English, at least in the home but only to a varying extent in the neighbourhood;[8] (2) students who use French and English more or less equally in both these settings; and (3) students who are predominant users of English in both settings. As concerns the home setting, it was found that, while relatively high proportions of students used French often to communicate with their parents, considerably fewer students did so with their siblings, and even fewer with their friends. This kind of finding, illustrating the influence which the wider sociolinguistic environment exerts on the younger generations of linguistic minorities, has often been reported in studies of language maintenance/shift (see Williamson and Van Eerde 1980 for a summary of such studies). Furthermore, Heller (1984) and Mougeon, Brent-Palmer, Bélanger, and Cichocki (1982) found that use of English by the students in the home and neighbourhood increased significantly with age. This finding may be attributed to the fact that, as students get older, their networks expand into the wider community and their parents exert less of an influence on their behaviour (linguistic or other). Again, this finding is well in line with similar findings reported in studies devoted to minority-language retention/abandonment (Williamson and Van Eerde 1980). This pattern of incremental use of English is also in keeping with the age grading in the acquisition of bilingualism which we noted when examining the census data on bilingualism (see Table 2.3). Further along this line, the survey by Mougeon, Brent-Palmer, Bélanger, and Cichocki (1982) revealed that, in the weaker francophone minorities, the predominant users of English with peer-group members actually outnumbered (and by far) the other two categories of students.

Very few studies have systematically examined Franco-Ontarian students'

[8] More specifically, it was found that the extent to which the students used French in the neighbourhood was a function of the local level of francophone concentration (i.e. only in the stronger minorities did the students make any extensive use of French in the neighbourhood).

language-use patterns in the schools. Recent ethnographic studies (Heller 1984; Heller 1989; Heller and Swain 1985) provide one source of data for Toronto; another study (Canale, Mougeon, Heller, and Bélanger 1987) provides data for kindergarten and first-grade students in Ottawa and Cornwall. Generally speaking, these studies show that opportunities for use of French outside school (i.e. at home, in the community, and elsewhere) have a significant impact on students' use of French inside the school milieu. In other words, the extent to which French represents a language which is useful for a variety of authentic activities outside the confines of the school, and is not merely associated with the authority figures which parents and teachers represent, is directly related to students' identification with and use of the language in the school. More specifically, this ethnographic research revealed that the students' language choices in school are directly related to their integration into primarily English- or French-speaking networks inside and outside school.

As we have seen, students can be grouped into three categories according to their preferred modes of language use outside the school: French, English, or both.[9] The latter two categories of students tend to prefer to speak English amongst themselves at school, although those who are at ease in both languages will speak French to teachers, students, or other individuals who are known to be more comfortable in French. Indeed, the students who are comfortable in French and English may act as brokers for their less French-proficient peers, translating or explaining for them, since otherwise they have difficulty gaining access to and participating in activities (mainly classroom activities) where the only language used is French. More generally, the students who are at ease in both languages have been observed to engage in 'special purpose' (as opposed to 'smooth') code-switching (see Poplack 1985 on the use of these labels) in situations of linguistic conflict, i.e. where the norms of language choice clash, as when, for instance, they have to communicate with their teachers (authority figures who must be spoken to in French) in the presence of peers with whom they would naturally communicate in English (e.g. side comments geared to the class while making an oral presentation in French, talking back to the teacher in English, etc.). According to Heller (1989),

---

[9] Predominant users of French tend to have spent most of their lives in a majority francophone area (such as Quebec or France) and to be very recently arrived in Toronto. Many arrive unable to speak any English at all. As indicated above, these students form part of recent and ongoing migration trends. Students who use French and English roughly equally may be of a variety of backgrounds: they may be of French or mixed origin, but have lived for most of their lives in a predominantly English-speaking milieu; they may be of non-francophone background, but have attended French-language schools for many years, and may have contacts with francophones outside the English milieu in which they live (e.g. time spent in a French-majority area due to parents' occupation). Predominant users of English may have received some education in French, but the majority of their contacts outside school are in English. The vast majority are of mixed or non-francophone background (see earlier section 3.1.2 regarding the presence of children of anglophone couples in the French-language schools).

such switches are the bilinguals' way of coping with the conflict which they perceive between their own dual-linguistic identity and the school as a setting which enforces the use of French. This behaviour can be interpreted as a particular instance of the more general phenomenon of linguistic divergence which is also observable in monolingual settings. A particularly appropriate parallel to the Franco-Ontarian case is mentioned by Beebe (1988: 63): 'Adolescents frequently fail to converge toward the more standard language of their parents and teachers, especially in the presence of their peers. Thus, a black teenager in class may use nonstandard Black English and incur the disapproval of the teacher simply because this cost is outweighed by the reward of gaining approval from other students in the room who prefer to use Black English.'

3.1.4. Language proficiency

We have seen in the preceding section that French-language schools are unable to ensure that all the students communicate in French inside the school context, let alone in the neighbourhood and in the home (such use being largely determined by wider demographic and sociological factors). It is understandable, therefore, that certain differences in grammatical competence which the students initially bring to school are not ironed out by the end of secondary school, though they do get levelled to a varying extent. This is exemplified by Table 3.1, which provides the results of a study (Mougeon 1982) of the mastery of a basic feature of French grammar, i.e. reflexive pronouns (e.g. *je me lève* literally 'I get myself up' vs. **je lève* 'I get up'), by grade level and locality for Franco-Ontarian students differing in level of retention of French at home. It is striking that in both Pembroke and North Bay the students who are predominant users of English at home do not reach the level of mastery of reflexive pronouns achieved by *grade 2* students from French-speaking homes in Cornwall!

These findings have led Mougeon, Bélanger, Heller, and Canale (1984) to characterize the differences in level of mastery of spoken French observable between the predominant users of English and the predominant users of French at home in terms of a second language–first language contrast (relatively speaking of course). They have also argued that it is possible to draw a parallel between the relative failure of French immersion to bring English-Canadian students to a first-language level of proficiency in French (Harley 1984; Swain and Lapkin in press), and the fact that Ontario's French-language schools are not capable of fully bridging the gap between the spoken French proficiency of the frequent vs. infrequent users of French at home, both within and across communities. What these two situations illustrate is that it is unrealistic to expect that schooling in a minority/second language will on its

TABLE 3.1. *Mastery of the reflexive pronouns as a function of Franco-Ontarian students' locality of residence, frequency of use of French at home, and grade level*

Grade	Locality of residence (% francophone)						
	Hawkesbury (85%)	Cornwall (35%)		North Bay (17%)		Pembroke (8%)	
	Frequency of use of French at home						
	High	High	Low	High	Low	High	Low
Grade 2							
N†	77	57	22	24	45	25	37
%‡	96	90	78	63	36	64	35
Grade 5							
N	72	77	29	23	44	27	40
%	96	99	80	96	72	86	33
Grade 9							
N	117	51	42	36	38	30	43
%	100	97	88	95	83	74	70
Grade 12							
N	82	62	30	77	26	45	20
%	100	100	94	100	89	89	75
TOTAL							
N	348	370		313		267	
%	99	92		80		64	

† N = number of obligatory contexts for use of reflexive pronouns.
‡ % = per cent use of reflexive pronouns.

Source: adapted from Mougeon (1982: 117)

own ensure full development of skills in that language.[10] This was already apparent to Mougeon and Canale (1979), who gave a negative answer to the question phrased in the title of their study: 'Maintenance of French in Ontario: Is Education in French enough?'

Turning to the learning of English, Franco-Ontarian parents, as we have seen, concur in thinking that the acquisition of very good skills in that language by their children is of primary importance, given the predominance of English

[10] Such a statement should not be taken as an endorsement of the view that all of the parents who do not communicate in French with their children at home have such an expectation. In fact, preliminary analysis of data gathered during a survey of parents who had enrolled their children in French-language schools in Welland revealed that a number of these Franco-Ontarian parents were of the opinion that the schools should give priority to the full development of *English*-language skills rather than to the full development of French-language skills, in order to maximize the students' chances of obtaining better jobs.

in Ontario. Many Franco-Ontarian educators, however, think that to a large
extent the wider environment plays a major role in the successful attainment of
such a goal and hence that, by placing too much emphasis on the learning of
English in the French-language schools, there is a risk of unnecessarily
diverting precious pedagogical time which could otherwise be spent on the
teaching of French. The strength with which the latter view is professed by
Franco-Ontarian educators is to some extent conditioned, once more, by the
demographic concentration of francophones at a local level: the weaker the
francophone community, the stronger and more widespread such a view. This
view is shared to some extent by Franco-Ontarian parents, especially those
who strongly support the goal of French-language and culture maintenance.
Other Franco-Ontarian parents (especially, but not exclusively, in strong
francophone communities), however, feel that the French-language schools
are not doing enough in the area of English-language teaching and/or are
doing too much in the area of French-language teaching (see n. 10 and
Mougeon and Beniak 1989a). In the Franco-Ontarian community of Welland,
for instance, the determination of parents who hold these views was such that
they were able to convince school authorities that the local French-language
high school should offer the option of English-medium instruction for selected
courses, especially scientific and technical subjects.

Research on the mastery of English-language skills by Franco-Ontarian
students is much less developed than research on their mastery of French-
language skills. Two studies (Hébrard and Mougeon 1975; Mougeon, Canale,
and Carroll 1979) focused on the minority francophone communities of
Welland and Sudbury, and revealed that, as far as oral proficiency is
concerned, in the elementary grades, students who are raised in mainly
French-speaking homes lag considerably behind students who are raised in
mostly or only English-speaking homes. This finding is reminiscent of that
concerning the impact of home language use on the development of French-
language skills. Another study (Mougeon, Hébrard, and Sugunasiri 1979),
based on data gathered via semi-directed, semi-formal taped interviews,
revealed, however, that, by the end of secondary schooling, Franco-Ontarian
students from the two communities mentioned above as a whole make *very few*
errors in their spoken English, a remarkable achievement given that the norm
used in that study was standard spoken Canadian English. In a provincial study
of written proficiency among Franco-Ontarian students, Desjarlais and
Carrier (1975) observed a similar phenomenon in several weak francophone
minority communities. It would seem, then, that, in predominantly English-
speaking localities, a large proportion of the initially sizeable differences in
English-language skills exhibited by the English-dominant and French-
dominant students dwindle considerably in the upper-school grades, a finding
which can be attributed to the primary role played by the wider environment.

A substantially different picture seems to obtain in majority francophone communities. Our impression (corroborated by self-report data—see next chapter), from having gathered a corpus of spoken English among grades 2, 5, 9, and 12 Franco-Ontarian students in Hawkesbury, is that most students come to school with very limited spoken English skills, and that, if by the end of high school the students have made considerable progress, English clearly remains their weaker language. In their research on the written English of Franco-Ontarian students from eastern Ontario (where Hawkesbury is located), Desjarlais and Carrier (1975) arrived at the same conclusion. The limited research devoted to English proficiency among Franco-Ontarian students confirms that the wider environment plays a major role in their linguistic development. The finding that in predominantly anglophone localities students from French-speaking homes tend to catch up with students from English-speaking homes is perhaps the best illustration of this fact.

3.1.5. Language pedagogy

Until recently, the most salient feature of current French-language pedagogy in Franco-Ontarian schools was its normative orientation, i.e. it aimed at eradicating the typical features of the students' vernacular from their oral and written expression. Furthermore, such pedagogy involved the practice of a very limited range of communicative functions and was based largely on the assumption that all the students could speak or write French as a first language (see Cazabon and Frenette 1982 for an extensive treatment of this question). We saw earlier that certain school boards have taken measures which are not based on this latter assumption (e.g. the Frenchification classes); however, such school boards are still in the minority. Furthermore, at the level of ministerial guidelines, the fact that Ontario's French-language schools include varying proportions of students for whom French is a 'second' language and who have specific linguistic needs has received little recognition to date. The same guidelines, however, which have just been revised, now place considerable emphasis on the teaching of oral skills, recognize the need for students to develop a mastery of language registers, and above all advocate a strict communicative approach. The current ministerial guidelines should have a beneficial impact not only on the learning of French by Franco-Ontarian students, but perhaps also on the students' desire to maintain French, a desire which may have been dampened by the normative approach (see Dorian 1987 for a similar assumption on the negative impact of the imposition of a foreign norm on the desire for mother-tongue maintenance in several minority settings).

English-language pedagogy differs markedly from French-language pedagogy in connection with the three problematic aspects mentioned above regarding the teaching of French. Thus, more recognition has been given to the fact that certain French-language schools include students for whom English is definitely a second language, not only at the classroom level, in the form of special remedial English classes, but also at the level of ministerial guidelines, which clearly identify the special needs of these students. Similarly, attention has been given to the presence in the French-language schools of students whose proficiency in English is native-like, again not only at the classroom level but also at the level of ministerial guidelines. The teaching of English which is geared to these students is quite similar to that which is geared to anglophone Ontarian students. Finally the orientation of the guidelines, and to a non-negligible extent of classroom practice, has long been much more communicative than was the case for French-language pedagogy. The fact that, in Canada, French-as-a-first-language pedagogy and English-as-a-first-language pedagogy have, until recently, had largely independent histories and traditions probably explains the contrast described above. In any case, it so happens that in the French-language schools the teaching of the minority language is much less in tune with the sociolinguistic reality in which Franco-Ontarian students are immersed than the teaching of the majority language. It is to be hoped that such an imbalance will disappear in the near future.

3.2. Status of French in other high domains of society

3.2.1. Mass media

Before the 1970s all that was available in the way of French-spoken media was a local radio station—and only in localities with sufficiently high numbers of francophones. Now, almost everywhere in Ontario, it is possible to listen to a radio station broadcasting in French exclusively (usually affiliated with the French network of the Canadian Broadcasting Corporation) and to watch two television channels also broadcasting exclusively in French (one channel is affiliated with the French CBC, the other with the provincial educational TVO network). Moreover, in the very near future it will be possible to tune in to a third French-medium television channel (the new Quebec/Canada television consortium: TV5), which will be available through cable television. So, just like French-medium education, the French spoken media have undergone significant expansion over the last twenty years or so. The parallel stops there, however, since Franco-Ontarians (especially the younger generations) do not make extensive use of the French spoken media, whereas there is a large measure of community support for and participation in the French-language schools. Several reasons can be offered for the greater loyalty to the schools. First, schools play a more important role in the transmission of the minority's linguistic and cultural heritage than the media. Second, whereas in the case of the schools the younger generations do not have much of a say in the matter of enrolment (especially at the elementary level), they can exercise much greater freedom of choice in the case of the media. Third, both the French CBC and particularly the French educational television network tend to cater more to intellectuals and hence are unlikely to appeal to a wide spectrum of the Franco-Ontarian community. Finally, in major urban centres, especially near the US border, the French spoken media are outnumbered by a much wider selection of competing English-language radio and television stations.

French has not expanded as much in the written media. There is only one French daily in Ontario. It is published in Ottawa, has a small circulation, and is readily available only within a fifty-mile radius. It is possible to subscribe to this paper, but there is not much point in doing so, since Canada Post is unable to ensure speedy delivery of the mail! Most French-language newspapers in Ontario are weeklies, available mostly through subscription (this is less of a problem since speed of delivery is not as crucial). There is also, of course, the possibility of subscribing to Québécois, national, or international magazines, although such publications tend to cater to a more restricted readership.

3.2.2. Community organizations

Overall, Franco-Ontarians have been quite successful in their efforts at setting up a wide variety of church- or government-sponsored social, cultural, or economic institutions, such as *maisons de la culture*, clubs for the elderly, sports clubs, co-operatives—including credit unions, etc. (see Lapointe, Poulin, and Thériault 1987; Robertson 1980; Welch 1988). However, drawing on the findings of several surveys carried out in Welland, it would seem that in localities where francophones are in the minority there is not sufficient interest among the younger generations in sustaining a high level of participation and leadership in socio-cultural activities. This may be due to the fact that the younger generations' cultural values have changed (i.e. moved closer towards the English North-American mainstream culture). But it is also noteworthy that many of them know English very well or better than French and hence may feel ill at ease in institutions which stress maximal use of French and/or which promote the maintenance of the traditional French-Canadian culture. This being said, there is currently a feeling among Franco-Ontarian community leaders or activists that at least three types of cultural activities—music, poetry, and theatre—are not disfavoured by the younger generations. In fact, there is a sense and hope that these activities will serve as new rallying points for the assertion and cultivation of Franco-Ontarian cultural and linguistic distinctiveness (see Lapointe, Poulin, and Thériault 1987).

3.2.3. Government services

At the end of 1986 the Ontario government passed a law (French Language Services Act) which reiterates the official status of French in education and in

the courts and recognizes the right of Franco-Ontarians to be served in French
by the government's agencies (i.e. ministries, boards, commissions, and
corporations under its jurisdiction). The law's preamble (Government of
Ontario 1986: 2) is the most forceful and explicit assertion to date of the
government's will to ensure the maintenance of French in Ontario:

Whereas the French language is an historic and honoured language in Ontario and
recognized by the Constitution as an official language in Canada; and whereas in
Ontario the French language is recognized as an official language in the courts and in
education; and whereas the Legislative Assembly recognizes the contribution of the
cultural heritage of the French speaking population and wishes to preserve it for future
generations; and whereas it is desirable to guarantee the use of the French language
in institutions of the Legislature and the Government of Ontario, as provided in this
Act . . .

The French Language Services Act is backed up by a series of policies and
concrete measures to ensure the implementation of the principle which it
enshrines. Among such measures can be mentioned a provincial commission to
oversee the implementation of the Act, the establishment of a French-language
services committee in each government agency, the hiring of a co-ordinator of
French-language services in each agency, etc. The most important fall-out
from the law at this stage has been the creation of a growing number of new
bilingual positions in the government agencies and the increasing visibility of
French on signs, notices, forms, etc. used in or by these agencies. It should be
pointed out, however, that, as was the case for the provision of French-medium
education before 1984, the application of the French Language Services Act is
restricted by a 'where numbers warrant' clause to designated areas (i.e. areas
where francophones number 5,000 or more or make up at least 10 per cent of ·
the population). It could be argued that such a limitation reveals that the
Ontario government, in spite of its official stance in favour of the preservation
of the French language in the province (see the above-quoted preamble), is
(still) driven by electoral concerns in the formulation and implementation of
French-language services policies. Where francophones represent a sizeable
group (i.e. a sizeable electoral base), it is worth wooing them with French-
language services, but where they are demographically weak (i.e. electorally
insignificant), there is no need to provide French-language services. This is
unfortunate because, as we have already pointed out, it is precisely in the weak
minority francophone communities that the French language is in greatest
danger.

3.3. Conclusion

As we have seen, there has been a considerable spread of French in(to) the
public domains of Ontarian society over the last twenty years or so. The

expansion of French-language schooling is undoubtedly the most important aspect of this phenomenon, since it can play a key role in intergenerational language transmission. The nature and importance of its role depends on (1) the extent to which French can be used in the community, and (2) the prior contribution of the home to the transmission of French. Table 3.2 provides a summary of the different combinations of these two factors (with French-language schooling a constant). These are not just theoretical possibilities, since, in the last twenty years of expansion, the French-language schools have not only spread to localities where francophones form very small minorities but have also admitted increasingly large proportions of students from 'English-speaking homes', whether the two parents are of French-Canadian extraction or make up a mixed marriage.[11]

Looking at Table 3.2 from top to bottom, it can be seen that the less French is used in the home and community, the more the school becomes the main provider of exposure to and opportunities to use French. It would be unrealistic to expect that in situations where the home and community contribute little to French-language transmission (e.g. combinations E, E, F; E, F < E, F; F < E, E, F; F < E, F < E, F), the replacement generations will be able to achieve as high a level of French-language mastery as when the near-ideal combination of a French-speaking home, a predominantly francophone neighbourhood, and a French-language school obtains (e.g. combinations F, F, F; F, F > E, F; F > E, F, F; F > E, F > E, F). The reader will recall the results on the mastery of the reflexive pronouns presented earlier.

What we do not know, however, is whether the lower levels of linguistic competence in French exhibited by the students who are raised in predominantly English-speaking homes and communities (the first set of combinations) are actually sufficient to bring about a reversal of the process of language shift which was initiated by their parents. In other words, will these children, as they become adults, transmit the French language to their offspring? Only long-term longitudinal studies will be able to provide an answer to this important question. Should the answer be negative (and our hunch is that this is the case), then the question would have to be raised as to the appropriateness of the presence of such students in the French-medium schools. Are they not linguistic deadwood or, worse still, sources of anglicization, as some community leaders contend? This is by no means an easy question to answer. Everybody would agree that the goal of linguistic revival is a noble one; however it is not obvious that the French-language schools can achieve this goal without shortchanging the students who are sent to those schools to obtain linguistic-maintenance education. Perhaps the solution of separate streams or

---

[11] It would also be of interest to consider the combinations involving less than categorical schooling in French, i.e. education in a bilingual school or in an English school. Since we did not gather our speech samples among Franco-Ontarian adolescents who had received this type of education, we shall not be considering these other combinations.

TABLE 3.2. *Patterns of language use in home, community, and school*

Home	Community	School
F	F	F
F	F > E	F
F	F = E	F
F	F < E	F
F	E	F
F > E	F	F
F > E	F > E	F
F > E	F = E	F
F > E	F < E	F
F > E	E	F
F = E	F	F
F = E	F > E	F
F = E	F = E	F
F = E	F < E	F
F = E	E	F
F < E	F	F
F < E	F > E	F
F < E	F = E	F
F < E	F < E	F
F < E	E	F
E	F	F
E	F > E	F
E	F = E	F
E	F < E	F
E	E	F

even schools, as has been tried recently in a few communities (e.g. Sault Saint Marie), is the most sensible approach under the circumstances.

Apart from the two opposite situations described above, there are intermediary ones where either the home and/or the neighbourhood contribute partially to French-language learning. In the latter situations the school builds on what these two domains have already achieved in the way of French-language transmission (e.g. widens the students' sociolinguistic repertoire, gives them access to the wider world of *la francophonie*, etc.), and thus wards off the danger of assimilation. In our opinion, this is the most positive contribution of Franco-Ontarian schools, more so than whatever measure of success they can achieve in Frenchifying students from predominantly English-speaking homes and communities.

In a recent paper, Fishman (1987) observed that in situations of language shift some community leaders deploy considerable efforts in lobbying for or directly implementing policies of minority-language spread aimed at the domains of modernity, officialdom, etc., while the minority language is losing on the home and neighbourhood fronts. In fact, Fishman wonders whether the expansion of the minority language into high domains of society while it is being abandoned in the private domains does not amount to a misspending of energy and resources. We do not think that it does. If our analysis of the importance of the role of perceived or objective lack of prestige and usefulness of French in English language shift is correct, then the spread of French into the high domains of Ontario society should help maintain French, since it will increase the prestige and instrumental value of that language. That does not mean, as Fishman advocates, that community leaders should not try to convince members of the linguistic minority to maintain their language in the primary domains of language transmission by invoking non-instrumental arguments (e.g. the invaluable worth of the community's linguistic and cultural heritage). However, we do believe that, in the case of linguistic minorities, instrumental factors are of prime importance and that it would be unwise to forgo opportunities for expansion into those high domains of society which can have a direct bearing on the usefulness of the minority language. Second, it should be remembered that English language shift has not reached an irrevocable stage among Franco-Ontarians. There are still a substantial number of French-mother-tongue individuals for whom it matters that they be given the fullest opportunity to use their mother tongue and who, one might argue, are entitled to receive services in their mother tongue on constitutional or philosophical grounds.

One important point needs to be made in connection with the provision of French-language services to which Franco-Ontarians are now entitled. A large proportion of the adult generations have either not been schooled in French or been only partially schooled in that language. This, coupled with the fact that French was virtually absent in nearly all key public-sector domains before the 1970s, means that adult Franco-Ontarians have not had much of a chance to become familiar with Standard French (even in its Canadian guise). French-language services (in the broadest sense) currently available in the public sector (and in several private institutions as well, e.g. banks) tend to be offered in Standard French (especially when the written medium is involved). As a result, adult Franco-Ontarians (who for the most part know English quite well—see Chapter 2) may not make maximal use of the French-language services available to them. Gérard Raymond, who has just been appointed to replace the previous chairman of the commission responsible for overseeing the implementation of the French Language Services Act, sees the commission's toughest challenge as the problem of sensitizing Franco-Ontarians to the need to change their well-ingrained habit to consume services in English (interview by Beaupré 1988). To assist them in gaining the habit of using French-medium services, attention will have to be given to the variety of French in which the services are dispensed. In our opinion, it should be (1) native or as close to native as can be, since most Franco-Ontarians have the capacity to switch to English if they sense that their interlocutor is anglophone and having problems with French, and (2) not overly standard or aligned on European French, given that Franco-Ontarians tend to experience a high degree of linguistic insecurity.

Finally, let us consider the possibility for further expansion of French into the high domains of Ontarian society. One measure which would carry much weight from a symbolic viewpoint and which might bring about further French-language expansion is the legal recognition of French as an *official* language of Ontario. Franco-Ontarian community leaders have been lobbying for such a measure since at least the 1960s. However, the various provincial governments have refused to satisfy this request, fearing that by so doing they would engender a backlash movement among the more conservative elements of Anglo-Ontarian society, which again could translate into electoral losses.[12] The French Language Services Act is the closest step to granting French official status that the current provincial government has so far been willing to take.

As concerns post-secondary education, a solution to the inadequacy of the present situation which is currently supported within the Franco-Ontarian community is the establishment of an autonomous network of French-medium university services which would include the services already available as well as new French-medium services provided by the designated bilingual universities or by other universities. Alternatively, other community leaders have called for the establishment of one or several full-fledged French-medium universities.

There is still room for some improvement even at the elementary and secondary levels. At the moment, French-speaking trustees and school-board administrators share the supervision of public or Catholic school boards with English-speaking counterparts. This situation is particularly deleterious to the adoption of measures for the expansion, improvement, etc. of the system of French-medium schools, since such measures must be fought for or negotiated by the French-Canadian trustees and administrators with their English-Canadian 'colleagues'. One alternative which has been implemented in Ottawa is to regroup, under one common administrative structure, French-language schools from the public and Catholic systems. Another alternative is to pull out the French-medium schools and administrators from the Catholic and public

[12] This fear is not completely unfounded, since the passing of the French Language Services Act has indeed brought about a backlash reaction (notably in rural Ontario). By using crude scare tactics involving notably the propagation of alarmist and false statements on the need for all anglophones working for the Ontario government to know French, they have successfully lobbied for the adoption of by-laws in several predominantly anglophone municipalities which are meant to put a halt to the 'spread' of French by declaring the municipality officially unilingual in English.

school boards and form independent francophone public or Catholic school boards (this alternative has been implemented in Toronto as concerns the public school sector). Although most Franco-Ontarian educators would agree that autonomous French-language school boards regrouping Catholic and public schools are desirable, they have yet to reach a consensus on how exactly to administer such boards, since, as we have seen, the public and Catholic school systems are currently not on the best terms. Finally, and most crucially, the provincial government needs to be convinced that it is worth taking the risk of further restructuring the educational system.

4

Methodology

IN this chapter we shall provide a description of the speech corpus which we drew on in the sociolinguistic studies which are featured in Chapters 5–11, examine the general theoretical hypotheses which guided our research, and finally say a word about our method of data analysis. As the corpus was drawn from two previous sociolinguistic surveys not entirely identical in terms of sampling procedures, interview schedules, questionnaires, etc., we shall consider each of these surveys separately. For additional details concerning the corpus, the reader is referred to Mougeon, Brent-Palmer, Bélanger, and Cichocki (1982).

4.1. The Hawkesbury survey

To understand the central place the Hawkesbury survey has come to occupy in the sociolinguistic research programme of the Centre for Franco-Ontarian Studies (CFOS), it is necessary to supply a minimum of historical information. In 1973 the Advisory Committee to the CFOS recommended that linguistic surveys be carried out among students enrolled in Ontario's French-language schools. These surveys were to have two main goals: (1) to assist in the evaluation of the students' proficiency in French, and (2) to provide data which could be used to develop materials for the teaching of French—mother-tongue pedagogy being looked upon as a priority concern by the Advisory Committee. In compliance with this recommendation, the CFOS gathered data on the spoken and written French of students attending the French-language schools of Welland (southern Ontario) and Sudbury (central Ontario) (see points 3 and 13 on Map 2.1). The analysis of the students' linguistic performance consisted in a series of descriptive/diagnostic studies which provided valuable data for the development of pedagogical materials meeting the specific needs of Franco-Ontarian students and teachers (see, e.g., Mougeon 1985 and 1986; Mougeon and Beniak 1979). These descriptive/diagnostic studies turned out to be the first stage of what would become a systematic investigation of the variety of French spoken by younger Franco-Ontarians. In 1976 the CFOS gathered supplementary data on the spoken and written French of students, enrolled this time in the French-language schools of Hawkesbury (eastern Ontario) (see point 8 on Map 2.1). By contrast with Welland or Sudbury, Hawkesbury was a predominantly French-speaking locality located in a region where francophones were well represented. These additional data were originally obtained so as to confer a broader geographical scope to the pedagogical materials which were being developed by the CFOS. But the Hawkesbury corpus was also used from the outset as a baseline comparison to gauge the spoken French performance of the *minority* community students. It has continued to perform this role in all subsequent research and especially in that reported on in this book.

The Hawkesbury survey involved, at the secondary level, a total of twenty students and was stratified as a function of speaker gender, grade (10 and 12), and social class (middle, lower-middle, and working). As it was quite apparent that few, if any, francophone students in attendance at Hawkesbury's French-language schools exhibited signs of restriction in the use of French, it was not felt necessary to stratify the sample along the frequency-of-use-of-French dimension. None the less, we did obtain information on the students' language-use patterns during the semi-directed oral interviews. This information confirmed our first impression as to the staunch maintenance of French by the Hawkesbury adolescents (see section 4.4).

4.2. The francophone-minorities survey

In the late 1970s the CFOS was contracted by the Ontario Ministry of Education (OME) to investigate the dual phenomenon of French-language maintenance and English language shift among Franco-Ontarian students, as revealed by their language-use patterns, and to see how these patterns related to their proficiency in spoken French. Ten years had already elapsed since the legalization of French as a medium of instruction in the public-school system. The OME felt it was time to find out whether the greater availability of French-medium education was having a measurable impact on French-language maintenance and French-language competence among the younger generations, especially in localities where francophones have *minority* status and where, consequently, the school constitutes the chief locus of French-language use in the public domain (see conclusion to Chapter 3). The survey was carried out in seven such localities, i.e. Cornwall, North Bay, Ottawa, Pembroke, Toronto, Welland, and Windsor (see Map 2.1 for locations). At the secondary level a total of 1,177 grades 9 and 12 students attending nine French-language high schools located in these seven localities participated in the survey. They were administered a written questionnaire (see Appendix B in Mougeon, Brent-Palmer, Bélanger, and Cichocki 1982: 119–26) eliciting information on their personal backgrounds, current patterns of interpersonal language use, current patterns of non-interpersonal language use (e.g. television viewing, book reading, etc.), and projections as to their future language-use patterns and perceptions of the utilitarian value of French. The nine French-language high schools were exhaustive of the number of such schools in the localities surveyed, just as the 1,177 participants represented the totality of grades 9 and 12 students in attendance at the high schools in question. Based on the information provided by the questionnaire, a sub-sample (stratified according to speaker gender, grade, social class, but also frequency of use of French) of forty high-school students per locality was selected for purposes of follow-up tape-recorded interviews (see Appendix B in Mougeon, Brent-Palmer, Bélanger, and Cichocki 1982: 114–18). Constraints of time and financial resources precluded the possibility of transcribing and analysing the full set of interviews. Only the 120 conducted in the three localities of Cornwall, North Bay, and Pembroke were retained.

4.3. The speech corpus

It is these 120 interviews, together with the twenty from the Hawkesbury survey, which formed our initial speech corpus. However, due to the particular nature of the OME survey, it proved necessary to 'clean up' the corpus before it could be submitted to the kind of sociolinguistic analysis we had in mind, namely a description of the variety of French spoken by Ontario adolescents of French-Canadian extraction (i.e. students with at least one French-Canadian parent). The inclusion of subjects of mixed parentage in our sample was motivated by the fact that exogamy is a key sociological characteristic of the Franco-Ontarian community (see Chapter 2) and that it might prove useful to investigate the linguistic effect of such marriages on the speech of the offspring. (Still, the majority, i.e. 76 per cent, of our subjects were the offspring of non-mixed marriages; see further Table 4.1). Some of the students who had been interviewed in the context of the OME survey failed to meet the require-ment that at least one of their two parents be of French mother tongue and so were excluded. Others either had not been born in or had not resided long enough in the communities under investigation for their speech to be deemed representative of the local varieties of French and thus were also excluded. As a result of 'tightening up' the selection criteria in these ways, the number of minority-locality subjects was pared down to ninety-seven. The number of subjects from the Hawkesbury survey remained unchanged.

The interviews conducted in both surveys were quite similar in content and format. They lasted from about thirty minutes to one hour and aimed at tapping as natural and unreflecting a style of speech as could be obtained in the context of a semi-directed face-to-face interview on the school premises. This was achieved through a series of open-ended questions covering such topics as the students' leisure activities, home and school life, personal experiences and aspirations, etc. The interviews also included a series of simple sentences and a passage of connected text which the students were asked to read after the open-ended questions. The sentences and passage were designed to elicit a shift in phonological style. The interviews ended with a series of closed questions on the students' language-use patterns and linguistic aptitudes in and attitudes to French and English. The interviews (excepting the twenty from Hawkesbury) were transcribed on to computer files, from which an alphabetical concordance of all word-tokens with some left- and right-hand context was produced. This greatly facilitated the search for occurrences of the linguistic variables selected for sociolinguistic investigation.

4.4. Student characteristics

Although the final sample of 117 speakers was stratified by grade level (9, 10, and 12), we decided not to investigate the possible effect of this parameter on linguistic variation as the age differences were considered too small. However, we controlled sex and social class, as is traditional in sociolinguistic research. Social class was determined on the basis of the occupation of the father or of the mother, whichever was judged higher. Admittedly, it is not difficult to come up with an equally good reason for proceeding in reverse fashion and ascribing social class on the basis of the lower occupation. Be that as it may, the number of such contentious cases was quite small and so we were not overly concerned about settling the question one way or the other. Three social classes were distinguished: (1) middle (i.e. professionals or semi-professionals such as doctors, lawyers, teachers, etc.), (2) lower-middle (i.e. small store owners, office workers, self-employed craftsmen, etc.), and (3) working (i.e. skilled and unskilled workers).

Having selected speakers residing in four different localities, we decided to control this factor as well with a view possibly to capturing geographical variation (Mougeon, Beniak, and Côté 1981). A speaker was deemed to be representative of the speech of his community if he had resided there at least since the age of eight, which is midway through what Labov (1972: 304–5) considers to be the 'formative period for a native speaker', that is, years 4–13 approximately. Locality of residence has a very obvious effect on the socio-logical level. Specifically, linguistic exogamy is particularly advanced in francophone communities that have minority status. This is well reflected in our speaker sample, as shown in Table 4.1. Those informants who were raised in mixed-marriage households are all resident in the three localities where francophones are largely outnumbererd by anglophones.

Given that linguistic exogamy among the French-Canadian minorities practically always amounts to the abandonment of French in the home by the francophone parent (see Chapter 2), it is no wonder that our sample includes speakers who have received little exposure to French at home and who use French sparingly (see further in this section). It remains to be seen, however, to

TABLE 4.1. *Correlation between locality of residence and linguistic exogamy*

Locality of residence	Francophone concentration (%)	Informants (N)	Informants of mixed parentage†	
			N	%
Hawkesbury	85	20	0	0
Cornwall	35	38	12	32
North Bay	17	31	7	23
Pembroke	8	28	9	32
TOTAL		117	28	24

† Linguistic exogamy was determined on the basis of information provided by the informants regarding the mother tongue of their parents.

what extent low values on the index of frequency of use of French are found for speakers who were born of homogeneous French marriages.

Last but not least, French-language-use restriction as measured by frequency of use of French in interpersonal communication was of course the central parameter whose effect we wished to study. As previously mentioned, information on the students' language-use patterns was gathered through oral (Hawkesbury) or written (Cornwall, North Bay, and Pembroke) self-reports. The questions focused on language use in a variety of settings (home, community, and school) and with different interlocutors (parents, siblings, and peers). The students were asked to rate their language use on a five-point scale ranging from 'always in French' to 'always in English'. The students were also asked to provide information on their parents' frequency of use of French with each other and with them, again using the same five-point rating scale. All of this information was compiled to arrive at global indices of frequency of use of French per individual.[1] The indices thus obtained ranged from 1 or exclusive use of French to near 0 (the lowest was .05) or almost exclusive use of English. The questions on which the index is based were attributed the same weight, irrespective of the setting (familial or extrafamilial), interlocutor (parents, siblings, or friends), and directionality of the interaction (informant → interlocutor or interlocutor → informant). On the five-point rating scale, students would score from 0 to 4 points depending respectively on whether they spoke (or were spoken to) always in English (0), mostly in English (1), as often in English as in French (2), mostly in French (3), or always in French (4).

[1] 'Frequency of use of French' is a more convenient than accurate label for the index. Indeed, as we have just seen, some of the questions which were used in its construction refer to the informant only as a passive participant in the interaction (i.e. the questions on parent → informant interaction), while others do not refer to him or her at all (i.e. parent ←→ parent interaction).

The reader should bear in mind that a very low index value does not, of course, signify English monolingualism, for the simple reason that all of the subjects were schooled in French (see Chapter 3 for a discussion of some of the reasons why Ontario's French-language schools cater for students who use French only minimally at home). We were satisfied that all were sufficiently fluent in French to go through a semi-structured interview situation without too much difficulty. Conversely, a high index value does not indicate poor fluency in English, at least not for the speakers who are resident in the three localities where anglophones make up the majority of the population; in such localities there certainly is no shortage of opportunities to be exposed to, learn, and use English outside one's family and circle of friends. For purposes of quantification and statistical analysis, three levels of frequency of use of French were distinguished: high or unrestricted (.80–1.00), mid or semi-restricted (.45–.79), and low or restricted (.05–.44). It is because we wanted (1) to limit the number of categories of users of French to three, (2) to have an adequate representation of speakers in each portion of the frequency continuum, and (3) to try to capture qualitative differences in patterns of language use (see next section) that we were forced to make more or less unequal cuts. The distribution of the speakers in our sample is given in Table 4.2.

The empty cells in the sample (indicated by a zero) mostly reflect the rarity of certain types of speakers given the concentration of francophones in the different localities. Thus the empty cells in the low and mid-portions of the frequency-of-use-of-French continuum for the Hawkesbury sample are consonant with the strong majority status of francophones in that locality. Similarly, the empty cells in the high portion of the frequency index for the Pembroke and North Bay samples reflect the weak minority status of francophones in those localities. The few remaining empty cells are the result of our having streamlined the corpus for the reasons mentioned above.

At this point we should try to do justice to the full complexity of the sociolinguistic reality which the index of frequency of use of French represents. There are at least two kinds of qualitative differences between the speakers which are blurred and which should be brought out. One difference has to do with whether language use is of the patterned or unpatterned type; in other words, are French and English each allocated to different situations of communication or do they overlap in their distribution? Another concerns language-acquisition histories. The index, clearly, is purely synchronic. The questions on which it is based asked the respondents to indicate their frequency of use of French at the time of the survey. No specific information was obtained concerning the respondents' previous language use, although reconstruction is possible to a certain extent (see further in this section).

Table 4.3 breaks down the frequency-of-use-of-French index by speaker and situation of communication. The speakers are ordered by decreasing index value, as are the situations of communication. (Speakers with the same index

TABLE 4.2. *Composition of speaker sample*

Locality of residence	Sex	Social class	Index of frequency of use of French		
			.05–.44	.45–.79	.80–1.00
Hawkesbury (N = 20)	M (N = 7)	Middle (N = 2)	0	1	1
		Lower-middle (N = 2)	0	0	2
		Working (N = 3)	0	0	3
	F (N = 13)	Middle (N = 4)	0	0	4
		Lower-middle (N = 5)	0	0	5
		Working (N = 4)	0	0	4
Cornwall (N = 38)	M (N = 24)	Middle (N = 3)	0	1	2
		Lower-middle (N = 10)	3	5	2
		Working (N = 11)	6	2	3
	F (N = 14)	Middle (N = 3)	1	1	1
		Lower-middle (N = 8)	2	5	1
		Working (N = 3)	0	2	1
North Bay (N = 31)	M (N = 16)	Middle (N = 4)	2	1	1
		Lower-middle (N = 8)	2	4	2
		Working (N = 4)	1	2	1
	F (N = 15)	Middle (N = 1)	0	1	0
		Lower-middle (N = 6)	2	4	0
		Working (N = 8)	1	6	1
Pembroke (N = 28)	M (N = 16)	Middle (N = 4)	1	3	0
		Lower-middle (N = 8)	5	2	1
		Working (N = 4)	0	4	0
	F (N = 12)	Middle (N = 1)	1	0	0
		Lower-middle (N = 6)	4	2	0
		Working (N = 5)	2	2	1
TOTAL N = 117	M = 63 F = 54	M = 22 LM = 53 W = 42	33	48	36

value were arbitrarily ordered according to locality of residence and number.) The breaks in the table correspond to the points where cuts were made on the index of frequency of use of French. Our discussion will be organized around the three portions of the index.

The top portion of the index comprises 36 speakers all of whom save one (N33; .82) come from non-mixed marriages. The first 16, all residents of the majority francophone locality of Hawkesbury, are categorical users of French (indicated on Table 4.3 by F) across the 11 situations of communication and thus have an index value of 1.00. Fourteen of the remaining 20 speakers in the

TABLE 4.3. *Scalar tabulation of language-use patterns, all informants (N = 117)*

Speaker characteristics†				Situations of communication‡											Speaker index value
Loc.	Sex	Class	Marr.	1	2	3	4	5	6	7	8	9	10	11	
Ho1	F	LM	NM	(F)§	F	F	F	F	F	F	F	(F)	F	F	1.00
Ho4	F	LM	NM	(F)	F	F	F	F	F	F	F	(F)	F	F	1.00
Ho5	M	W	NM	(F)	F	F	F	F	F	F	F	(F)	F	F	1.00
Ho6	M	LM	NM	(F)	F	F	F	F	F	F	F	(F)	F	F	1.00
H11	F	LM	NM	(F)	F	F	F	F	F	F	F	(F)	F	F	1.00
H12	M	M	NM	(F)	F	F	F	F	F	F	F	(F)	F	F	1.00
H13	M	W	NM	(F)	F	F	F	F	F	F	F	(F)	F	F	1.00
H14	F	W	NM	(F)	F	F	F	F	F	F	F	(F)	F	F	1.00
H15	F	M	NM	(F)	F	F	F	F	F	F	F	(F)	F	F	1.00
H17	F	W	NM	(F)	F	F	F	F	F	F	F	(F)	F	F	1.00
H18	F	M	NM	(F)	F	F	F	F	F	F	F	(F)	F	F	1.00
H19	F	LM	NM	(F)	F	F	F	F	F	F	F	(F)	F	F	1.00
H20	F	LM	NM	(F)	F	F	F	F	F	F	F	(F)	F	F	1.00
Ho2	F	W	NM	(F)	F	*	*	F	*	*§	*	(F)	?§	?	1.00
Ho3	F	W	NM	(F)	F	F	?	F	F	F	F	(F)	F	F	1.00
Ho9	F	M	*	(F)	F	F	F	F	F	F	F	(F)	F	F	1.00
C23	M	M	NM	F	F	F	F	F	F	F	F	f	F	F	.98
Ho7	M	W	NM	(F)	F	F	F	F	F	F	F	(F)	F	f	.97
Co9	F	W	NM	F	F	F	F	F	F	F	F	F	f	f	.95
No7	F	W	NM	F	F	F	F	F	F	F	F	F	f	f	.95
Co6	F	M	NM	F	f	F	F	F	F	F	f	F	f	f	.93
H16	M	LM	NM	(F)	F	F	F	fe	F	F	F	(F)	fe	fe	.91
C10	M	LM	NM	F	F	F	F	F	F	F	F	F	fe	fe	.91

Table 4.3 *(cont.)*

Speaker characteristics†				Situations of communication‡											Speaker index value
Loc.	Sex	Class	Marr.	1	2	3	4	5	6	7	8	9	10	11	
C17	M	W	NM	F	F	F	F	F	F	F	F	F	fe	fe	.91
C26	M	W	NM	F	F	F	F	F	F	F	f	F	f	fe	.91
N03	M	LM	NM	F	F	F	F	F	F	F	f	f	f	fe	.91
N35	M	LM	NM	?	F	F	F	F	F	F	f	F	f	fe	.91
H10	F	M	NM	?	F	F	F	F	F	F	F	?	fe	fe	.89
C01	M	LM	NM	fe	F	F	F	F	F	F	F	fe	F	fe	.86
C30	M	M	NM	?	F	F	F	F	F	F	F	fe	fe	fe	.86
P02	F	W	NM	?	F	F	F	F	F	F	F	?	fe	e	.86
P30	M	LM	NM	?	F	F	F	F	F	f	f	?	fe	fe	.86
C35	M	W	NM	F	F	F	F	F	F	f	f	fe	fe	fe	.82
N01	M	M	NM	F	F	F	F	F	F	F	f	F	E	E	.82
N33	M	W	M	F	F	F	F	F	F	F	F	E	fe	E	.82
C21	F	LM	NM	F	F	F	F	F	F	F	F	E	fe	e	.80
H08	M	M	NM	?	f	F	f	f	f	f	f	?	f	f	.78
C16	M	W	NM	F	F	f	F	f	f	F	F	E	fe	fe	.77
C20	F	LM	NM	F	f	f	F	F	f	fe	fe	F	fe	fe	.77
N19	F	M	NM	F	F	F	F	F	F	fe	fe	F	e	e	.77
N21	M	W	NM	F	f	F	F	F	F	fe	fe	fe	e	e	.77
N30	F	W	NM	F	f	F	f	f	f	f	f	fe	f	f	.77
C33	M	LM	NM	F	f	f	F	f	f	f	f	F	f	f	.75
C12	F	LM	NM	F	F	F	F	F	F	*	*	F	fe	fe	.75
N11	F	LM	NM	F	f	f	f	f	f	f	fe	F	e	e	.75
N36	F	W	NM	F	F	F	F	F	F	fe	e	F	e	e	.75

Case	Sex	Region	Status	R1	R2	R3	R4	R5	R6	R7	R8	R9	R10	Score
Po9	F	LM	NM	fe	fe	e	f	f	f	F	F	f	F	.73
C39	M	LM	NM	E	e	E	f	f	f	F	F	F	F	.70
N22	M	W	NM	E	E	F	E	f	f	F	F	F	F	.70
N25	M	M	NM	E	E	e	f	f	F	F	F	F	F	.70
Co3	F	W	M	fe	fe	F	f	f	fe	f	f	fe	f	.68
Co8	M	W	NM	fe	fe	E	f	f	F	f	f	f	f	.68
Co5	M	LM	M	e	e	E	f	f	f	f	f	f	f	.66
C13	F	LM	NM	e	e	fe	f	f	f	F	F	F	F	.66
C34	F	W	NM	e	e	f	fe	fe	f	f	f	f	fe	.66
C36	F	LM	M	e	e	F	fe	fe	fe	fe	f	f	f	.66
No5	F	LM	NM	fe	fe	E	fe	f	f	f	f	f	f	.66
P35	M	M	NM	E	E	e	fe	fe	fe	F	F	F	F	.66
No4	M	LM	NM	E	E	E	fe	fe	F	fe	fe	F	F	.64
P15	M	W	NM	fe	fe	E	fe	e	F	F	F	F	F	.64
P18	F	LM	NM	e	e	E	e	e	F	fe	e	f	f	.64
N24	M	LM	NM	e	e	fe	e	fe	f	F	F	f	f	.61
N17	M	LM	NM	E	E	F	fe	f	f	f	f	F	F	.59
N16	F	W	NM	E	E	E	f	fe	F	F	F	f	fe	.57
N18	M	LM	NM	fe	fe	e	e	fe	f	f	fe	f	f	.57
C37	M	LM	NM	e	fe	fe	fe	fe	f	F	fe	f	f	.55
No8	F	W	NM	E	fe	E	e	fe	fe	fe	F	F	F	.55
N34	F	M	NM	e	e	E	E	E	F	fe	fe	fe	fe	.55
P12	M	LM	NM	E	E	E	fe	fe	F	F	F	F	F	.55
P17	M	LM	NM	E	E	F	e	e	f	f	f	f	f	.55
P31	M	W	NM	E	E	E	e	fe	f	f	f	f	f	.55
P29	M	W	NM	f	f	E	E	fe	fe	fe	fe	fe	fe	.53
C31	M	M	NM	e	e	e	E	E	f	f	f	f	f	.52
P20	M	LM	NM	E	E	E	E	e	f	f	F	f	f	.52
C25	F	M	NM	e	e	E	fe	e	f	fe	fe	fe	F	.50
Po7	F	W	NM	E	E	e	*	*	f	f	F	f	e	.50

Methodology

T ABLE 4.3 (*cont.*)

Speaker characteristics†				Situations of communication‡											Speaker index value
Loc.	Sex	Class	Marr.	1	2	3	4	5	6	7	8	9	10	11	
C18	F	LM	NM	fe	fe	fe	fe	fe	fe	fe	e	fe	fe	fe	.48
P16	M	W	NM	E	F	F	fe	F	F	e	E	E	E	E	.48
C40	M	LM	M	E	f	f	f	fe	fe	e	fe	E	fe	fe	.45
N12	F	LM	M	F	e	fe	fe	e	fe	E	e	F	E	e	.45
N26	F	W.	M	F	f	f	F	fe	fe	fe	E	fe	E	E	.45
N31	M	LM	NM	F	fe	fe	fe	fe	fe	fe	e	f	E	E	.45
P19	M	M	NM	f	f	f	f	F	fe	E	E	e	E	E	.45
P22	F	W	NM	E	F	F	F	F	F	E	E	E	E	E	.45
N28	F	LM	M	F	fe	E	E	fe	E	*	*	F	fe	fe	.44
C27	M	W	M	f	fe	fe	fe	fe	e	e	e	fe	fe	e	.43
C19	F	M	M	F	fe	fe	fe	e	e	E	E	F	e	e	.41
C32	M	LM	NM	F	f	e	f	fe	fe	E	E	fe	E	E	.41
N32	F	LM	NM	F	fe	e	fe	fe	e	e	e	f	e	e	.41
P25	F	W	NM	e	f	f	f	e	fe	fe	e	E	e	e	.41
C22	M	W	NM	fe	fe	fe	e	fe	e	e	e	e	e	e	.39
N10	F	W	M	F	fe	e	e	fe	e	e	e	fe	e	e	.39
P28	M	LM	M	e	f	fe	f	fe	fe	fe	fe	e	e	e	.39
C02	M	W	NM	fe	fe	fe	e	fe	e	e	e	E	E	E	.36
N20	M	W	M	F	fe	e	e	e	e	e	e	f	e	e	.36
N06	M	LM	NM	F	fe	fe	fe	fe	fe	E	E	E	E	E	.34
C04	M	W	NM	F	E	fe	E	E	e	E	E	fe	fe	E	.32
P06	M	LM	M	F	E	e	E	E	e	e	e	fe	fe	fe	.32

	Sex	Class	Marriage												Index
N13	M	LM	NM	f	e	e	e	e	e	e	E	fe	e	e	.30
C24	F	LM	M	f	e	E	E	e	E	e	e	fe	e	fe	.27
Co7	M	LM	M	f	e	E	E	E	E	E	E	e	fe	fe	.25
C38	M	W	M	F	fe	E	E	E	E	e	e	E	fe	e	.25
P23	M	LM	NM	?	f	fe	fe	e	e	E	E	?	E	E	.25
Po5	F	LM	M	fe	fe	fe	E	E	E	e	e	fe	E	E	.23
P24	F	LM	M	?	e	e	E	e	e	E	e	?	fe	fe	.22
N29	M	M	M	E	E	E	E	E	E	E	E	f	E	E	.20
P14	F	W	NM	e	fe	fe	fe	fe	e	e	f	E	E	E	.20
P27	F	LM	M	fe	e	e	e	e	E	e	e	E	e	e	.20
C11	M	W	M	F	E	E	E	E	e	E	E	E	e	e	.18
P13	F	LM	NM	E	E	E	E	E	E	fe	E	E	E	E	.18
C28	F	LM	M	E	E	E	E	E	E	e	E	E	E	E	.14
Po1	F	LM	M	e	e	E	E	E	E	e	E	E	E	E	.11
Po8	F	M	M	E	E	E	E	E	E	E	E	E	E	E	.09
P10	M	LM	M	E	E	E	E	E	E	E	E	E	E	E	.09
No2	M	M	M	?	e	e	E	e	E	E	E	?	E	E	.06
C29	M	LM	M	E	e	E	E	E	E	E	E	E	E	E	.05
P21	M	M	M	E	e	E	E	E	E	E	E	E	E	E	.05
Column index value:				.80	.75	.72	.72	.72	.68	.56	.52	.52	.38	.37	.61

† Under 'speaker characteristics' we indicate locality of residence (*Hawkesbury*, *Cornwall*, *North Bay*, or *Pembroke*) and informant number, sex (*Male* or *Female*), social class (*Middle*, *Lower-Middle*, or *Working*), and type of marriage (*Mixed* or *Non-Mixed*).

‡ Under 'situations of communication' we indicate settings and interlocutors: (1) informant → friends at school in class; (2) mother → informant; (3) father → informant; (4) mother ←→ father; (5) informant → mother; (6) informant → father; (7) informant → siblings at home; (8) informant → siblings outside the home; (9) informant → friends at school in corridors; (10) informant → friends at home; (11) informant → friends outside the home. Language-use patterns: F = always in French; f = mostly in French; fe = as often in French as in English; e = mostly in English; E = always in English.

§ Asterisks indicate inapplicable questions, question marks unavailable data, and parentheses inferred information.

top portion of the index use French categorically in the situations of communication involving members of the family (situations 2–8). Though the other 6 speakers variably use English in some of these situations, they still use French most of the time (indicated by f), except in one case (H16; .91; situation 5) where it is used on a par with English (indicated by fe). This slight penetration of English in family situations seems to be largely limited to communication between siblings outside the home (situation 8) and is probably the result of an extension of the pattern of variable language use with peers (situations 9–11). This is indicative of an incipient trend towards language shift, since, in accordance with our definition of shift, communication with siblings outside the home is a situation which does not force English upon the francophone. Where these 20 speakers differ most from the previous 16 is in their patterns of language use with friends at school in the corridors, at home, and outside the home (situations 9–11). As one descends the top portion of the figure from speaker C23 (index value .98) to speaker C21 (index value .80), it can be seen that frequency of use of English increases steadily. Understandably, to the extent that these speakers have English-speaking friends, they will use English with them, especially outside the confines of the school. However, linguistic accommodation to unilingual peers is not the only explanation, since seven (or 35 per cent) of these 20 speakers use English more often than expected in 'unsupervised' peer-group interactions (situations 10 and 11), considering the proportion of anglophone friends that they report.[2] Such 'overuse' of English—especially if it goes as far as predominant use (indicated by e) or categorical use (indicated by E)—is also evidence of an incipient trend towards language shift. The classroom, finally, is practically the sole preserve of French (situation 1).

The .80+ speakers, then, exhibit either pervasive use of French or language compartmentalization according to interlocutor, with some influence of setting; French is used categorically with family members (parents and siblings) at home, but only variably with peer-group members (siblings and friends) outside the home. It is only normal that, as the number and variety of situations of language use increase in the course of an individual's socialization, French should enter into competition with English for allocation to some of these new situations of communication. Thus, even if strict compartmentalization of the languages is achieved by an individual from an exclusively French-speaking home, his or her frequency of use of French will perforce decline from childhood to adolescence. We might want to refer to this as *language restriction without shift.* Examples are provided by speakers P02 (index value .86) and C21 (index value .80), whose preponderant use of English with

---

[2] Information on the ratio of francophone vs. anglophone friends was obtained in the course of the oral interviews with the minority-community students. We reasoned that, if the informant's average frequency of use of French in situations 10 and 11 was appreciably lower than the proportion of his or her francophone friends, we had evidence of shift to English.

friends simply reflects the fact that most of them are anglophone, and nothing else.

As concerns the language-acquisition histories of the 36 speakers that make up the top portion of the index, it can be safely assumed that all acquired French as a mother tongue, given that at adolescence they still reported categorical use of French within the family at home.

Fourteen of the 48 speakers in the middle portion of the index also show patterned language use, although the patterning is not as favourable to French as was that of the high-frequency users of French (.80 ≤ index value ≤ .98), because the number of situations of communication allocated to French is smaller by one. While for these 14 speakers communication with parents remains categorically French (situations 2–6), English is now used to a variable extent with siblings in the home (situation 7), in what looks like a carry-over of language-use patterns with siblings outside the home (situation 8) and more generally with peers (situations 9, 10, and 11). Furthermore, when frequency of use of French with peers (situations 10 and 11 only) was examined as a function of reported proportion of francophone vs. anglophone friends, 12 (or 86 per cent) of the 14 speakers in question were found to be doing more than just accommodating unilingual peers; they were in fact using English when they did not have to with French-speaking peers. (Recall that the proportion for the .80–.98 speakers was only 7 out of 20 or 35 per cent.) If we were to speculate about these speakers' language-acquisition histories, we would have to suppose that they too acquired French as a mother tongue by being exposed to it in the home but only learned English later through socialization in the wider, mainly English-speaking community.

The remaining 34 speakers making up the middle range of the index (five of whom are of mixed parentage) may be said to exhibit uncompartmentalized language use. It is the parents themselves who seem to have been responsible for introducing English in the home in the first place, since they speak it to one another and/or to their children (situations 2–4) most of the time to some of the time. None, however, has gone as far as totally abandoning the use of French in these situations. It may be surmised that these 34 speakers, contrary to the previous 14, were exposed to French *and* English at home at an early age and thus acquired the two languages simultaneously as opposed to sequentially. Twenty-two (or 65 per cent) overuse English in 'unsupervised' peer-group interactions (situations 10 and 11), in view of the proportion of francophone vs. anglophone friends that they report. We may observe finally that the classroom (situation 1) no longer escapes English-language penetration.

It is interesting to note that the dividing line between the middle and bottom portions of the index falls after a speaker (P22; .45) who exhibits perfect language compartmentalization. In contrast, none of the 33 speakers in the bottom portion of the index shows such patterned language use. The home, normally a minority-language sanctuary, has been thoroughly penetrated by

English. Twenty-two are the offspring of linguistically mixed marriages. Thus exogamy by itself suffices to explain two-thirds of the cases of low index values. Not only that, 15 of the 18 informants who have the lowest scores on the index (<.30) are of mixed parentage, meaning that exogamy accounts for over 80 per cent of these cases! Language choice in these 22 mixed households has taken place very much in the way Castonguay's (1979) findings would lead one to predict. Indeed, the average frequency of use of French between parents (situation 4) is only .09 for the speakers located in the bottom portion of the index who have mixed parents. However, as we had more or less suspected (see Chapter 2 n. 20), the situation is not quite as sombre if one looks at the total subsample of the 28 students of mixed parentage (see Table 4.4).

First, 8 (or 29 per cent) of the 28 adolescents reported that their parents use French categorically, predominantly, or on a par with English when communicating with each other at home (situation 4), with an average frequency of use of French of .22 for this situation. The reader will recall that Castonguay found that only 10 per cent of Franco-Ontarians who had contracted a mixed marriage in 1971 reported French as their main language of communication at home. The discrepancy between the provincial proportion and that revealed by our sample may be due to the fact that the latter was drawn in only four localities and thus is hardly representative of the province as a whole. More interestingly, it may also reflect the fact that it is only made up of couples who have children and who have chosen to send them to a French-medium school. Such couples represent a 'select' subsample of the universe of linguistically mixed marriages that seems to exhibit a higher than average level of motivation to maintain French at home.

In contrast to mixed parents, homolinguistic ones generally draw the line at equal use of French and English at home. Only speakers N13 (index value .30) and P13 (index value .18) have non-mixed parents who have moved beyond this threshold and given up French almost entirely when interacting with their children or with each other (situations 2–4 in bottom portion of Table 4.3).

As concerns language use in peer-group interactions in 'unsupervised' settings (situations 10 and 11), a shift to English was detected once more, as 23 (or 70 per cent) of the 33 speakers located in the bottom portion of the index failed to use French as often as they could have based on the reported ratio of francophone vs. anglophone friends. In short, the speakers in the bottom portion of the index tend toward pervasive use of English, especially if they are the offspring of linguistically mixed couples. The one situation which resists the intrusion of English, relatively speaking, is the classroom (situation 1). In terms of language-acquisition histories, it is clear that the speakers with the feeblest index values are comparable to second-language learners of French, having barely been exposed to this language in the home. Others in the bottom portion of the index probably acquired both languages in the home.

Having examined the language-use patterns of the speakers who make up the three portions of the language-use index, we need to examine the relationship that holds between levels of French-language use and bilingualism. In theory, the relationship will be one of communicating vessels: knowledge of English should be inversely proportional to French-language use. Table 4.5 shows that it is precisely such an inverse relationship which holds at the upper and lower ends of the French-language-use continuum. Without exception, informants with an index value greater or equal to .80 and residing in Hawkesbury reported that they spoke French better than English (74 per cent said they had a lot of difficulty speaking English). Conversely, 85 per cent of the informants located at the bottom of the continuum (index lower or equal to .44) reported that they spoke English better than French, although only 9 per cent said they experienced a lot of difficulty speaking French. This quite obviously is a reflection of the positive influence that French-language schooling has had on their capacity in this language. The remaining 15 per cent reported balanced bilingualism. It is clear, then, that the sample does not include any speakers 'suffering' from extreme minority-language-use restriction, such as are found in situations of language death without educational support in the threatened language (e.g. the case of East Sutherland Gaelic investigated by Dorian 1981).

The relationship between French-language use and bilingualism is a lot less clear-cut as concerns the mid-portion of the index (.45–.79) and the higher portion (.80–1.00)—not including the Hawkesbury informants. One may suppose that it is the milieu (predominantly English-speaking) which is responsible for the fact that 47 per cent of the minority-locality speakers who have an index value of .80 or higher evaluated themselves as being balanced bilinguals, in spite of the fact that all come from homes in which English has made no penetration at all. We may infer from the fact that none of these informants reported bilingualism of the English-dominant type that being raised in a genuine French-speaking home—and possibly also attending school in that language—are necessary conditions for mother-tongue maintenance in a minority environment. If these conditions are fulfilled, subsequent development of bilingualism in the majority language will be of the 'additive' kind. Thus for them French truly remains a mother tongue. As concerns the informants whose index value is comprised between .45 and .79, Table 4.5 shows that, if a majority of them reported French-dominant or balanced bilingualism, more than one-third (37 per cent) evaluated themselves as dominant in English. Three explanations may be offered: (1) incipient English penetration in the home (a total of 13 per cent come from homes where English is used as often as or more often than French), (2) widespread use of English with friends, and, of course, (3) influence of the mainly English-speaking milieu, which presents numerous domains where the interlocutors of our informants are unilingual in English and where the latter must perforce interact in English. The environmental factor is particularly evident in the city of Pembroke, where

TABLE 4.4. *Scalar tabulation of language-use patterns, minority-community informants from mixed marriages* (N = 28)

Speaker characteristics†				Situations of communication‡											Speaker index value
Loc.	Sex	Class	Marr.	1	2	3	4	5	6	7	8	9	10	11	
N33	M	W	M	F	F	F	F	F	F	F	F	F	E	E	.82
Co3	F	W	M	F	f	fe	fe	fe	fe	f	f	F	fe	fe	.68
Co5	M	LM	M	F	f	F	f	f	F	f	f	E	e	e	.66
C36	F	LM	M	F	f	f	f	f	f	fe	fe	F	e	e	.66
C40	M	LM	M	E	f	fe	f	fe	fe	e	fe	E	fe	fe	.45
N12	F	LM	M	F	e	fe	fe	e	fe	e	e	F	e	e	.45
N28	F	LM	M	F	fe	E	E	fe	E	*§	*	F	fe	fe	.44
C27	M	W	M	f	fe	fe	fe	fe	e	E	e	fe	fe	e	.43
C19	F	M	M	F	fe	fe	fe	fe	e	E	E	F	e	e	.41
N10	F	W	M	F	fe	fe	e	fe	fe	fe	fe	fe	e	e	.39
P28	M	LM	M	e	fe	fe	e	fe	e	e	e	e	e	e	.39
N20	M	W	M	F	E	e	E	e	e	e	e	f	e	e	.36
P06	M	LM	M	F	e	E	E	E	E	e	e	fe	fe	fe	.32
C24	F	LM	M	f	e	E	E	e	E	e	e	fe	e	fe	.27
C07	M	LM	M	f	e	E	E	e	E	e	E	e	fe	fe	.25

	Sex	Class	Marr.	1	2	3	4	5	6	7	8	9	10	11	Index
C38	M	W	M	F	fe	E	E	e	E	e	e	E	e	e	.25
Po5	F	LM	M	fe	fe	E	E	fe	E	e	e	fe	E	E	.23
P24	M	LM	M	?§	e	E	E	e	E	e	e	?	fe	fe	.22
N29	M	M	M	F	E	e	E	E	e	E	E	f	E	E	.20
P27	F	LM	M	e	fe	e	E	e	E	e	e	E	e	e	.20
C11	M	W	M	fe	E	e	E	E	e	e	e	E	e	e	.18
C28	F	LM	M	E	E	E	E	e	E	fe	fe	E	E	E	.14
Po1	F	LM	M	e	e	e	E	E	E	e	e	E	E	E	.11
Po8	F	M	M	E	E	E	E	fe	E	e	e	E	E	E	.09
P10	M	LM	M	E	fe	E	E	e	E	E	E	E	E	E	.09
No2	M	M	M	?	e	E	E	e	E	E	E	?	E	E	.06
C29	M	LM	M	E	e	E	e	E	E	E	E	E	E	E	.05
P21	M	M	M	E	e	E	e	e	E	E	E	E	E	E	.05
Column index value:				.62	.38	.28	.22	.33	.25	.29	.28	.41	.22	.22	.32

† Under 'speaker characteristics' we indicate locality of residence (*Cornwall*, *North Bay*, or *Pembroke*) and informant number, sex (*Male* or *Female*), social class (*Middle*, *Lower-Middle*, or *Working*), and type of marriage (*Mixed*).

‡ Under 'situations of communication' we indicate settings and interlocutors: (1) informant → friends at school in class; (2) mother → informant; (3) father → informant; (4) mother ←→ father; (5) informant → mother; (6) informant → father; (7) informant → siblings at home; (8) informant → siblings outside the home; (9) informant → friends at school in corridors; (10) informant → friends at home; (11) informant → friends outside the home. Language-use patterns: F = always in French; f = mostly in French; fe = as often in French as in English; e = mostly in English; E = always in English.

§ Asterisks indicate inapplicable questions, question marks unavailable data.

TABLE 4.5. *Correlation between French-language-use index and language skills, linguistic exogamy, and exposure to French at home (%)*

	French-language-use index			
	.80–1.00 (H)†	.80–1.00	.45–.79	.05–.44
Degree of bilingualism				
French-dominant	100	53	23	0
Balanced	0	47	40	15
English-dominant .	0	0	37	85
Difficulty speaking French				
None	100	76	25	15
Little	0	24	60	76
Much	0	0	15	9
Difficulty speaking English				
None	0	59	54	88
Little	26	29	42	12
Much	74	12	4	0
Type of marriage				
Mixed	0	6	10	67
Non-mixed	100	94	90	33
Home exposure to French‡				
French only	100	100	53	0
Mostly French	0	0	34	10
French = English	0	0	12	28
Mostly English	0	0	1	62

† H = Hawkesbury.
‡ Average frequency of use of French in parent-to-informant and parent-to-parent interactions (situations 2, 3, and 4 in Table 4.3).
Source: adapted from Beniak and Mougeon (1989: 75)

Franco-Ontarians make up only a small minority. In fact, in the bottom part of the middle range of the index (.45–.55), there are proportionally more students from this locality (47 per cent) than from the other two localities, Cornwall and North Bay (26 per cent in each).

4.5. Theoretical hypotheses

Restriction in the use of French was controlled under the general assumption that, if it was significant or allowed to go over a critical threshold, there would be imperfect learning, the latter manifesting itself in the form of (1) simplification of certain features of the language (presumably ones which could independently be shown, on the basis of structural arguments, to be 'complex', i.e. irregular, infrequent, opaque, etc.), and (2) interference of various types.

Our broad assumption about the the relationship between language restriction and structural simplification was very much in accord with that formulated by Andersen (1982: 91), although he was dealing more with the specific case of language loss, of which incomplete acquisition—that which we are specifically studying—is a special case: 'When a person's use of a language diminishes [is restricted] in such a way as to cause a break in that person's participation in the linguistic tradition that he previously had full participation in [if he ever had full participation in it], he is thus removed from the type and quantity of linguistic input and linguistic interaction necessary to maintain [acquire] the full lexical, phonological, morphological, and syntactic distinctions that are made by fluent speakers of this language' (our additions). Our goal was not only to uncover those distinctions which are incompletely acquired under conditions of restricted use of a language but also to determine the thresholds of language disuse which are necessary for acquisition to fall short of the mark. Thus to quote Andersen (1982: 91–2) further:

When the amount and type of linguistic input and linguistic interaction become [are] inadequate for a person to maintain [acquire] all the lexical, phonological, morphological, and syntactic distinctions in that language, not all linguistically marked distinctions will be affected equally. Some distinctions will be maintained for a long time [acquired] in spite of the inadequate input and linguistic interaction; others will begin to be eroded very early [will not be acquired] in the change in use of the language; and all other linguistically marked distinctions will fall somewhere in between these two extremes. In other words, there will be a continuum or hierarchy of linguistically marked distinctions ranging from early erosion [non acquisition] of these distinctions to full maintenance [acquisition] in spite of the change in input and interaction [our additions].

By adopting this research framework, we wanted to arrive at a more realistic characterization of the notion of 'degree of difficulty' of linguistic structures. We were and still are personally in favour of an empirical rather than a theoretical approach to this problem, because the former seems to comprise a smaller risk of error. We shall see in Chapter 6, for example, that the child may operate morphological restructurings which are nothing short of stunning in that they apply to forms which in appearance are perfectly regular! This suggests that there is not a one-to-one correspondence between ease of learning and structural complexity.

Our general assumption about the relationship between language-use restriction and interlingual transfer was also in accord with Andersen's (1982: 109) broad hypothesis about morphosyntactic transfer, which predicts that an 'LA [language-attrited speaker] will produce in language X morphological and syntactic constructions based on his stronger language' (our addition).

   Thus we formulated the hypothesis that those of our subjects who reported clear cases of English-language dominance and concomitant French-language-use restriction (i.e. most of the subjects with an index value of .44 or lower) would exhibit various forms of morphosyntactic and, we might add, lexical transfer from English. The reader will recall, however, that our sample includes an intermediary category of semi-restricted speakers who exhibit mid-level French-language use (i.e. speakers with an index value of .45–.79) and who reported either balanced bilingualism, French-, or English-dominant bilingualism. In her research on the spoken Spanish of Puerto Ricans residing in Harlem, Poplack (1982) found that the speech of her balanced (both in terms of frequency of use and mastery of Spanish and English) bilingual subjects was immune to interference. However, her investigation was limited to verbal morphology and her sample had been drawn (unlike ours) in a community that exhibited little shift to English (a situation of stable bilingualism). Therefore, at the outset of our research, it was not obvious to us whether the spoken French of those of our informants who had mid-level indices of French-language use would or would not exhibit interlingual transfer, and, if it did, what form such transfer would take. Chapters 9, 10, and 11 will provide answers to this two-faceted question—at times rather startling ones!

   Finally, as concerns the phenomenon of sociolectal reduction, we derived our general hypothesis from previous studies which had investigated the similar topic of stylistic reduction (e.g. Gal 1984; J. Hill and K. Hill 1977). Our assumption was that the speech of those of our subjects who exhibited the highest level of functional restriction in the use of French (i.e. who had an index value of .44 or less and who tended to confine their use of French to the school domain) would exhibit a significant decline or even total loss of non-standard variants of vernacular Ontarian French.

4.6. Limitations

A limitation of our corpus is that, since it is not constructed with an 'apparent time' dimension, we shall not be able to say much at all about whether the cases of linguistic variation under study are stable or changes in progress (Labov 1981). None the less, as others have done, we might still wish to speak of 'change' in at least two other senses: (1) in the sense of departure from an external standard monolingual norm (Trudgill 1976–7), or (2) in the sense of departure from an internal-community norm (Haugen 1977). In a bilingual setting such as the one we are investigating, the internal-community norm or bench-mark would be that which the speech of the high-frequency users of French from Hawkesbury embodies, that is, the most 'conservative norm' in Dorian's words (1981: 116). It is in this second sense that we shall be employing the word 'change' in this book when referring to developments in the speech of the adolescents from the minority francophone communities. As Trudgill (1983: 124–5) himself acknowledges, the first criterion for establishing change seems less than satisfactory, since there is no telling whether the external *vernacular* monolingual norm does not itself exhibit the same departures from the Standard as does the contact variety. Worse still, when the contact variety has had a prolonged independent existence (as is the case of Arvanítika, the Albanian dialect of Greece studied by Trudgill), to take the non-contact variety (i.e. mainland Albanian) as the norm of comparison is all the more unwarranted (Dorian 1986).

Be that as it may, if it is true that turning to the most conservative local speech form as norm of comparison allows the sociolinguist to avoid the all-too-common pitfall of taking the standard variety as a base-line comparison, it has to be admitted that it may only amount to displacing the problem, for the developments which the local conservative norm enable him to identify will risk in turn being perceived as *deviations* from an ideal language state (negative perception which will only add to the already numerous prejudices of which minority-language groups are the butt). Which is why, we think, sociolinguists investigating minority languages should make a special effort to examine the linguistic developments which they reveal from a functional point of view. More specifically, they should attempt to tease apart those (if there are any) that are dysfunctional because they constitute cases of loss (without compensation) of means of encoding ('destructurings'—our translation from the French original—in Valdman's 1979*a*: 10 terminology), and those which simply correspond to alternative ways of structuring the system. Only changes of the first type might be legitimately considered 'bad' to the extent that they entail an inadequacy in the language (see Trudgill 1983: Chapters 5 and 6 for a discussion of the conceptually clear but empirically difficult to prove distinction between structural simplification and reduction).

4.7. Data analysis

Wherever possible (i.e. quantity of data permitting), we resorted to the VARBRUL 2S programme as a tool for statistical analysis (Sankoff 1979). This programme does a stepwise regression analysis, yielding an ordered selection of the factor groups (e.g. speaker gender) which are significant predictors of variant choice. It also provides the effect on variant choice of each one of the factors (e.g. male, female) belonging to a significant factor group. The effects vary between 0 and 1, with values greater than .5 favouring rule application (i.e. the realization of the linguistic variable as one variant in preference to another) and values less than .5 inhibiting it. The VARBRUL 2S programme also gives two more general measures, one of the overall goodness of fit (log likelihood), the other of the variable rule's probability of application irrespective of the contribution of the factor groups (input probability). Only for two linguistic variables were we unable to perform such a variable-rule analysis. In both cases the data were simply insufficient for the number of factor groups considered, the problem being compounded by the existence of knockout factors. Thus for these two variables we had no other recourse but to present and interpret frequency data expressed in the form of percentages.

We should point out one other aspect of the VARBRUL 2S programme. Having been designed for the analysis of binary variables (i.e. variables realized as either one of two variants), multi-variant variables such as the ones we shall be examining in Chapters 8 and 11 pose a problem of token classification, i.e. that of determining which of the possible sets of binary oppositions to which the variable must be reduced allows the best prediction of variation (Sankoff and Rousseau 1989). In the case of a three-variant variable, the possible token classifications are V_1 vs. (V_2 and V_3), (V_1 and V_2) vs. V_3, and (V_1 and V_3) vs. V_2. Once the data are classified in this way, a normal binary analysis of one variant vs. the other two combined can be performed, followed by a second binary analysis of the two previously combined variants. The log likelihoods are added to get the overall log likelihood. These same two steps are repeated for the other sets of token classifications, with the lowest overall log likelihood indicating the best token classification.

An alternative way of analysing a multi-variant variable is to consider each variant separately and perform a variable-rule analysis with the VARBRUL 3 programme (Rousseau 1983). However, unlike VARBRUL 2S, the VARBRUL 3 programme (in its current guise at least) has the drawback that it does not select and order the significant factor groups. The output merely consists in a log likelihood, input probabilities (one for each variant), and factor effects. Note also that the neutral factor effect in a three-variant analysis is no longer .5 but .333. Details regarding the exact statistical treatment of the data will be provided in the relevant chapters.

5

Simplification

In this chapter we shall examine a case of simplification relating to subject–verb number concord in the third person plural. Subject–verb agreement in the third person plural has been the focus of several recent quantitative studies in sociolinguistics, most prominent among these being that of Naro (1981). Naro has shown that in Brazilian Portuguese there is a rather marked tendency for the 3pl. forms of verbs to be replaced by their 3sg. counterparts in the speech of the lower uneducated classes (e.g. *eles dão* 'they give' > *eles dá* 'they gives'). In other words, the rule of subject–verb agreement is undergoing a process of elimination from the grammar of popular Brazilian Portuguese. Naro's study is important because it proposes a model of syntactic change based on the notion of 'saliency'. According to this model, a syntactic change starts at a point in the grammar where it produces the least noticeable result. Thus he shows that the 3pl. verb forms are levelled in inverse proportion to their degree of phonetic saliency (i.e. material difference with respect to their 3sg. counterparts). However, no convincing explanation is given for why this should be so.[1] Kiparsky (1980: 413) has pointed out furthermore that *phonetic* saliency is just one aspect of a broader saliency hypothesis encompassing, among other factors, frequency of occurrence:

An innovation progresses through the system beginning with the least salient circumstances, where saliency is a function of how different the old and new forms are phonetically, how monitored the speech is, and I would like to add, how frequent the form is and how much the innovation deviates from the canonical syntactic or phonological pattern of the language. This accounts for the well-known tendency for 'small' morphological alternations to be leveled out before 'big' ones, for innovations to progress relatively further in informal speech and marked morphological categories . . .[2]

This chapter is based on a paper originally entitled 'Leveling of the 3sg./pl. Verb Distinctions in Ontarian French' which the authors presented at the Eleventh Annual Linguistic Symposium on Romance Languages held at the University of Texas at San Antonio, 11–13 March 1981. It was published the following year as part of the selected proceedings edited by James P. Lantolf and Gregory B. Stone, *Current Research in Romance Languages* (Bloomington, Ind.: Indiana University Linguistics Club), 126–44.

[1] A natural explanation which immediately suggests itself is that perceptually less salient distinctions would be harder to hear and thus easier to miss than perceptually more salient ones. For a recent attempt at understanding the role of perception in constraining linguistic variation and change, see Guy (1988a).

[2] Naro first began sketching his model of syntactic diffusion along the axis of phonetic saliency in Naro and Lemle (1976). It is to this earlier article of Naro's that Kiparsky refers.

The problem, however, is that phonetic saliency and frequency of occurrence are often confounded, morphologically salient oppositions usually being best preserved in high frequency lexical items. Is it possible to tell, then, whether it is phonetic saliency or frequency of occurrence which is the real factor guiding the diffusion of a syntactic change such as loss of subject–verb agreement (see section 5.3.1)?

Poplack (1980a, b) has studied the variable phonological rule of word-final -n deletion in Puerto Rican Spanish as it is spoken in the United States. Since -n is the regular 3pl. inflection, rule application results in a form which coincides exactly with the 3sg. one (e.g. *ellos hablan* 'they speak' > *ellos habla* 'they speaks'). Let us clarify right away a point about the Puerto Rican Spanish data which will be of crucial importance later, in the conclusion to this chapter. Subject–verb concord remains categorical whenever the 3sg./pl. verb oppositions involve more than just absence vs. presence of inflectional -n. Thus there is no evidence that in New York City Puerto Rican Spanish the rule of word-final -n deletion has triggered an analogical generalization of 3sg. verb forms at the expense of their 3pl. counterparts (e.g. *hablá* 'they spoke' instead of *hablaro(n)*). In other words, loss of subject–verb agreement in the 3rd person is coterminous with the output of the phonological rule of word-final -n deletion. However, it should be said that, in Spanish, contrary to Portuguese, the 3pl. verb forms practically always differ from their 3sg. counterparts by just this additional -n (the only exception is in the preterite, see above example). A tendency towards replacement of 3pl. by 3sg. verb forms has also been observed outside the Romance family in a study by Lefebvre (1980) on Peruvian Quechua (e.g. *miku-n-ku* 'they eat' > *miku-n* 'they eats').

In this study we shall look at how the 3pl. forms of the few verbs which still maintain a 3sg./pl. distinction are faring in the speech of our subjects. It will be shown that these morphologically marked forms tend to give way to the unmarked 3sg. ones (e.g. *ils veulent* 'they want' > *ils veut* 'they wants'; *ils savent* 'they know' > *ils sait* 'they knows'). The levelling process under study in Ontarian French can be looked upon as a case of variation whereby the 3pl. variable is actualized via two variants, a morphologically 3pl. verb form (very often but not always in agreement with the prescribed standard) or a morphologically 3sg. one (in which case the form is always non-standard). Using quantitative methodology, we set out to provide answers to three basic questions concerning this levelling process. First, is it conditioned by certain linguistic factors? In particular, how does Naro's notion of phonetic saliency fare as an explanation? Second, is it correlated with certain social characteristics of the speakers? In particular, is lower-class speech the social locus of levelling, as it is in the case of Brazilian Portuguese? And third, how did it originate in Ontarian French? The purpose of these questions is to contribute to our understanding of the mechanism of linguistic change in a language-contact situation involving restriction in the use of the minority language.

Ideally, we would want to come up with an explanation which encompasses the various sociolinguistic settings in which levelling has been attested, at least the settings involving Romance languages. Thus an explanation which would be valid for Ontarian French but not for Brazilian Portuguese, or vice versa, would have to be regarded as possibly suspect because of its lack of generality. This is not to deny, on the other hand, that dissimilar social conditions may give rise to similar linguistic developments, nor that such developments may be structurally constrained in different ways. Still, an explanation which misses a generalization will be less elegant and possibly even wrong in the particular sociolinguistic setting to which it is meant to apply in the first place.

5.1. History, scope, and nature of the 3sg./pl. distinctions

Old French was characterized by a conjugation which distinguished person and number via alternating verb stems and endings which made the use of subject pronouns redundant. The number of distinctive stems and endings progressively diminished, however, as a result respectively of analogical levelling and phonetic 'erosion', at the same time as the use of subject pronouns became obligatory (Wartburg 1962: 101, 127, 130–1). This transformation (analogical restructuring + phonetic erosion) of the verbal morphology never reached completion, however, as certain persons are still marked by an inflectional ending (e.g. *nous voul-ons* /vul-ɔ̃/ 'we want', *vous vul-ez* /vul-e/ 'you (pl.) want') and certain verbs still preserve stem alternations, especially across tenses (e.g. *je veux* /vø/ 'I want', *je voud-rai* /vud-re/ 'I shall want'), but also within the same tense, especially the present indicative (e.g. *je veux* /vø/ 'I want', *nous voul-ons* /vul-ɔ̃/ 'we want', *ils veulent* /vœl/ 'they want').

As revealed by a detailed consultation of *Le Nouveau Bescherelle* (1980), a very useful dictionary of the conjugations of all of the 12,000 or so verbs of contemporary Standard French, outside the future indicative it is only in the present that there still exists a surface morphological opposition between 3sg. and 3pl. verb forms. Further, while all verbs show such an overt opposition in the future, this tense is rarely used in spoken French, having come to be largely replaced by the periphrastic future (conjugated form of *aller* 'go' + infinitive, e.g. *je vais y penser* 'I am going to think about it'). Finally, in the present tense only 600 and some odd verbs out of the total of 12,000 or so verbs in the language show morphological covariation as a function of number in the third person. The scope of the 3sg./pl. distinctions is clearly restricted in the verb system of modern Standard French.

Essentially the same situation as that described for Standard French holds for Ontarian French. More specifically, most of the verbs which were found (variably) to show a morphologically marked form in the 3pl. are a subset of the 600-odd verbs which have distinctive 3pl. forms in Standard French. However, paradoxically enough, Ontarian French also includes a handful of verbs which (variably) display a distinctive form in the 3pl. whereas in Standard French they do not![3] Some belong to the so-called 'first' or regular group (i.e. the *-er* verbs), which in Standard French includes only verbs with non-distinctive 3pl. forms. For instance, *jouer* 'to play' is variably realized as *jousent* /ʒuz/ in the 3pl., instead of the standard form *jouent* /ʒu/; another such verb is *continuer* 'to continue', which variably gives *continussent* /kɔ̃tinys/ instead of standard *continuent* /kɔ̃tiny/ in the 3pl. Some also belong to the so-called 'irregular' groups, like *rire* 'to laugh', which variably displays *risent* /riz/ instead of standard *rient* /ri/, or *s'assire*, a non-standard variant of *s'asseoir* 'to sit', which variably features *s'assisent* /sasiz/ instead of the standard non-distinctive form *s'asseoient* /saswa/. These 'overmarked' forms have been countenanced in descriptive works on Canadian French for a long time and are thus not innovations of Ontarian French. Although intriguing, they had to be excluded from the present study since we were interested in exactly the opposite phenomenon, namely undermarking. Also excluded were overmarkings involving the use of a 3pl. verb form with a semantically plural but morphologically singular subject (e.g. *c'est une famille qui ont des problèmes* 'it is a family that have problems' H18–1).[4]

Concerning the nature of the 3sg./pl. oppositions, two main facts can be pointed out. The oppositions are highly regular and predictable in the future and highly diverse and unpredictable in the present. In the future all French verbs end in *-ra* in the 3sg. and in *-ront* in the 3pl. (e.g. *il finira* 'he will finish' vs. *ils finiront* 'they will finish').[5] In the present the 3sg. and 3pl. forms can be best characterized as morphologically indivisible wholes, i.e. as separate stems of the verb (Martinet 1969: 91–120). The reader will find a sample of the range of present tense 3sg./pl. oppositions in Table 5.1, which shows the high degree of morphological diversity displayed by the oppositions. Two involve totally different forms: e.g. 3sg. *est* 'is' vs. 3pl. *sont* 'are'; others are related only minimally: e.g. 3sg. *sait* 'knows' vs. 3pl. *savent* 'know'; still others involve only an additional final consonant in the 3pl. However, for the five verbs which belong to this category, i.e. *dire* 'to say', *connaître* 'to know', *vivre* 'to live', *devoir* 'must', and *mettre* 'to put', there are no fewer than four different final consonants.

Again, Ontarian French differs only minimally from the standard variety in terms of the nature of the 3sg./pl. oppositions. A small number of verbs may

---

[3] The paradox, of course, is that non-standard speech varieties are expected to be further along the path of morphological levelling than the Standard.

[4] The alpha-numeric code following each example identifies the speaker by locality and indicates the line number (or page number for Hawkesbury) of the example in the interview transcript.

[5] This is not to say that speakers never face any problems forming the future. Stem-changing verbs may occasion hesitations as to which is the appropriate future stem. Our corpus contained the following example: *i' t' comprenneront* /kɔ̃prɛnrɔ̃/ *pas* 'they won't understand you', instead of *comprendront* /kɔ̃prãdrɔ̃/ (N30–476).

now and then appear with a morphologically marked 3pl. form which is different from the standard one. Thus, for instance, a verb like *aller* 'to go' is normally realized as *vont* in the 3pl. (the standard form), but also sometimes appears as *allent* /al/. An actual occurrence in our corpus was the following: *Même si y'allent à 'a messe, ils pensent pas* . . . 'Even if they go to mass, they don't think . . .' (C13–077).[6] *Faire* 'to do' is another such verb: its standard 3pl. form in the present is *font*, but we also find *faisent* /fɛz/ in Ontarian French (e.g., *Quand qu'ils se rendent là ben ils le faisent pas pis . . . t'sais . . .* 'When they go there well they don't do it . . . you know . . .' C10–239). Both look like obvious regularizations based on the conjugational model of the dominant *-er* verb group. These non-standard 3pl. forms (which incidentally also occur in Quebec French) were included in the present study since they constitute evidence that the speaker has applied the rule of subject–verb agreement. However, they were grouped together with the 'normal' (i.e. standard) 3pl. forms, such that no separate analysis was done in their case.

5.2. Linguistic parameters

We identified several linguistic parameters which, in theory, could act as constraints on the levelling process. These are:

5.2.1. Verb

In previous studies of variation in the verb system of Ontarian French, e.g. replacement of the irregular auxiliary *être* by *avoir* (Canale, Mougeon, and Bélanger 1978) and omission of the reflexive pronoun of pronominal verbs (Beniak, Mougeon, and Côté 1980), we discovered that there was a considerable amount of variation in the rates of replacement or omission from one verb to the other, and that this variation could be accounted for in terms of a number of linguistic and/or functional properties of the verbs (e.g., notably, frequency of occurrence). In this study we wanted to see whether similar verb-by-verb variation in the rate of levelling of the 3pl. variants obtained, and, if so, to examine what properties of the verbs could account for such variation.

5.2.2. Subject position

In his study of popular Brazilian Portuguese, Naro (1981) found that the position of the plural subject was correlated with the use of 3pl. variants. The rule of concord applied more frequently when the plural subject was

---

[6] The examples are transcribed in such a way as to preserve the 'flavour' of informal spoken Canadian French, especially its numerous deletion or contraction rules (e.g. *l*-deletion, as in the example: *à la > à 'a*).

immediately or closely preposed to the verb than when it was distantly preposed, and more frequently in the latter case than when the subject was postposed. In order to test the effect of subject position on subject–verb agreement in Ontarian French, we distinguished between immediately preposed subjects, closely preposed ones (i.e. those separated from the verb by object clitics or the liaison element /z/), and distantly preposed ones (i.e. those separated from the verb by a sentence, a prepositional phrase, or an adverb). There were no cases of postposed subjects in our data. The subject was sometimes deleted, but, instead of considering this as a special case of subject position, we considered it as a case of absence of plurality in the subject (see next section).

5.2.3. Marking of plurality in subject

Following Lefebvre (1980) and Poplack (1980*a*), we considered the hypothesis that levelling might be blocked or at least significantly reduced when plurality is not already overtly marked in the subject, failing which, singularity rather than plurality would be conveyed. In order to test this functionalist hypothesis, we distinguished between four types of subjects: (1) deleted subjects, almost always *ils* before *sont* (e.g. *(ils) sont après bâtir le gros Simpson* 'they are building the big Simpson's store' C03–182); (2) subjects which are phonetically identical in the sg. and in the pl. (e.g. personal pronouns like *il(s)* /i(l)/ 'he, they (masc.), they (fem.)'[7] and the relative pronoun *qui* 'who, that, which'); (3) subjects which are morphologically plural (e.g. nouns preceded by a plural determiner and pronouns like *eux-autres* 'them', *ceux-là* 'those', etc.); and (4) subjects which consist of a semantically plural quantifier with or without its nominal head (e.g. *la plupart* 'most', *beaucoup de monde* 'many people', etc.).

5.3. Results and discussion

Table 5.1 presents the results of the VARBRUL 2S analysis of concord probability, i.e. use of 3pl. variants. The factor groups appear in order of decreasing statistical significance. With the exception of subject position and plural marking in subject,[8] the factor groups were all found significantly to affect variant choice. In order of diminishing importance they are: verb, locality of residence, French-language-use restriction, social class, and sex.

[7] In popular Canadian French *elles* 'they (fem.)' is non-existent. The fem./masc. opposition is thus neutralized in the 3pl.

[8] For the purpose of testing the effect of subject position, the 287 cases of deleted subjects were coded as part of the 3,750 cases of immediately preposed subject, since this is the surface structure position where subjects can undergo deletion. Naro (1981) proceeded differently by considering deleted subject as a separate subject position. His results for Brazilian Portuguese support our amalgamation, however, as the 3pl. variants were used with nearly equal probability when the subject was immediately preposed (.71) as when it was deleted (.65) (see his Table 10, p. 85).

TABLE 5.1. *Variable-rule analysis of 3pl. subject–verb concord*

Factor groups		3sg. (N)	3pl. (N)	Total	3pl. (%)	Factor effects
Verb	3sg./3pl.					
être	*est/sont*	15	1,254	1,269	99	.976
avoir	*a/ont*	28	1,067	1,095	97	.945
aller	*va/vont*	34	475	509	93	.840
future	*-ra/-ront*	7	39	46	85	.619
faire	*fait/font*	32	110	142	77	.518
comprendre	*comprend/comprennent*	23	68	91	75	.446
savoir	*sait/savent*	30	57	87	66	.409
apprendre	*apprend/apprennent*	10	23	33	70	.399
dire	*dit/disent*	58	122	180	68	.396
connaître	*connaît/connaissent*	7	10	17	59	.388
vouloir	*veut/veulent*	58	142	200	71	.379
vivre	*vit/vivent*	13	16	29	55	.361
venir	*vient/viennent*	41	88	129	68	.344
others		39	89	128	70	.327
prendre	*prend/prennent*	12	30	42	71	.318
pouvoir	*peut/peuvent*	64	77	141	55	.248
devoir	*doit/doivent*	8	12	20	60	.217
mettre	*met/mettent*	13	13	26	50	.210
Locality of residence						
Hawkesbury		7	533	540	99	.658
Cornwall		82	1,428	1,510	95	.671
North Bay		106	908	1,014	90	.490
Pembroke		297	823	1,120	73	.210
French-language use						
Unrestricted		19	1,194	1,213	98	.844
Semi-restricted		270	1,627	1,897	86	.369
Restricted		203	871	1,074	81	.240
Social class						
Middle		68	662	730	91	.561
Lower-middle		199	1,847	2,046	90	.600
Working		225	1,183	1,408	84	.343
Sex						
Male		309	1,880	2,189	86	.389
Female		183	1,812	1,995	91	.611
Subject position						
Immediately preposed		449	3,301	3,750	88	not
Closely preposed		37	348	385	90	sig.
Distantly preposed		6	43	49	88	

TABLE 5.1 *(cont.)*

Factor groups	3sg. (N)	3pl. (N)	Total	3pl. (%)	Factor effects
Plural marking in subject					
Deleted subject	5	282	287	98	
Unmarked pronoun	381	2,680	3,061	88	not
Marked noun or pronoun	103	658	761	86	sig.
Quantifier (+ noun)	3	72	75	96	
TOTAL	492	3,692	4,184	88	.873

5.3.1. Verb

We observed levelling of the 3pl. variants in both tenses (i.e. present and future indicative) in which verbs still exhibit a 3sg./pl. opposition. Consistent with our earlier observation (see section 5.1), the future was quite infrequent in our corpus (only 46 occurrences). Thus we decided to group together all the verbs which were used in that tense into one category, 'future', and to calculate a general rate of use of the 3pl. variants for the future tense. In contrast, it was possible to calculate individual rates for verbs used in the much more frequent present tense. We did so whenever an individual verb had 15 or more occurrences. Verbs with fewer than 15 occurrences were grouped together in the category 'others'. What we have done in Table 5.1 is to provide the 3sg. and 3pl. variants of the verbs which were used 15 or more times in the present tense.[9]

As can be seen from Table 5.1, individual verbs vary widely in their effect on use of the 3pl. variants, a finding which ties in well with our previous discovery of similar verb-by-verb variation in the verb system of Ontarian French. One explanatory factor which we would like to propose is the frequency of the 3pl. variables. It has often been observed that levelling processes tend to affect infrequent elements more than frequent ones, other things being equal (see, among others, Canale, Mougeon, and Bélanger 1978; Hooper 1976; Kiparsky 1980; Martinet 1969: 115ff.). In keeping with this observation, it can be seen that it is *être* and *avoir*, the verbs with the highest frequencies in the 3pl. (1,269 and 1,095 respectively), which have the highest favouring effects on use of the 3pl. variants (.976 and .945). *Aller* has the next highest frequency (509) in the 3pl. and

---

[9] As can be seen, the list of verbs is already long (N=16). F ≥ 15 was a compromise frequency ensuring that we would have a sufficient number of verbs to test the hypothesis of verb-by-verb variation in levelling rate, while at the same time preserving the meaningfulness of the individual rates.

the next highest favouring effect (.840). All the other verbs have much lower frequencies in the 3pl. (≤ 200) and all of them except one (*faire* .518) have disfavouring effects (< .5) on use of the 3pl. variants. In sum, there is definitely a relationship between frequency of agreement and frequency of occurrence of the 3pl. variables. The relationship seems to be characterized by at least two thresholds. There is an upper threshold which separates those highly frequent verbs which strongly inhibit the levelling process (*être* and *avoir*) from that less frequent verb (*aller*) which is not as inhibiting, and a lower threshold which separates these three verbs from those 13 remaining infrequent verbs which are even less inhibiting. The frequency argument is also supported by the behaviour of the 'others' category. The low-frequency verbs grouped in this category display one of the lowest effects (.327) on subject–verb agreement. A high or even an intermediary effect would have been damaging for the frequency explanation.

Only 'future', which we have not yet considered (and which, interestingly, occupies an intermediate position between the high- and low-frequency verbs in terms of its effect on the use of 3pl. variants), seems to be incompatible with the frequency explanation, since it has a relatively high favouring effect (.619) despite a low frequency of occurrence (46). However, as mentioned earlier in section 5.1, the 3pl. future variants are morphologically regular as far as the inflectional ending is concerned (always -*ront*). This property apparently overrides what otherwise should be a negative effect of the low frequency of occurrence of the future tense. In contrast to the 3pl. future variants, the present tense ones do not display a common inflectional ending (see section 5.1). This in turn would explain why, as noted above, the most frequent ones (*sont, ont,* and *vont*)—and thus the most habitualized ones—are undergoing the least amount of replacement by the 3sg. variants.

The finding of verb-by-verb variation is consonant with Conwell's and Juilland's (1963: 157) observations on the levelling of the 3sg./pl. distinctions in the present indicative in Louisiana French, also a contact variety of French.[10] Like us, they noticed that *sont, ont, vont,* and *font* showed more resistance to replacement than the 3pl. variants of the other verbs. Interestingly, however, Conwell and Juilland attributed this greater resistance to the suppletive or near suppletive character of the 3pl. variants *sont, ont, vont,* and *font* rather than to their superior frequency. In a similar vein, Naro (1981) argued that the degree

---

[10] Louisiana French is not to be confused with the variety of French known as 'Cajun', spoken by the descendants of the Acadians who were deported to Louisiana in 1755 following the British conquest of the French colonies in the Maritimes. Louisiana French was originally spoken by French immigrants who came directly from France in the eighteenth century. However, the present-day situation shows much cross-influence between Cajun French, Louisiana French, and even Louisiana French creole (Phillips 1979). In the specific area of verbal morphology, however, Louisiana French appears never to have had the common indicative present 3pl. -*ont* inflectional ending so typical of Acadian and Cajun French: e.g. *ils mangeont* 'they eat' (see conclusion to this chapter).

of levelling of the 3sg./pl. oppositions in popular Brazilian Portuguese depends on the phonetic saliency of these oppositions. Phonetic saliency was defined in terms of stress, phonetic features, and segments not shared by the two verb forms realizing the 3sg./pl. opposition. Naro's findings fitted the phonetic-saliency hypothesis as, the more the 3pl. verb form differed from the 3sg. one, the more frequently it was used by the lower-class Brazilian-Portuguese speakers. It matters, then, that we examine how phonetic saliency fares as an alternative to frequency of the 3pl. variables in accounting for the verb-by-verb variation in the rate of use of the 3pl. variants in Ontarian French.

Using Naro's definition of phonetic saliency (stress excepted as it is fixed in French), it is possible to categorize the oppositions listed in Table 5.1 into four groups. The first group includes the oppositions *est/sont* and *a/ont*. These two oppositions are characterized by the highest degree of phonetic saliency, since they are realized by totally distinct verb forms (cases of suppletion). Ranking second in phonetic saliency is a group which is made up of the oppositions of the verbs *prendre* 'to take', *comprendre* 'to understand', *apprendre* 'to learn', *venir* 'to come', *vouloir* 'to want', *pouvoir* 'can', and *savoir* 'to know'. These 3sg./pl. oppositions involve a difference in vowel quality and an additional consonant (e.g. 3sg. *prend* /prã/ vs. 3pl. *prennent* /prɛn/). The third group includes the 3sg./pl. contrasts of *aller*, *faire*, and the verbs in the future. These oppositions are characterized by a difference in vowel quality only (e.g. 3sg. *va* /va/ vs. 3pl. *vont* /vɔ̃/). The fourth group comprises the 3sg./pl. oppositions of the verbs *mettre*, *dire*, *vivre*, *devoir*, and *connaître*. These oppositions also involve only one element, namely an additional consonant (e.g. 3sg. *met* /mɛ/ vs. 3pl. *mettent* /mɛt/). This last group was judged by the two co-authors (both native speakers of French) to involve a less salient type of opposition than the third, on the grounds that the adjunction of a consonant is perceptually less noticeable than a change in vowel quality.

With this classification in mind, we can now see whether the phonetic saliency of the 3sg./pl. oppositions correlates well with the rate of use of the 3pl. variants. Examination of this question reveals several serious incongruities which raise doubts concerning the explanatory power of the phonetic-saliency principle for Ontarian French. A first incongruity concerns the third group of oppositions. Since the three oppositions of this group all involve the same or a very similar vocalic alternation, we would expect them to have a similar effect on the use of 3pl. variants. This is obviously not the case (*aller* .840, 'future' .619, *faire* .518). Furthermore, the fact that the latter effects are significantly higher than those associated with the 3sg./pl. oppositions of the verbs belonging to group two (the highest effect is .446 for *comprendre)* also contradict the prediction that the lesser phonetic saliency of the oppositions associated with *aller*, 'future', and *faire* should have a negative effect on the use of the 3pl. variants. A third inconformity concerns the oppositions in group two in comparison to those in group four. The greater saliency of the group-two oppositions should correlate with higher effects on the use of 3pl. variants. Yet, as was reported earlier, the effects of the twelve oppositions which make up groups two and four all disfavour subject–verb concord in the 3pl.

In fairness to the principle of phonetic saliency, it correctly predicts that the *est/sont* and *a/ont* oppositions should have the highest effects on the maintenance of 3pl. variants, since they are the most salient ones. However, we have just seen that frequency of the 3pl. variables makes the same predictions for *sont* and *ont* but is not plagued with inconsistencies in the predictions that it makes concerning the 3pl. variants of the other verbs, as is the principle of phonetic saliency. We conclude, therefore, that frequency of the 3pl. variables is a superior explanation for the observed variation in subject–verb agreement in Ontarian French.

5.3.2. Locality of residence and French-language-use restriction

The results concerning these two factor groups are presented and discussed in the same section because of their interrelatedness, as will be demonstrated below. It will actually facilitate things to begin with French-language-use restriction, even though this factor group was selected after locality of residence. Table 5.1 shows that unrestricted use of French has a strong positive effect (.844) on the use of 3pl. variants, whereas semi-restricted and restricted use have strong negative effects (.369 and .240). This result ties in with and amounts to extralinguistic evidence in favour of the previously invoked explanation regarding the effect of individual verb frequency in the 3pl. on the rate of use of 3pl. variants. More precisely, we would like to argue that French-language-use restriction brings about a general decrease in the frequency of use of all the verbs examined here, and that this is why we have found the levelling process to be limited, to all intents and purposes, to the speech of the restricted and semi-restricted users of French. In other words, frequency as a property of individual lexical items is conditioned by a more general property, i.e. frequency of use of the minority language as a whole. This rather obvious truth (now that we have uncovered it!) stands to be obscured so long as one has in mind monolingual speech communities. The finding of a correlation between 3pl. levelling and language restriction is consonant with similar results found in several previous studies of ours on processes of simplification operating in the verbal system of Ontarian French (Beniak, Mougeon, and Côté 1980; Canale, Mougeon, and Beniak 1978), in its prepositional system (Mougeon, Beniak, and Côté 1981), and in its system of demonstrative pronouns (Mougeon, Beniak, and Bélanger 1982). It is also consonant with observations on processes of simplification in 'dying' non-Latin languages such as East Sutherland Gaelic in Scotland (Dorian 1978) and a dialect of German in the valley of Aosta in Italy (Giacalone Ramat 1979). Both studies showed that the simplification processes investigated were non-existent or much less advanced in the speech of the strongest maintainers of the dying minority language.

Why locality of residence turned out to have a significant effect on the rate of use of the 3pl. variants in addition to—indeed ahead of—French-language-use restriction is rather difficult to explain without going into statistical details. It can be better understood by comparing some of the effects associated with each factor group (see Table 5.1). One is especially struck by the fact that the effect associated with residence in Pembroke (.210) is actually lower than the effect associated with restricted use of French (.240)! This is telling us that Pembroke speakers, regardless of their level of use of French, are heavily inclined to level the distinctive 3pl. verb forms. On the other hand, that the effect associated with residence in Hawkesbury (.658) is lower than the effect associated with unrestricted use of French (.844)—in spite of the fact that all but one of the Hawkesbury speakers were precisely *unrestricted* users of French—also needs to be commented upon. Let us mention that, when the factor group locality of residence was considered alone at level one of the statistical analysis, or together with the previously selected factor group (i.e. verb) at level two of the analysis, the effects associated with Hawkesbury were very high (.851 and .880). They dropped as soon as the factor group French-language-use restriction was added at level three of the analysis, thereby suggesting that the effect of residence in Hawkesbury tends to be neutralized (i.e. move toward the .5 value) when the effect of unrestricted use of French is taken into account. One possible explanation for the interlocality differences is that, because our measure of restriction was based on the students' reported frequency of use of French in an appreciable but still limited number of situations (eleven all told; see Chapter 4), it fails to reflect the fact that overall French-language use is higher among the Franco-Ontarian adolescents residing in the strong majority locality of Hawkesbury, which in turn is higher than among those residing in the strong minority locality of Cornwall, and so on. Thus it could very well be that locality of residence compensates, as it were, for the lack of comprehensiveness of the French-language-use measure.[11]

It is possible, however, that this 'technical' explanation is insufficient. We have in mind the very interesting community effect uncovered recently by Poplack (1989) in her study of English code-switches and lexical borrowings into Ottawa–Hull French. She found that speakers, depending on their community of residence, will code-switch and borrow more often or less often than their individual characteristics (i.e. degree of bilingualism and social class) would lead one to expect. The contrasting norms of communication in Ottawa vs. Hull are in fact so strong as to make it possible for speakers resident in Ottawa, where French has minority status, but who have no other characteristics that would make them prone to code-switch into or borrow from the

---

[11] Of course, no measure of language use will ever be exhaustive of the possible situations of communication.

majority language, actually to code-switch and borrow more often than speakers with all the right characteristics, but resident in Hull, where French has majority status! In our case, levelling might be expected to be tied not only to individual degree of French-language-use restriction, but also to the proportion of restricted and semi-restricted speakers in a given community. Thus, the restricted and semi-restricted speakers in Pembroke might be expected to level more than their North Bay counterparts, and the latter more than their Cornwall equivalents, due to differential exposure to their own norm and to the conservative norm of the unrestricted speakers. The hypothesis of a community effect *à la* Poplack (1989) will be examined again in Chapter 10 in connection with an interference-based development.

5.3.3. Social class

The results of Table 5.1 show that working-class background has a disfavouring effect (.343) on the use of 3pl. variants, while middle- or lower-middle class backgrounds have slightly favourable effects (.561 and .600 respectively). The relatively small spread between the three effects may be taken as an indication that 3pl. levelling is not a strong 'indicator' of social-class membership (in the sense in which Labov 1972: 178 has used this term). On the other hand, the slight but nevertheless real working-class connection of 3pl. levelling lends credence to the hypothesis entertained by Labov (1980a: 253)—and others before him—that 'the lowest social class, which is most isolated from the influence of the standard language, would be most free to innovate in a direction distinct from the standard'.

What the results do not tell us, however, is whether a working-class background on its own (that is, without the added contribution of restricted or semi-restricted use of French) is sufficient to trigger levelling. In order to investigate this question, we proceeded to cross-tabulate the data on social class and level of restriction in the use of French (see Table 5.2).

There is some very tentative evidence in the literature that lower-class status is a factor which, on its own, i.e. independently of language restriction, is apparently sufficient to induce 3pl. levelling. For example, Frei (1971) occasionally observed the phenomenon in the French of monolingual European adult francophones with little education. Bauche (1929) also reports a few examples in popular Parisian French. To judge by these reports, however, 3pl. levelling is quite sporadic in the speech of these lower-class European monolinguals. It logically follows that, when both language restriction and absence or low levels of schooling in French are present, 3pl. levelling is likely to be more advanced. Such seems to be the case for the varieties of French spoken in the Franco-American enclaves (Old Mines, Missouri, and Frenchville, Pennsylvania) examined by Valdman (1980). In fact, in these

TABLE 5.2. *Levelling as a function of language restriction and social class*

French-language use	Social class	Use of 3pl. variants (%)
Unrestricted	Middle	0.95
	Lower-middle	1.58
	Working	1.97
Semi-restricted	Middle	13.91
	Lower-middle	11.60
	Working	19.91
Restricted	Middle	17.18
	Lower-middle	16.14
	Working	26.59

varieties the 3sg. is used as an invariant verb form for all the persons of the singular and the plural, including 2pl.

The results presented in Table 5.2 support the idea that the weak exposure and low sensitivity to the standard language characteristic of lower-class milieux tend to favour levelling. As can be seen, the speakers from a working-class background consistently display higher levels of levelling than those from the other two social classes, irrespective of how restricted their use of French is. However, consistent with the above reports in the literature, language restriction seems to be necessary in order to elevate 3pl. levelling beyond the status of mere 'performance error', as its incidence in unrestricted working-class speech remains extremely low (only 1.97 per cent). The correct conclusion appears to be that lower-class status and, more generally, isolation from the influence of a standard, can only play a secondary, mediating role in 3pl. levelling once this process has been touched off by language restriction. The persistence of a class effect, in itself, is a particularly interesting finding, especially as regards the restricted speakers. At first sight, language restriction and social stratification of speech seem at odds. Why would restricted users of a minority language continue to monitor their speech and self-correct (as best they can)? Mougeon (1982) made a similar finding in connection with another case of simplification of the morphology of the verb system of Ontarian French, namely levelling of the distinction between pronominal and simple verbs via reflexive pronoun omission. Chapters 10 and 12 will again address the problem of the restricted speakers' differential capacity to 'avoid' non-standard innovations depending on their social background.

5.3.4. Sex

Of all the parameters which were found to have an effect on the use of 3pl. variants, speaker gender makes the smallest contribution. This is reflected in the small spread between the slightly disfavouring effect of male sex (.389) and the slightly favouring effect of female sex (.611). It would seem, then, that the variable under study is also only weakly indicative of the speaker's sex. That the female adolescents were found to use the 3pl. variants slightly more frequently than the male adolescents probably reflects a greater sensitivity (Labov 1972) and a more positive orientation (Hudson 1980) to the standard language. Furthermore, it is in keeping with the finding of a weak effect as well of social class.

5.3.5. Subject position

The results of Table 5.1 indicate that the variation in the rate of use of 3pl. variants as a function of the position of the subject is not significant. This contrasts with Naro's (1981) results for popular Brazilian Portuguese. Although less than significant, the subject-position results for Ontarian French were none the less qualitatively in line with those for popular Brazilian Portuguese, as is shown by the effects of the three subject positions on the rate of use of the 3pl. variants: immediately preposed subject (.560), closely preposed (.541), and distantly preposed (.400). As can be seen, concord probability increases as the distance between the subject and the verb lessens. It is possible that the discrepancy is a consequence of the fact that we did not distinguish exactly the same subject positions (see section 5.2.2), but it is more likely attributable to the very unequal distribution of the data by subject position (i.e. the great majority of subjects were immediately preposed). According to Sankoff (1988), uneven distribution of variable tokens may occur in corpus-based socio-linguistic research, since the number of token occurrences per context depends on the relative frequency of each context in discourse and hence can be highly variable. Such a skewed distribution may have the effect of making it difficult to prove the existence of statistically significant differences.

5.3.6. Plural marking in subject

Like the previous one, the present factor group does not have a significant effect on the levelling of the 3pl. variants. This suggests that the functionalist hypothesis examined by Lefebvre (1980) and Poplack (1980a) does not hold for the levelling process which applies in Ontarian French. Again, although not significantly different from each other, the effects of the different types of subjects on the rate of use of the 3pl. variants in Ontarian French are none the less qualitatively consistent with the functionalist hypothesis, since concord probability increases as overt plural marking in the subject decreases: marked noun or pronoun (.402), quantifier (+ noun) (.461), morphologically unmarked pronoun (.482), and deleted subject (.651). Perhaps the reason why the levelling process was not found to be sensitive to plural marking in the subject is that the plurality of the unmarked or deleted subject is recoverable in a straightforward manner from the plurality of its nominal antecedent. In any case, the formal ambiguity resulting from the levelling process under study is not new, since it already prevails elsewhere in the verb system of modern French as we saw in section 5.1, i.e. for the great majority of verbs not displaying a 3sg./pl. opposition when used in the present indicative with an unmarked subject (e.g. *i' mange(nt)* /mãʒ/ 'he eats, they eat').

5.4. Origin of the levelling process

We now have a good idea of the linguistic and social constraints of 3pl. levelling, but how exactly did the variable replacement of 3pl. verb forms by their 3sg. counterparts originate in Ontarian French? This is the third question we said we would try to answer in this chapter.

In his longitudinal study of the acquisition of French, Grégoire (1968) observed that the first verb forms which his two young subjects attempted to produce were 3sg. ones. He also observed that his two young subjects sometimes used the 3sg. forms of some of the verbs under study here instead of their 3pl. counterparts, but not vice versa. We may infer from Grégoire's observations that there is a developmental stage in the acquisition of the 3pl. verb forms during which the latter are variably replaced by the previously acquired 3sg. ones. Children's prior acquisition of the 3sg. verb forms is not surprising when one considers that they are much more frequent (see Juilland, Brodin, and Davidovitch's 1970 frequency dictionary) and are phonetically identical with other forms, whereas their 3pl. counterparts are not.[12] Children's generalization of the 3sg. forms to 3pl. contexts is hardly surprising either, since the 3sg. forms are the only ones at their disposal for the expression of the concept of 3pl. that they have already grasped but whose verb forms they have yet to internalize due to their infrequency (both in terms of occurrence and paradigmatic 'presence'). As children grow aware of the existence of special verb forms for 3pl. contexts, they will enter a stage of variable use of the 3sg. and 3pl. forms, such as the one which can be deduced from Grégoire's data. It

---

[12] In the present, the 3sg., 2sg., 1sg., and 1pl. forms of practically all verbs are identical. Three verbs (i.e. *aller*, *avoir*, and *être*) represent minor exceptions to this pattern as their 1sg. forms are distinct (i.e. *vais*, *ai*, and *suis*)—although *aller*, as we shall see in Chapter 8, is very often realized as *vas* in the 1sg., a form which is phonetically identical with 3sg. *va* /va/. In the future, the 3sg., 2sg., and 1pl. forms of all verbs are identical. As concerns the 1pl. forms, it must be pointed out that, in modern spoken French, the 3sg. subject pronoun *on* has all but come to replace *nous* (e.g. *nous disons > on dit* 'we say').

is possible to speculate that, as children's capacity to draw analogies increases, the absence of 3sg./pl. distinctions for the majority of the verbs that they hear (see section 5.1) may militate against their attainment of the categorical use of 3pl. forms for the minority of verbs which still display such a distinction. Another inhibiting linguistic factor is the one we have identified in the present study (i.e. low verb frequency in the 3pl.).[13]

As we saw in Chapter 4, the language-use patterns of our subjects suggest that all but the most severely restricted began acquiring French in infancy (along with English in some cases). So it may be that the subjects who acquired French as a mother tongue have not completely outgrown the stage of variable replacement of the 3pl. forms by 3sg. ones. In other words, the rule of subject–verb agreement in the 3pl. never became completely automatic due to more or less pronounced French-language-use restriction. That such fossilization is intimately tied to language restriction is underscored by the extreme rarity of 3pl. levelling in the speech of the unrestricted speakers (whether or not they reside in the majority francophone locality of Hawkesbury).

The levelling process under study is also typical of the interlanguage of second-language learners of French (Harley 1986; Kenemer 1982). In other words, the order of learning of 3sg. vs. 3pl. verb forms is the same for the native child as it is for the older second-language learner. As we saw in Chapter 4, the most severely restricted speakers have language-use patterns which suggest that they acquired French primarily as a second language at school. Fossilization of an *interlanguage* developmental stage is thus likely to be at the root of 3pl. levelling in their speech, again due to French-language-use restriction.

5.5. Conclusion

The generalization of 3sg. verb forms at the expense of 3pl. ones in Ontarian French represents the last stage of the levelling of a morphological distinction inherited from the Latin verb system and originally present in all tenses of all French verbs. There are other varieties of Canadian French in which levelling of the 3sg./pl. distinction has not yet reached this final stage and is in fact even less advanced than in Standard French. In French Acadia, for example, there are still isolated francophone communities where speakers not only maintain the 3sg./pl. distinction for the minority of verbs which have kept it in Standard French, but also preserve it for the regular -*er* verbs, i.e. verbs which in Standard French no longer have the distinction in the present (see Gesner 1979

---

[13] Grégoire's data are mute regarding the problem of order of acquisition of the morphologically marked 3pl. verb forms. It would be interesting to see whether children do not acquire them precisely in the order of decreasing frequency of occurrence in their input. Thus *sont* and *ont* would be acquired first, then *vont*, and so on. A similar order of acquisition could also be looked for in second-language data (see further in this section).

and Flikeid 1989, among others). However, in the case of Acadian French, the
3pl. forms have something going for them, namely perfect regularity (all 3pl.
verb forms in the indicative present take the common inflectional ending *-ont*
/ɔ̃/, e.g. *ils mangeont* 'they eat'). This property may well explain Flikeid's (1989)
finding that, even where Acadian French is in intensive contact with English,
the 3pl. verb forms are not significantly affected by levelling (it only occurs in
the same context in which it has been sporadically observed in popular
European French, namely after relativizer *qui*—which disfavours concord in all
persons, as Bauche 1929 and Frei 1971 observed: e.g. *c'est moi qui a fait ça* 'I'm the
one who did that', instead of standard *c'est moi qui ai fait ça*).[14]

It is our contention that in every francophone community successive generations of children learning the language go through a stage where they
generalize the 3sg. forms at the expense of the 3pl. ones. The extent to which
such overextension is likely to prolong itself beyond the language-acquisition
phase *per se* and into adult speech will largely depend on extralinguistic factors
such as mother-tongue restriction (in bilingual communities) and social-class
background (in monolingual as well as in bilingual communities). There is
reason to believe that learners of (Brazilian) Portuguese and (Puerto Rican)
Spanish may also go through a stage where they generalize the 3sg. forms, for
Grégoire (1968) has observed that, even in languages having morphologically
distinct verb forms for each singular and plural person, the 3sg. verb forms are
again the first to be produced by the child (this is in fact confirmed by the work
of Hooper 1980). This opens up the possibility that the same child-language
generalization lies at the root of 3pl. levelling in Brazilian Portuguese. This
view of things has the merit of providing an account of an unexplained
development in Brazilian Portuguese. Naro (1981) argued that levelling of the
3sg./pl. verb distinctions in popular Brazilian Portuguese started out as the
output of a variable phonological rule of denasalization of word-final vowels
(e.g. *eles comen* /komĩ/ 'they eat' > *eles come* /komi/ 'they eats'). What remains
unelucidated, however, is how the levelling process then managed to spread to
verbs whose 3sg./pl. oppositions show more than just a difference in vowel
nasalization (e.g. *eles fizeram* 'they did' > *eles fez* 'they dids'). As Naro (1981: 90)
himself is forced to concede, 'the process appears to be strictly one of generalization of privilege of occurrence of the singular morphemes at the expense of
their plural equivalents'. It is precisely the same generalization that the French
child makes and that we assume the (Brazilian) Portuguese child makes as well.
This would not mean that the variable phonological rule of denasalization of

---

[14] The reader will recall that we found the regular *-ont* ending of the future tense also to be quite
resistant to levelling. When levelling does occur outside relative clauses in Acadian French, it may
in fact be standardization instead (e.g. *ils mangeont* > *ils mangent* 'they eat'). True levelling can only
be established with certainty for verbs which in Standard French maintain a morphologically
marked 3pl. form. For example, if Acadian French *ils perdont* 'they lose' is replaced by *ils perd* /pɛr/
'they loses', that would constitute a clear instance of levelling, since the Standard French form
perdent /pɛrd/ is marked.

word-final vowels had nothing to do with the rise of 3pl. levelling in Brazilian Portuguese, only that it played a secondary role of reinforcement rather than the primary role of actuation which Naro attributes to it. The absence of examples (Poplack, p.c.) of levelling of irregular 3sg./pl. distinctions in Puerto Rican Spanish (e.g. *hablaro(n)* 'they spoke' > *hablό* 'they spokes') similarly constitutes support for considering the variable phonological rule of word-final -*n* deletion as insufficiently powerful on its own to trigger, via analogy, the generalization of 3sg. verb forms at the expense of their 3pl. counterparts.

As concerns 3pl. levelling in Ontarian French, we cannot assert that it solely originates in child language for two main reasons: (1) the speakers who level the 3sg./pl. distinctions have markedly dissimilar language acquisition histories (L1 vs. L2), and (2) both infant first-language learners and older second-language learners of French have been observed to level 3sg./pl. verb distinctions.

A final point which emerges from this and other studies which have documented the phenomenon of 3pl. levelling (in Romance and non-Romance languages) is that the functional load carried by the 3sg./pl. distinctions is not very high, even in the case of a pro-drop language like Spanish, or a language like French, which often fails to distinguish 3sg. from 3pl. clitic pronouns. Marking of the sg./pl. distinction on NPs and on non-clitic pronouns, together with situational cues, seems to provide enough information for the distinction to be conveyed. In the case of French, the combined factors of high frequency of the verbs which maintain distinctive 3pl. forms, formal schooling, and mono-lingualism seem to be capable of preventing the natural tendency to level from spreading any further. Only time will tell how long the stalemate will last.

6

Children and Linguistic Change

FOR some time now linguists have been struck by parallels between historical changes and child language. One of the best illustrations of this parallelism is to be found in Hooper (1980). Hooper shows how several generalizations about child morphology arrived at in the literature on language acquisition (e.g. the indicative mood is acquired before the subjunctive) have counterparts in the literature on historical change (e.g. other moods have been restructured on the analogy of the indicative). The repeated observation of correspondences between historical developments and language-acquisition processes has quite naturally given rise to a tradition in linguistics of grounding change in language acquisition (see Baron 1977 for a critical review). Unfortunately, it cannot be proved that yesterday's children were actually responsible for certain historical changes, because we obviously lack data on what the speech of children was like at the time the changes were taking place. It follows that the problem of adducing proof of a causal relation between child language and linguistic change is best tackled in synchrony.

Assuming that, as linguists interested in synchronic variation, we have observed variants in the speech of adults which we know or suspect to be developmental features arising during language acquisition, it would be tempting indeed to conclude that the presence of these variants in the speech of adults is the result of their having 'internalized' (to use Kiparsky's 1980: 414 terminology) their own childhood innovations. However, this may be jumping to conclusions, for, as Martinet (1969) and Hooper (1980) have commented, it could very well be that the adults themselves *actively* produce the innovations for the same structural reasons as the child. In other words, there may well be innovations whose structural motivation is constant, i.e. not age-related. The levelling of 3sg./pl. verb distinctions examined in the preceding chapter has all the appearances of such a type of innovation. We saw that it has been attested in child speech and in the speech of second-language learners of French who acquired this language beyond early childhood (the second-language learners of French who participated in the study by Kenemer 1982 mentioned in the preceding chapter were actually university students). The latter attestation clearly underscores the fact that it is not just young children who can produce

This chapter is based on a paper by the same title originally presented at NWAVE XII, Montreal, 27–9 October 1983. It later appeared in the selected proceedings edited by David Sankoff, *Diversity and Diachrony* (Amsterdam/Philadelphia, John Benjamins, 1986), 347–58. It reappears here in an expanded and updated version.

the innovation in question. This in turn suggests that the sporadic attestation of 3pl. levelling in the speech of adult speakers of French from popular milieux is due not to their having been unable to get rid of a child error, but probably to the fact that they too can now and then succumb to the force of this particular levelling process.

Our specific goal in this chapter is to try to argue that there are, however, innovations which are the *sole responsibility* of children. In other words, that there are innovations which are intimately linked with the way linguistic competence is acquired by the child (which excludes their production by second-language learners) and therefore which, should they be attested in adult speech either as variants or as cases of completed change, could only be interpreted *à la* Kiparsky as internalizations of childhood errors. The demonstration will be based on the verbal form *sontaient*, a non-standard variant of *étaient* 'were', the standard third person plural imperfect form of the verb *être* 'to be'. We shall first take a look at *sontaient*'s distribution among our adolescent speakers to see just who uses it. We shall go on to show that *sontaient* is an analogical formation which young children create (as opposed to imitate) during acquisition. Given the observed parallel between child and adolescent speech, we shall ask whether children are the sole party responsible for creating *sontaient*. We shall provide developmental linguistic evidence to suggest that they are and return to a fact about *sontaient*'s social distribution which, in retrospect, amounts to extralinguistic support in favour of grounding this analogical creation solely in child language. We shall end by discussing several questions raised by the case of variation under investigation (e.g. Why is *sontaient* apparently retained by some children as they grow older? Is the variation stable or is it a change in progress? When did *sontaient* first emerge in (Canadian) French?).

6.1. The variable

Since we encountered only eleven examples of *sontaient* in our corpus, it will not take up too much space to list them all for the benefit of the reader who might not be familiar with this rather striking non-standard variant:

1. *C'était heu . . . c'était bon voir comment le monde . . . l'atmosphère du monde dans ce temps-là, comment* sontaient 'It was uh . . . it was good to see how the people . . . the atmosphere of the people in those days, how they were' (C17–037).
2. *J'pensais qu'i'* sontaient *corrects* 'I thought they were all right' (C23–146).
3. *Pis i' l'ont vendu à d'autres gars qui* sontaient *des spécialistes pour ces autos-là* 'Then they sold it to some other guys who were specialists in those cars' (C08–074).

4. *Y'avait toute une 'gang' heu . . . gars et filles qui* sontaient *en bateau* 'There was a whole gang uh . . . guys and girls who were in a boat' (C16–020).

5. *C'est . . . les tours que je jouais* sontaient *pas méchants . . .* sontaient *jusse comme . . .* 'It's . . . the tricks that I played weren't mean . . . they were just like . . .' (C39–081).

6. *C'est . . . les tours que je jouais* sontaient *pas méchants . . .* sontaient *jusse comme . . .* 'It's . . . the tricks that I played weren't mean . . . they were just like . . .' (C39–082)

7. *Sont toute faite garrocher dehors à cause qu'i'* sontaient *jusse là pour niaiser* 'They all got thrown out 'cause they were just there to fool around' (C03–040).

8. *Ben j'ai acheté une . . . des cordes de guitare puis heu . . . c'était pas les heu . . . le paquet était bon . . . mais les cordes* sontaient *pas* 'Well I bought a . . . guitar strings and uh . . . it wasn't the uh . . . the package was good . . . but the strings weren't' (C39–115).

9. *J'savais pas de quand qu'*sontaient *pour venir me . . . mais j'savais pas de quand qu'*sontaient *pour venir me voir* 'I didn't know when they were going to come and see me . . . but I didn't know when they were going to come and see me' (C03–202).

10. *J'savais pas de quand qu'*sontaient *pour venir me . . . mais j'savais pas de quand qu'*sontaient *pour venir me voir* 'I didn't know when they were going to come and see me . . . but I didn't know when they were going to come and see me' (C03–203).

11. Sontaient *toute dans une heu . . . toute dans une maison* 'They were all in a uh . . . all in a house' (C03–028).

Sociolinguists have sometimes been accused of not always paying sufficient attention to linguistic detail, with the consequence, for example, that forms are claimed to be variants when they are not in reality, or that possible variants of a variable are overlooked (Léard 1983). While the linguistic equivalence of *étaient* and *sontaient* hardly needs any demonstration (*sont-* is a third person plural stem of the verb *être* and *-aient* an imperfect ending), the question of whether the variable might have other variants besides *étaient* and *sontaient* is somewhat more problematic. The *Glossaire du parler français au Canada* (La Société du parler français au Canada 1968) attests a form *I's étiont* 'they were' in Canadian French as it was spoken around the turn of the century, but *étiont* failed to show up in our own corpus. It appears to be an archaic feature, perhaps now restricted to Acadian French. Since no other variants came to our attention during the interview transcription phase, and furthermore since Deshaies, Martin, and Noël (1981) and Drapeau (1982) all report the same 'binary' variable in Quebec City French and in Montreal French, we feel reasonably certain that it is composed of just *étaient* and *sontaient*.

6.2. Social distribution

Our intention was originally to carry out a variable-rule analysis, but the existence of several knockout factors left too few occurrences of the variable in the remaining contexts to warrant such an analysis. As can be seen in Table 6.1 and as the astute observer may already have noticed from the eleven examples provided above, only the Cornwall speakers used *sontaient*.

For the time being, we will leave aside the problem of apparent categorical geographical variation and continue instead to examine the correlations between the variable and the other factor groups. Of necessity, this examination will be conducted on the basis of just the data for the Cornwall speakers. These data are presented in Table 6.2.

Table 6.2 indicates that French-language-use restriction and social class are two factor groups which seem to have an effect on the variable use of *sontaient*. Given the small size of the data base, we decided to cross-tabulate these two factor groups to check for the possibility of a confounding effect between them. This cross-tabulation (see Table 6.3) reveals that the data are distributed in a way which supports the idea that French-language-use restriction and social class are two independent predictors of the variable use of *sontaient*.

TABLE 6.1. *Social distribution of* sontaient, *all localities*

Factor groups	*sontaient* (N)	*étaient* (N)	Total	*sontaient* (%)
Locality				
Hawkesbury	0	17	17	0
Cornwall	11	38	49	22
North Bay	0	44	44	0
Pembroke	0	58	58	0
French-language use				
Unrestricted	2	34	36	6
Semi-restricted	9	68	77	12
Restricted	0	55	55	0
Social class				
Middle	1	27	28	4
Lower-middle	3	87	90	3
Working	7	43	50	14
Sex				
Male	7	72	79	9
Female	4	85	89	4
TOTAL	11	157	168	7

TABLE 6.2. *Social distribution of* sontaient, *Cornwall*

Factor groups	sontaient (N)	étaient (N)	Total	sontaient (%)
Locality				
Cornwall	11	38	49	22
French-language use				
Unrestricted	2	12	14	7
Semi-restricted	9	14	23	39
Restricted	0	12	12	0
Social class				
Middle	1	3	4	—†
Lower-middle	3	22	25	12
Working	7	13	20	35
Sex				
Male	7	25	32	22
Female	4	13	17	24
TOTAL	11	38	49	22

† Per cent of *sontaient* not calculated due to paucity of data.

TABLE 6.3. *Distribution of* sontaient *by language restriction and social class*

French-language use	Social class	sontaient (N)	étaient (N)
Unrestricted	Middle	1	1
	Lower-middle	0	7
	Working	1	4
Semi-restricted	Middle	0	2
	Lower-middle	3	7
	Working	6	5
Restricted	Middle	0	0
	Lower-middle	0	8
	Working	0	4
TOTAL		11	38

Table 6.2 reveals that the semi-restricted speakers are by far the primary users of *sontaient*. The restricted speakers, on the other hand, do not seem to have *sontaient* in their speech repertoire. The significance of this finding will be brought out below.

Table 6.2 also shows that *sontaient* is mostly concentrated in the speech of the working-class adolescents, a finding which corroborates those of Deshaies, Martin, and Noël (1981) for Quebec City French, and Drapeau (1982) for Montreal French. We now have at least a partial explanation for the absence of *sontaient* in the speech of the Hawkesbury adolescents. Of the seventeen occurrences of the variable produced by these speakers (see Table 6.1), only three were by working-class members. The non-attestation of *sontaient* in the speech of the Hawkesbury students could be due to this artefact of the data, coupled with the fact that all but one of these speakers, given the preponderance of francophones in their locality of residence, are unrestricted users of French (see Chapter 4). These are speakers who, as we have just seen, are very infrequent users of *sontaient* to begin with.[1]

As to the final factor group, speaker gender, it can be seen from Table 6.2 that the proportions of *sontaient* use are almost identical for the male and female adolescents, a finding which suggests that *sontaient* does not differentiate the speech of the two sexes. This is rather surprising, as one might have expected females to shun *sontaient*, given its strong connection with working-class speech. Note, however, that the expected sexual differentiation of speech is observable in the more general Table 6.1, where the final column shows that males are more than twice as likely to use *sontaient* as females are—9 per cent vs. 4 per cent. Because of the paucity of data in Table 6.2 (only 49 cases), we should perhaps reserve judgement on the role of sex as regards *sontaient* in Cornwall.

In sum, *sontaient* would appear to be typical of working-class adolescent speech in Cornwall, just as it is in Montreal and Quebec City. But in Cornwall, where the French-speaking community is in intensive contact with English, this non-standard variant is especially frequent in the speech of the adolescents whose use of French is semi-restricted and altogether absent in the speech of those whose use of French is restricted. If we compute *sontaient*'s frequency for the Cornwall speakers who are the most likely users of this form, namely the semi-restricted working-class adolescents, it reaches 55 per cent! This is quite analogous to what Drapeau (1982) found for her adolescent working-class speakers in Montreal. As a group, their frequency of use of *sontaient* was 47 per cent. This goes to show that *sontaient* is far from being a negligible phenomenon in adolescent working-class speech.

---

[1] Similar explanations appealing to skewed data distributions cannot be offered for the non-attestation of *sontaient* in the speech of the subjects residing in Pembroke and North Bay. We are at a loss to explain this absence. However, we doubt very much that it reflects reality.

6.3. Child language

It seems that the acquisition of the imperfect in French has not been well investigated, probably on account of the low frequency of occurrence of this tense in the speech of children (Bronckart 1976; Grégoire 1968). It is true that Gagné and Barbaud (1981) observed *sontaient* in the speech of six- and seven-year-old Montreal children, but the young age of the speakers is not sufficient on its own to prove that its source is language acquisition. It could be, after all, that the children simply imitated their parents' speech. We know for a fact that *sontaient* is used as a variant of *étaient* by certain adult speakers of Montreal French (Drapeau 1982). This left us no other recourse but to rely on our own observations of child speech. In this connection, the first author's two children were observed as early as approximately age two to produce *sontaient*, though he and his wife never use this form themselves. The children could not have picked up *sontaient* from other francophone children (or even adults for that matter), since their family resides in an English-speaking neighbourhood. Denise Deshaies (p.c.) has also caught her own children sometimes saying *sontaient* instead of *étaient*, in the absence again of any evidence of imitation of the speech of others. Thus we must admit that French children seem to be able to construct *sontaient* on their own. But how do they do it?

The findings of several studies of the acquisition of verbal morphology in various languages concurs to show that the third person singular verb forms are acquired ahead of the forms of other person and number combinations (Grégoire 1968; Rúke-Dravina 1959; Simões and Stoel-Gammon 1978; Chapter 5 in this volume). This order of learning would seem to hold tense by tense, so that the third person singular present is learned before, say, the first person singular present, the third person singular imperfect before the first person singular imperfect, etc. Also, the present is learned sooner than the imperfect. This acquisitional chronology provides the basis for a plausible explanation of the genesis of *sontaient*.

We surmise that upon learning *était* /etε/ 'was', the third person singular and first acquired imperfect form of *être*, the French child takes cognizance of the phonetic identity of the previously learned third person singular present form of *être*: *est* /e/ 'is', and the initial vowel /e/ of *était*.[2] The perception of this phonetic identity then leads the child to hypothesize that *était* is composed of the present tense form *est* to which is affixed the inflection *-tait*. In other words, in the eyes of the child *était* might well be *est* + *tait*. We speculate that, as

---

[2] The phonetic identity is of course no coincidence. Historically, the imperfect stem of *être* had an /s/—the same /s/ that is still graphically represented in *est*, as is evidenced by the following Middle French imperfect forms (taken from Brunot and Bruneau 1969: 295):

Sing.			Plur.		
	1.	*esteis* 'was'		1.	*estiienz* 'were'
	2.	*esteies* 'were'		2.	*estiiez* 'were'
	3.	*esteit* 'was'		3.	*esteient* 'were'

children move on to learn the other imperfect forms of *être*, they are guided by the same hypothesis: that they involve affixing -*tait* to the corresponding present tense forms.[3] We believe that *sontaient* (i.e. *sont* + *taient*) is the product of just such an hypothesis. Some of the other imperfect forms of *être* that children proceed to learn will actually lend support to their morphological hypothesis. Indeed, the second person singular imperfect form *étais* can be analysed as being built on the corresponding second person singular present form *es*. Likewise, the semantically first person plural imperfect form *on était* can be analysed as being built on the corresponding semantically first person plural present form *on est*.[4] This explanation would seem to receive strong support from the fact that another analogical imperfect form of *être* exhibiting the same pattern is heard in the speech of children: *suitais* (i.e. *suis* + *tais*), instead of the appropriate first person singular form *étais* (personal observation of the speech of the first author's two children once again). While we have not observed *suitais* in the speech of our Franco-Ontarian adolescents, Drapeau (1982) reports that the first person singular imperfect form of *être* in Montreal French is variably pronounced [ʃyta], in which the [y] comes from *suis*, variably pronounced [ʃy], and devoiced by a regular phonological rule applying to high vowels between voiceless consonants (Dumas 1977).[5]

Having just shown that *sontaient* is undeniably a feature of child speech and that it seems to be part of a more general restructuring of the morphology of the imperfect of *être* on the analogy of the previously learned present tense forms, the question now before us is whether it could also be an analogical creation of adults. Martinet (1969: 96) has opined that adults can continue to fall prey to the same analogical processes that lay in wait for them when they were still children, in which case children could not be attributed sole responsibility for introducing analogical formations in the language. Martinet gives the example of *je vas* for the standard form *je vais* in European French, a regularization which is observable in the speech of all children as well as in that of adults belonging to the lower class, and which he claims is determined by one and the same analogical process for both groups of speakers (*je vas* will be examined in more detail in Chapter 8). However, we have seen that the analogy underlying

---

[3] This would mean that children's initial morphological analysis of the imperfect of *être* does not match the linguist's, who would be more inclined to posit for *être* the same imperfect ending that he would for other verbs, namely /-ɛ/, not /-tɛ/. Thus Drapeau (1982) analyses the imperfect of *être* in Standard French as just mentioned:

Sing. 1. *étais* /et-ɛ/ 'was'   Plur. 1. *étions* /et-jɔ̃/ 'were'
      2. *étais* /et-ɛ/ 'were'   2. *étiez* /et-je/ 'were'
      3. *était* /et-ɛ/ 'was'   3. *étaient* /et-ɛ/ 'were'

[4] We remind the reader that, in informal French, the first person plural subject pronoun *nous* is never or hardly ever used; the third person singular (but semantically first person plural) pronoun *on* is used instead.

[5] The devoicing rule makes it very difficult to hear the /y/, which can even undergo complete syncope when it follows a fricative (Drapeau 1982). It is not impossible therefore that we overlooked instances of *suitais* in the speech of our subjects.

sontaient is intimately tied to the way (i.e. the order) in which children go about learning the present and imperfect forms of *être*. Children do not have all the present and imperfect forms of *être* in their purview at once and so are blinded to the morphological regularity of the imperfect conjugation of *être* and in particular to the invariance of the stem /e-/ or /et-/ (see n. 3). Unaware of this morphological regularity, they feel the impulse to create analogical forms like *sontaient* and *suitais*, which amount to a reintroduction of the suppletive stems of the present tense conjugation in the imperfect paradigm. To the linguist or adult this may appear to be a morphological complication, but to children, on the contrary, it is a regularization which is justified on the basis of the restricted set of data in their purview at what amounts to a very early stage of language acquisition (as early as age two, as we have seen). In our opinion, this casts serious doubt on the possibility that this analogy can continue to be operant as the learners grow older and the full set of data becomes available to them.

Had it been the case that *sontaient* was an analogical formation which older speakers could also produce (i.e. the kind of analogical formation that Martinet wrote about), we would have expected the restricted users of French to give evidence of knowing this form as well, even though many did not begin learning French as young children at home (see Chapter 4). It is also worth mentioning here that, to the best of our knowledge, *sontaient* has not been reported either in the speech of second-language learners of French (see in particular Harley 1986, whose study is devoted to the acquisition of the French verb system by anglophone immersion students). Together with the absence of *sontaient* in the speech of the restricted users of French, this bolsters the view that the analogy underlying *sontaient* is not available to older (i.e. cognitively and linguistically more mature) learners.

Interestingly enough, the restricted speakers of French, while seemingly incapable of creating *sontaient* on their own, could simply have picked up this form from the other, less restricted speakers. That they did not is quite reminiscent of other socially marked non-standard variants whose absence was also noted in their speech, such as the use of the preposition *à* to introduce possessive nominal complements (see next chapter), or the use of the preposition *su(r)* to indicate location at or movement to one's dwelling (see Chapter 9).

6.4. Discussion

Having just argued that the genesis of *sontaient* lies exclusively in child-language acquisition, a number of questions are raised. One of them is how to account for the fact that *sontaient* is found in the speech of adolescents and even adults. We have to admit along with Drapeau (1982: 132) that this finding means that '*sontaient* is not just an oddity of child speech which disappears as the child grows older like other developmental features' (our translation from the

French original). The answer must be that some children retain this analogical formation as they get older, in spite of the fact that it is no longer motivated. One linguistic explanation for *sontaient*'s persistence beyond the limits of the language-acquisition period is the infrequency of the imperfect, the unmarked past tense in French being the compound past (*passé composé*). More specifically, the young learners of French who produce *sontaient* have relatively little opportunity to learn the correct form *étaient*, since they will not hear it very often. To quote Hooper (1980: 178), 'less frequent forms tend to be regularized early because they are not reinforced to the same extent that the forms of frequent items are'. Thus children would retain *sontaient* as they grow older for lack of reinforcement of the standard form *étaient*. However, this linguistic explanation by itself is insufficient, since it is not all children who are equally likely to retain *sontaient*, but, as suggested by the sociolinguistic evidence, mostly those who belong to the working class and who, in a language-contact situation, have acquired French in infancy, but whose use of this language is semi-restricted. In the preceding chapter we quoted Labov (1980: 253) as saying that it is in social class milieux which are most isolated from the influence of the standard language that there is greatest freedom to innovate in a direction different from the standard variety. One reason for this hypothesis would be that, in working-class milieux, children's language errors are not or rarely corrected. Working-class children would therefore be more likely to get stuck with their linguistic innovations than children raised in families where parental filtering of language errors is more systematic (i.e. bourgeois families). Hence the possibility that such innovations may eventually make their way into the working-class vernacular. As for the reasons why semi-restricted language use in a minority setting should also favour the retention of *sontaient*, we believe they are as follows. One is that reduction in exposure to and use of French makes the reinforcement of the appropriate adult language form *étaient* even lower than it is under 'normal' conditions (i.e. little or no French-language-use restriction). The other is related to the explanation we have just invoked for the working-class child, namely that French-language-use restriction also entails a reduction in parental error correction. The reader will recall that the parents of the semi-restricted speakers interact with their children significantly less in French than the parents of the unrestricted speakers (see Chapter 4). Hence the former parents would have less time at their disposal and perhaps also less of an inclination for error correction.

Another question has to do with whether the variation between *étaient* and *sontaient* is stable or changing. As pointed out, an unfortunate limitation of our corpus is that it is not constructed with an apparent time dimension and so, strictly speaking, we cannot answer this question. However, Labov (1981) has argued that inferences about stability or change can be drawn from another indication, namely the social-class distribution of the variable, a linear distribution suggesting stability, a curvilinear one change in progress. In this regard, the fact that the variable is lined up with the social-class hierarchy is suggestive of stable variation. Drapeau (1982), on the other hand, found *sontaient*'s frequency decreased steadily from pre-adolescence to adolescence to young adulthood, with speakers over thirty-five never using this variant. Is this an indication that *sontaient* is a form which might be just emerging in working-class Montreal French, as Drapeau wonders? Labov (1981: 178) has warned against 'the naive interpretation of age distributions as evidence for change in real time without considering the possibility of stable age grading'. Indeed we are inclined to think that, ever since children have been producing *sontaient*, this form has tended to linger beyond the limits of the acquisition period and then slowly to dwindle in frequency until disappearance in young adulthood.[6] Its diminishing frequency as a function of age would be due to the speaker's tendency to correct salient non-standard forms as s/he leaves adolescence behind and with it the pressures towards peer-group solidarity. Deshaies, Martin, and Noël (1981: 416–17) provide evidence that the Quebec City adolescents in whose speech they noted *sontaient* maintain this form in spite of being quite conscious of its nonconformity to standard usage. One adolescent bore the following testimony: 'Yes, I sometimes turn my sentences backward, saying *i' sontaient* instead of *ils étaient* ; I will often say that' (our translation from the French original). However, given the ambiguity inherent in an apparent time study of *sontaient* (change in progress or stable age grading?), a study in real time should be carried out to get a better idea of whether this variant is on the rise or not in popular Canadian French.[7]

A further question is whether there are any other verbs in French which are affected by the same analogical process. The verb *avoir* 'to have' is a good candidate because, like *être*, its third person singular present form *a* 'has' is phonetically identical to the initial vowel /a/ of its third person singular imperfect form *avait* 'had'. Though it is true that the expected analogical third person singular imperfect form *ontvaient* /ɔ̃vɛ/ has, to our knowledge, yet to be attested in the speech of French-Canadian children or older speakers, Thogmartin (1979) reports the existence of such a form in the Franco-American dialect of Old Mines, Missouri, along with *fontsaient* /fɔ̃zɛ/ for *faisaient* '(they) did'. It is likely that these analogical creations could once be heard in Canadian French also.

[6] That *sontaient* has not been reported in any of the oft-consulted lexicographic works on past varieties of Canadian French, such as the *Glossaire du parler français au Canada*, is probably due to the fact that lexicographers have missed this form precisely on account of its diminishing frequency with age.

[7] Our prediction, for what it is worth, is that a real time study would show *sontaient* to be on the wane. Indeed Canadian French, ever since its beginnings back in the seventeenth century, has been characterized by a tendency toward standardization. This has been amply demonstrated, for instance by Juneau (1972), as far as the phonetic system is concerned. Further in this section we present historical evidence which suggests that *sontaient* was indeed probably more frequent in earlier stages of Canadian French than it is today.

We can no longer put off the question of the exact diachronic moment at which *sontaient* would have entered the French language. Happily for us, observers of the offshoots of Canadian French seem to have been less distracted than their Québécois counterparts. They have all amply attested *sontaient*, whether it be in Ontarian French (ourselves), in Western Canadian French (Papen 1984), or in the Franco-American dialect spoken in Old Mines, Missouri (Thogmartin 1979).[8] The commonality of this feature can mean only one thing, that it was already a feature of Canadian French before the various secondary diasporas took place which spread the language west and south. From this point of view, the attestation of *sontaient* in Old Mines is definitely the most instructive, as it allows us to date *sontaient* as far back as the early eighteenth century. But it looks as if we can push back *sontaient*'s diachronic emergence even further, since it has also been observed in the Franco-American dialect of Saint Thomas, US Virgin Islands (Highfield 1979). Now this dialect is unconnected to Canadian French, being the result of direct immigration from France to the Caribbean in the seventeenth century. If we again place our faith in the principles of comparative linguistics, we have no other alternative but to reconstruct a *sontaient* etymon in pre-colonial French. If it did exist, however, it would of necessity have disappeared soon after the beginning of the colonization of the New World, as none of the works on modern popular European French (Bauche 1929; Frei 1971) or past popular (and for that matter cultivated) European French countenance this form (Gougenheim 1951—sixteenth century; Haase 1969—seventeenth century; Vadé 1875—eighteenth century; Gougenheim 1929—nineteenth century). We ourselves are not as inclined to apply rashly the principle of linguistic reconstruction. Here is our scenario. *Sontaient*'s emergence coincided with the exportation of the French language to the New World. In the confusion of dialect contact that existed in all areas of French colonial expansion (be it in New France or in the Caribbean), children learning the language would have been given a freer rein to restructure it due to the absence, at the beginning of colonization at least, of a well-defined community norm (the pre-focusing stage of new dialect formation posited by Trudgill 1986). Not to mention that parents (and adults generally) had more pressing business to attend to than to correct the language errors of their children. Later, as French-Canadian society developed its own standardizing institutions, *sontaient* naturally got relegated to the speech of the lower classes, a position it still occupies today.

Finally, it is somewhat paradoxical that *sontaient* should be an analogical formation which is a counter-example to Hooper's (1980) theory of child morphology (see her n. 11). Hooper contends that verb stem generalization across tenses as is evidenced by *sontaient* (i.e. generalization of the present tense

---

[8] Acadian French and its Louisiana offshoot, Cajun French, are exceptional in that they do not have *sontaient*, a not so surprising fact considering other peculiar aspects of Acadian/Cajun French verb morphology (see previous chapter).

stem *sont-* to the imperfect) is supposed to be impossible. The normal generalization of verb stems is within the same tense from the third person singular to
other person and number combinations. There are indeed many examples of
the latter generalization in Ontarian French (e.g. *je vas* 'I goes' instead of *je vais*
'I go', which we shall examine in Chapter 8; *ils fait* 'they does' instead of *ils font*
'they do', which we examined in the preceding chapter; etc.). Yet the existence
of *sontaient* (and *suitais* for that matter) indicates that stem generalization across
tenses is possible, contrary to Hooper's theory. The problem has to do with the
fact that Hooper's argument is based on the acquisition of the present/
preterite pair of tenses by Brazilian Portuguese children. It just so happens to
hold for this pair of tenses in Brazilian Portuguese that the tense distinction is
made earlier than person and number distinctions within each tense, thus
effectively barring the possibility of stem generalization from the present to the
preterite. But, as Hooper herself points out, the imperfect is learned after the
present (and even the preterite) in Brazilian Portuguese. This order of learning
is true of French as well, considering the imperfect's infrequency. Thus, before
the imperfect is even used, the French child probably already knows *je suis*, *il
est*, and *ils sont*. Given this prior knowledge, there is nothing to prevent these
present tense forms from influencing the child in his attempts at learning the
imperfect forms of *être*, all the more as the third person singular imperfect *était*
gives the impression of being built on the third person singular present *est*. It
would appear, therefore, that Hooper's theory makes the right predictions only
in so far as the present and preterite are concerned, since the preterite begins to
be acquired before person and number distinctions are made in the present. Its
scope should then probably be restricted just to this pair of tenses.

6.5. Conclusion

The findings of this study would seem to warrant the conclusion that child
language is indeed a possible source of linguistic variation, hence of potential
linguistic change. Returning to diachrony, it may well be then that yesterday's
children initiated changes by virtue of having introduced innovations in adult
language. The general picture of how children go about creating and introducing innovations in adult language which emerges from the study of *sontaient*
rather supports Kiparsky's (1980: 414) notion of 'false analogies', that is, 'forms
projected by the optimal grammar based on a restricted set of data at an
intermediate stage of language acquisition which are *retained* even though they
force a complication in the final grammar based on the full data'. An original
aspect of this study worth underlining is that the presence in our subject
sample of restricted speakers who have learned the bulk of their French at
school (i.e. beyond infancy) put us in a strong position to ground *sontaient* in
children's speech. Finally, our study of *sontaient* suggests that certain crucial

extralinguistic conditions need to be present for the child-language innovations to become part of the vernacular, because child speech is not 'normally' expected to weigh very heavily in linguistic evolution. Two such extralinguistic conditions were identified or proposed here: (1) temporary absence of a well-defined community norm, and (2) semi-restricted exposure to and use of a language.

7

Sociolectal Reduction

THE breakdown of the Latin case system was offset in part by an expansion of
its prepositional system. Two prepositions which underwent considerable
expansion were *ad* and *de*. One aspect of their expansion saw them vie with one
another to introduce nominal complements expressing the idea of possession.
This rivalry developed in Vulgar Latin and is still extant today in marginal,
popular, or simply informal varieties of French on both sides of the Atlantic
(e.g. *la voiture à/de mon père* 'my father's car').[1] This long-standing case of
variation has been commented upon by many linguists, yet certain aspects of its
diachrony and synchrony remain unclear. An initial goal of our study is to
retrace the history of possessive *à*'s and *de*'s protracted rivalry. This will take
us from the origins of possessive *à* and *de* in Vulgar Latin to the seventeenth
century when *à* was proscribed by the French grammarians. From there we
shall move on to contemporary French and the other goal of our study, which is
to see how possessive *à* is faring in non-standard (i.e. marginal or popular)
varieties of French in general and in Ontarian French in particular. More
specifically, this study will explore the extralinguistic conditions under which
long-term linguistic variation may suddenly be tipped in favour of one of the
variants.

7.1. History of possessive *à* and *de*

As is well known, nominal complements expressing possession were in the
genitive case in Classical Latin (e.g. *liber Petri* 'Peter's book'). It is probably not
as well known, however, that they were sometimes in the dative case in Preclassical Latin if the possessor was a person (e.g. *Philocomasio amator*
'Philocomasius' lover') (Haadsma and Nuchelmans 1966: 46). According to

This chapter is based on a paper which was presented at the Twelfth Annual Linguistic
Symposium on Romance Languages, Pennsylvania State University, State College, 1–3 April 1982.
It was later published in the selected proceedings edited by Philip Baldi, *Papers from the XIIth
Linguistic Symposium on Romance Languages* (Amsterdam, John Benjamins, 1984), 15–36, under the
original title 'Possessive *à* and *de* in Informal Ontarian French: A Long-standing Case of
Linguistic Variation'. It reappears here with stylistic modifications, corrections, and improve-
ments over the previously published version.

[1] By 'marginal' we are referring to those non-standard varieties of French still spoken in the
various enclaves in North America (e.g. Frenchville, Pa.; Old Mines, Mo.) or in the Caribbean (e.g.
Saint Thomas, USVI; Saint Barthélemy—usually called Saint Barts—, FWI). 'Popular' is a
synonym for lower or working class.

Haadsma and Nuchelmans, the dative case was a more expressive exponent of possession than the genitive case. Indeed, the dative was a concrete case marking the semantic notion of recipient or experiencer of an action, whereas the genitive was a grammatical case marking the syntactic notion of inter-nominal complementation (Harris 1978: 41–2). In the previously cited example Philocomasius is the recipient of his lover's love, hence the use of the dative case in preference to the genitive case. This was not the only use of the dative case to signal possession. From the beginnings of Latin it marked possession with predicate complements of the copula *esse* (e.g. *liber est Petro* 'Peter has a book', literally 'a book is to Peter') and as the so-called 'dative of interest' (e.g. *militibus animos accendere* 'to inflame the soldiers' hearts', literally 'to inflame the hearts to the soldiers') (Herman 1967: 63). Thus, as Harris (1978: 65 n. 3) has observed, there was not an absolute distinction between the notions of possessor and experiencer. Absent throughout the Classical Latin period, the use of the dative case to mark possessive nominal complements resurfaces in a considerably fleshed-out guise in Vulgar Latin (Haadsma and Nuchelmans 1966: 46).[2] Thus the use of the dative case to mark possessive nominal complements probably increased steadily in the spoken language over the course of the Classical period, while Classical Latin continued to abide by the rule prescribing the use of the genitive case.

Another change that was incipient in Preclassical Latin and that developed in the course of time was the replacement of the dative case via a prepositional phrase introduced by *ad* (e.g. *dare alicui* > *dare ad aliquem* 'to give to someone') (Väänänen 1963: 120). Just as the dative case had begun to mark possessive nominal complements in Preclassical Latin, so *ad* began to introduce such complements in Vulgar Latin (Bloch and Wartburg 1950: 1; Harris 1978: 65 n. 3; Väänänen 1956: 13–14). The earliest known example of possessive *ad* appears in a Christian inscription dating from the sixth century (e.g. *Hic requiiscunt menbra ad duus fratres, Gallo et Fidencio, qui foerunt fili Magno* 'Here lie the remains of two brothers, Gallus and Fidencius, who were (the) sons of Magnus') (Nyrop 1899: 14). The inscription is felicitous in that it features another posses-sive nominal complement, this time in the dative case (i.e. *fili Magno* '(the) sons of Magnus'), the older alternative to the genitive case. The inscription is also noteworthy in that the possessive nominal complement introduced by *ad* and the one marked by the dative case both display a human possessor. We would not expect things to be otherwise considering that the notion of experiencer or recipient which the synthetic and analytic datives marked implies the notion of human being (or at least that of animate being). But the use of *ad* to introduce possessive nominal complements involving a human possessor was rare in Vulgar Latin (Väänänen 1956: 14–15). Let us now see how possessive *de* arose.

We said earlier that possessive nominal complements were in the genitive

---

[2] Expressiveness being a notable trait of popular speech, Vulgar Latin was a natural locus for the development of the dative case as an expression of possession.

case in Classical Latin. But possession was of course only one of many notions that this case could signal in Classical Latin. Ever since Preclassical Latin there was a growing tendency for one of these other notions, the partitive, to be expressed via a prepositional phrase introduced by *de* (e.g. *pars militum* > *pars de militis* 'part of the soldiers') (Väänänen 1963: 121). Like the use of *ad* to mark the notion of recipient or experiencer, which was semantically motivated by *ad*'s primitive meaning of 'direction towards', the use of *de* to mark the partitive notion was semantically motivated as well, by *de*'s primitive meaning of 'separation from' (Väänänen 1956: 4). From there *de* spread to the other notions expressed by the genitive case, first to those with which it shared some degree of semantic compatibility, then via analogy to the others (Cohen 1967: 145; Haadsma and Nuchelmans 1966: 45–6; Nyrop 1930: 99; Väänänen 1956). In short, generalizing along semantic lines and then grammaticalizing, *de* was taking over from the genitive case as the marker of internominal complementation. This is how *de* got to introduce possessive nominal complements. But similarly to *ad*, the use of *de* to introduce possessive nominal complements involving a human possessor was rare in Vulgar Latin (Väänänen 1963: 121). This was not so with inanimate possessors, which were much more susceptible to be introduced by *de* (Väänänen 1956: 12–13).

While at first sight the distinction appears to suggest that the spread of *de* to possessive nominal complements was controlled by the reference of the possessor (i.e. human vs. inanimate), it is our contention that it is not the reference of the possessor *per se* but rather the nature of the possessive relationship as determined by the reference of the possessor that was the controlling factor. Thus, when the possessor is inanimate, the possessive relationship is of the partitive type (e.g. *la poignée de la porte* 'the doorknob', literally 'the knob of the door'). But when the possessor is a person, the possessive relationship may be partitive (e.g. *le dos de mon père* 'my father's back') or either one of several other types: it may indicate a human relationship such as kinship or friendship (e.g. *la sœur de mon père* 'my father's sister'), ownership (e.g. *les outils de Jean* 'John's tools'), or a human attribute of some kind (e.g. *la fête de Marie* 'Mary's birthday'). Because of *de*'s semantic compatibility with the partitive notion, it is probably partitive possessive complements that this preposition first introduced. The fact that the possessive relationship is necessarily partitive with inanimate possessors but not with human possessors would explain why the former were more susceptible than the latter of being introduced by *de* in Vulgar Latin. Owing to the lack of examples provided by Väänänen, this account of the rise of possessive *de* in Vulgar Latin remains conjectural. However, we shall see that it is substantiated by what is known concerning possessive *de*'s situation in Old French, to which we now turn.

Väänänen (1956: 15) reports the results of an inventory of possessive *à* and *de* introducing human possessors in fourteen Old French texts written before the thirteenth century. The inventory yielded 1,645 examples of human possessors not introduced by a preposition (e.g. *li filz le rei* 'the king's son') in comparison to only 120 introduced by *à* and even fewer (18) by *de*. Judging by this inventory, *à* (< *ad*) and *de* had not gained much ground since Vulgar Latin as exponents of possessive nominal complements involving a human possessor, but it appears that *à* had made more inroads than *de*. The examples of *de* are ones where the possessee is a body part and as such they provide the awaited support for our contention that *de* began by marking partitive possessive complements in Vulgar Latin. The inventory also revealed that human possessive nominal complements were introduced by *de* if they happened to be generic rather than specific. The results of this inventory are very much in accord with those of Foulet's (1977: 14–27) own study of possessive nominal complements in Old French, which we shall consider here because of its attention not just to human possessors but to inanimate and animal possessors as well.

Foulet tried to show that possessive *à* and *de* were in complementary distribution in Old French depending on the reference of the possessor. He argued that the prepositionless possessive nominal complement was receding at the hands of *à* when the possessor was a person, but was doing so (or rather had already done so) at the hands of *de* when the possessor was an animal or a thing. What Foulet failed to appreciate, however, is that all the examples of *de* introducing animal or inanimate possessors are partitive in nature (e.g. *les cols de lor chevaus* 'their horses' necks'; *un pertuis de la posterne* 'a hole in the door'). As a result, he is led to treat the few examples of *de* with human possessors as exceptional, when in fact they convey precisely the same partitive notion (e.g. *l'ame de ton pere et de te mere* 'the soul of your father and of your mother'). What Foulet also failed to appreciate is that the few examples of *à* with non-human possessors all involve animal possessors, not inanimate ones (e.g. *les piez au cheval* 'the horse's feet'). We suggest that the correct interpretations are rather that, in the early stages of French, *de* was still restricted to marking just partitive possessive complements and *à* was still barred from marking possessive complements involving inanimate possessors. Thus in reality there was no complementary distribution between possessive *à* and *de*. In thinking that *de* was constrained by the reference of the possessor instead of by the nature of the possessive relationship, Foulet seems to have committed the very error that we cautioned against making based on Väänänen's description of possessive *de* in Vulgar Latin. In contrast to *de*, *à*, only barred as it was from introducing inanimate possessors, was free to mark all the different types of possible possessive relationships with animate possessors: kinship (e.g. *li oncles au buen chevalier* 'the good knight's uncle'), ownership (e.g. *la chambre a la pucele* 'the girl's room'), a human attribute of some kind (e.g. *la volenté au vaslet* 'the servant's will'), and the partitive notion or inalienable possession (e.g. *la main au vaslet* 'the servant's hand'). This is probably why human possessors were more susceptible of being introduced by *à* than by *de* in Old French. Lest it be forgotten, however, we saw that the prepositionless option (i.e. zero) was still the rule rather than the exception with human possessors (*de*, not *à*, nor zero, being the rule with inanimate possessors).

It is in the fourteenth century that *à* and *de* began to make significant headway with human possessors, *de* more so than *à* (Nyrop 1925: 134). It may be surmised that it is at this time that *de* started to mark more than just the partitive relationship with human possessors. It is also at this time that the two-case system (i.e. nominative vs. oblique) began breaking down (Foulet 1977: 34). It is not clear to us whether nor how this might have contributed to the rise of possessive *à* and *de*, especially since word order in internominal complementation was already fixed (i.e. possessee followed by possessor) (Foulet 1977: 17–19). In the fifteenth century the prepositionless possessive nominal complement was moribund and *de* had gained the upper hand on *à* (Nyrop 1925: 134). In the sixteenth century the prepositionless possessive nominal complement had all but disappeared (only a few frozen expressions remained) and, though *à* was still frequently in use in literary French, *de* was none the less much more common (Gougenheim 1951: 210–11). By the seventeenth century possessive *à* in its turn had all but disappeared from the literary language, surviving only in a few fixed expressions (Haase 1969: 281, 322). Those few seventeenth-century authors who still used possessive *à* were reprimanded by the prescriptive grammarians, who regarded *à* as archaic and popular (Brunot and Bruneau 1969: 379; Haase 1969: 322). Witness this quote from a seventeenth-century observer (De Boisregard 1689 and 1693/1972: 1): 'There are sometimes people who say *c'est le livre à mon frère* "it is my father's book", *c'est le cheval à mon cousin* "it is my cousin's horse" instead of *c'est le livre de mon frère, c'est le cheval de mon cousin.* It used to be that people spoke that way . . . but not any more, with the exception of the common people' (our translation from the French original).

By all appearances the prescriptive grammarians intervened at a time when possessive *de* was already more common than possessive *à* in the written language. We deduce from this that possessive *de*'s superiority was due to purely internal causes, having to do with the syntax of internominal complementation, rather than due to the external agent of grammatical prescriptivism. We believe that there must have been considerable analogical pressure on *de* to introduce possessive nominal complements, since such complements were the last hold-outs to the general syntactic pattern head noun + *de* + complement noun.

The prescriptivists, however, would certainly seem to have to be held responsible for bringing about the premature end of possessive *à* in the literary language. Indeed, as mentioned in the introduction, possessive *à* is still found to this day in so-called marginal varieties of French in the New World, such as St Thomas French (Highfield 1979), and in popular varieties of French in Europe (Bauche 1929: 141; Frei 1971: 194–5; Guiraud 1973: 73) as well as in Canada (La Société du parler français au Canada 1968: 1; Seutin 1975: 337).

Even members of the higher classes, when not having to put on their best linguistic behaviour, are not adverse to using possessive *à* occasionally (personal observation and experience!).

That the prescriptive grammarians abhorred variation is no secret. As Chaudenson, Véronique, and Valli (1986: 17) have written: 'The history of the prescriptive norm (which people tend to confuse too often with the history of the French language) includes instances of progressive and total elimination of variation involving several competing usages. One usage gets prescribed, the other gets proscribed and is rooted out of the standard language. However, the proscribed usage will often survive in informal, regional, or marginal varieties of the language' (our translation from the French original). The logic behind the interventionism of the prescriptive grammarians often seems to have been the desire to mark a clear distinction between 'cultivated' and popular speech. Thus we may speculate that, whenever they declared themselves in favour of this or that particular variant, the disfavoured one was probably perceived by them as characteristic of popular speech. In other words, there is good reason to believe that their prescriptivism was sociolinguistically as opposed to linguistically based. The above quote from De Boisregard certainly confirms this view of things for possessive *à* and *de*. We saw that the possessive dative was typical of popular Latin, otherwise more commonly referred to as Vulgar Latin. The common people, it may be surmised, preferred it because of its expressive force. That its successor, the analytic *ad* (> *à*) construction, should later emerge as a typical feature of popular French could not be a more natural development. It was probably so frequent as to be a stereotype of the popular language, hence the grammarians' preference for *de*, which, in addition (this may also have been a factor in their choice), was the successor of the Classical Latin genitive possessive. Be that as it may, the end result of the grammarians' prescriptivism was the eradication from the standard language of a case of linguistic variation which, according to all the available evidence provided by today's marginal, popular, or simply informal varieties/styles of French, they had no real business to meddle with. Indeed, possessive *à* has proven its vigour by surviving this long. Is this protracted existence solely attributable to its advantage of expressive force over the standard equivalent *de*? This question, as we shall see in the next section, will figure prominently in the discussion of the social distribution of possessive *à* and *de* in Ontarian French. The discussion will actually suggest a new and original view of the *raison d'être* of variation in language.

7.2. Synchrony of possessive *à* and *de*

Let us consider what other linguists have had to say about possessive *à* and *de* in popular Parisian French, in a regional variety of Quebec French, and in St

Thomas French as a prelude to the quantitative sociolinguistic description of these variants in Ontarian French. Consider the following quote from Guiraud's (1973: 73) book on popular Parisian French: 'The notion of possession is rendered by *à*: *la fille au boulanger* "the baker's daughter", *la bague à Jules* "Jules's ring". As can be seen from these examples, the possessor is a person; one normally uses *de* when the possessor is an animal or a thing: *la queue du chat* "the cat's tail", *la porte de la cuisine* "the kitchen door", etc.' (our translation from the French original). Guiraud, then, seems to be of the opinion that *à* and *de* are in complementary distribution in popular Parisian French: *à* is used when the possessor is a person, *de* when it is an animal or a thing. In an earlier book on popular Parisian French, Bauche (1929: 141) makes a similar observation with this difference—that *à* is not said to be categorical, but simply the more frequent of the two prepositions with human possessors: 'Possessive *de* is most often rendered in popular French by *à*, when the possessor is an animate being: *la femme à Eugène* "Eugene's wife", *la fille à Jacques* "James's daughter", *le livre à Paul* "Paul's book", *l'idée au capitaine* "the captain's idea". Otherwise *de* is used: *le bout de la canne* "the tip of the cane", *le tiroir de la commode* "the drawer of the dresser", as in Standard French' (our translation from the French original). Consider finally the following quote from Seutin's (1975: 337) book on the variety of French spoken on the island of L'Île-aux-Coudres, Quebec (located down-river from Quebec City on the St Lawrence):

Standard French is unlike informal or popular French in their use of *à* for *de* when the nominal complement refers to a person: *la fête à tante Aurore* 'aunt Aurora's birthday'. L'Île-aux-Coudres French conforms to the same popular usage: *la chienne à Jacques* 'James's dog'. However, euphony seems to play a role. Before a word starting with vowel *a*, one always finds *d'*; before a word starting with another vowel, one generally finds *d'*: *le frère d'Amable* 'Amable's brother'. It is possible that awareness of style level also plays a role. When the complement is not a proper noun, *de* alternates with *à*. It seems to us that *de* is more formal [our translation from the French original].

According to Seutin, then, there are two other constraints on possessive *à* in the spoken French of L'Île-aux-Coudres besides the reference of the possessor. One is the avoidance of hiatuses before vowel-initial words via the substitution of *d'* for *à*, categorical or variable depending on whether the vowel is *a* or not. The other is the avoidance of informality via the substitution of *de*, perceived as more formal, for *à* before nouns referring to persons with whom the speaker is not closely acquainted (i.e. whose proper names the speaker does not know). Barring these two new constraints, however, Seutin's comment would seem to suggest that *à* is categorical with human possessors in the French spoken in L'Île-aux-Coudres.

Consider finally the syntax of possession in the variety of French still spoken in St Thomas, US Virgin Islands. According to Highfield (1979: 62–3), the preposition *de* is the most common means of expressing possession (e.g. *les nasses de mon mari étaient toutes volées* 'all my husband's fish traps were stolen'). The preposition *à* is also employed in a way which is quite reminiscent of its use in L'Île-aux-Coudres French. Thus *à* is used to indicate possession by a specific individual known to the speaker (e.g. *les enfants à Alphonse est bien élevés* 'Alphonso's children are well raised'). Interestingly enough, Highfield claims that possession can also be expressed by simple juxtaposition (e.g. *le livre Alphonse* 'Alphonso's book'). The provenance of this prepositionless option is difficult to establish with certainty, however. If it really does represent an underlying zero preposition, then we are forced to revise our historical treatment (see section 7.1) and assume that the expression of possession via mere juxtaposition of possessee and possessor, which is said to have disappeared from the literary language in the sixteenth century (the century prior to the beginning of colonial expansion), may have lingered in the popular language and been brought over to the New World in the seventeenth century. It would then truly represent an archaism in St Thomas French, which Highfield (1979: 16) claims is 'the most archaic form of West Indian French still in existence'. The second possibility is that the prepositionless option is only a surface realization of an underlying *à* construction, *à* getting deleted before an *a*-initial noun in order to avoid creating a hiatus, as in L'Île-aux-Coudres French. The lone example provided by Highfield (*le livre Alphonse*) has us leaning in favour of this explanation. Finally, creole influence cannot be discounted either, as simple juxtaposition is the normal way of marking possession in French-based creoles. St Thomas French has been in more or less constant contact with French-based creoles spoken in the Lesser Antilles, including on the island of St Thomas itself. So has Old Mines, Missouri French been in contact with Louisiana French creole, and it too shows the prepositionless possessive construction (e.g. *la fille rouè-là* 'the king's daughter') (Thogmartin 1979: 115).

The above survey of the literature calls for a number of comments. First, it indicates that possessive *à* has not only survived but is generally more frequent than *de* with human possessors in the varieties of French in question. This adds fuel to our earlier argument that possessive *à* must have been quite frequent in the popular language of the seventeenth century. It should prove instructive to see whether possessive *à* is as vigorous in Ontarian French.

Second, no reference at all is made to the possessee. Does this mean that the possessee does not intervene in the selection of *à* vs. *de*? We shall explore this question with regard to Ontarian French.

Third, the quotes would have it that *à* can only be used with human possessors in the varieties of French examined. We saw, however, that Foulet (1977: 14–27) reports examples of *à* marking inalienable possession with animals in Old French. We have argued that such examples are to be expected, since animals are animate beings. As far as inanimate possessors are concerned, we found no historical evidence that they could be introduced by *à*. Nor do the above quotes provide any synchronic evidence that they can now. The influence of the possessor's reference on the selection of *à* vs. *de* is another question we shall explore with respect to Ontarian French.

Finally, the focus of the works surveyed is entirely on the linguistic distribution of possessive *à* and *de*. By restricting their observations to lower-class Parisian French, Bauche and Guiraud avoided altogether the question of whether possessive *à* is not also present to some extent in the informal speech of the more privileged classes. On the other hand, by observing as he did the spoken French of over one hundred islanders of L'Île-aux-Coudres, Seutin probably had people of different social backgrounds but did not take advantage of this to seek out possible social-class differences in the use of possessive *à* and *de*. The question of sociolectal variation was not pertinent in the case of St Thomas French, as the French-speaking islanders are all essentially fisherfolk and their families. Nor did any of these linguists consider the possibility of differences due to sex.

In short, what the above review of the literature on the synchrony of possessive *à* and *de* points to is the complete lack of a detailed sociolinguistic investigation of this case of variation. What follows should at least partly fill this gap in our knowledge of possessive *à* and *de*.

7.3. Possessive *à* and *de* in Ontarian French

All told we recorded 171 occurrences of the possessive variable, 21 of the variant *à* (or 12 per cent) and 150 of the variant *de* (or 88 per cent). Though there is no denying that possessive *à* is much the weaker of the two alternatives for our speakers as a group, we shall see that it may be even weaker than that or on the contrary much stronger than that, all depending on the subgroup of speakers and the linguistic context. As was the case for *sontaient* (see preceding chapter), the paucity of data combined with the existence of knockout factors precluded the possibility of carrying out a statistical analysis using the VARBRUL 2s programme. This of course takes some rigour out of the analysis, which was essentially conducted on a factor-group-by-factor-group basis (i.e. one factor group at a time).

7.3.1. Linguistic distribution

Table 7.1 shows the distribution of possessive *à* and *de* as a function of the reference of the possessor. As can be seen, we found possessive *à* only with human possessors (e.g. *les sœurs à ma mère* 'my mother's sisters' H04–5). However, because there are also no examples of possessive *de* with animal possessors, we cannot conclude that possessive *à* is barred from such contexts. In fact, based on our intuitions and on consultations with other native speakers

TABLE 7.1. *Distribution of* à *and* de *according to reference of possessor*

Reference of possessor	à (N)	de (N)	Total	à (%)
Human	21	143	164	13
Animal	0	0	0	0
Thing	0	7	7	0
TOTAL	21	150	171	12

of French, the use of *à* with animal possessors seems possible (e.g. *l'os à Fido* 'Fido's bone'), as we know it was in Old French. That we recorded only seven examples of *de* with inanimate possessors (e.g. *le capot de l'auto* 'the car's hood' C39–191) does not constitute a very solid statistical base from which to conclude that possessive *à* is barred from such contexts. However, when these results are coupled with the fact mentioned above that there is no historical nor any synchronic evidence that *à* ever introduced inanimate possessors, the conclusion seems warranted.

Table 7.2 shows the distribution of *à* and *de* as a function of whether the possessor is specific (one or several distinct individuals) or generic (a group of individuals). As can be seen, *à* was never used with generic human possessors (e.g. *les problèmes des jeunes* 'young people's problems' C21–128). This would seem to us to be a categorical constraint on the use of *à*, since it is the same one that Väänänen and Foulet identified for Old French. Recall that, according to these linguists, *de* was the preposition that was used to introduce possessors referring to a whole class of individuals. They report no exceptions to this rule in Old French.

Table 7.3 shows the distribution of *à* and *de* according to whether the specific human possessor is a personal acquaintance of the speaker or not. It can be seen that *à* was used almost twice as often with possessors known

TABLE 7.2. *Distribution of* à *and* de *according to specificity of human possessor*

Human possessor	à (N)	de (N)	Total	à (%)
Specific	21	109	130	16
Generic	0	34	34	0
TOTAL	21	143	164	13

TABLE 7.3. *Distribution of* à *and* de *according to speaker's relationship to human possessor*

Specific human possessor	à (N)	de (N)	Total	à (%)
Known personally to speaker	16	70	86	19
Not known personally to speaker	5	39	44	11
TOTAL	21	109	130	16

personally to the speaker (e.g. *des amis à ma mère* 'friends of my mother' N36–506) as with possessors unknown to the speaker. This is quite consistent with Seutin's and Highfield's observations that the speakers of L'Île-aux-Coudres and St Thomas tend to use *de* instead of *à* when talking about a person or persons whom they do not know personally. But, since the tendency to talk about personal acquaintances vs. strangers is probably dependent to some extent upon whether the speech situation is respectively informal or formal, and since *à* and *de* are respectively informal and formal variants,[3] the constraint on *à* is probably more the result of this coincidence than of any attempt on the part of the speaker to increase the level of formality, as Seutin seems to suggest.

Table 7.4 presents the results concerning the distribution of *à* and *de* before vowel-initial and consonant-initial words. Though we found no occurrences of possessive *à* before vowel-initial words, the number of occurrences of *de* in the same context is too low (only thirteen) to conclude that vowel-initial words block or otherwise restrict the use of *à*, not to mention the fact that in most of the thirteen examples of *de* the possessor is an indefinite person not known personally to the speaker (e.g. *le nom d'un jeune Noir* 'a young black's name' C23–018), factors which are not very conducive to the use of *à* in the first place.[4]

Finally, Table 7.5 presents the results concerning the distribution of *à* and *de* according to the type of possessive relationship as determined by the possessee. Not considering inalienable possession for the moment, *à* seems to be about equally distributed between human relationship (e.g. *beaucoup d'amis à mon frère* 'many of my brother's friends' N11–196), ownership (e.g. *l'auto à mes parents* 'my parents' car' N05–146), and human attribute (e.g. *l'anniversaire de mariage à mon père* 'my father's wedding anniversary' H01–12). Again, the problem of scarcity of data precludes us from concluding that *à* cannot mark

---

[3] Table 7.3 itself provides supporting evidence by showing that reference was made almost twice as often (86 cases) to personal acquaintances as to persons not personally known to the speaker (44 cases). As mentioned in Chapter 4, we believe we have captured an informal style of speech with the interviews (though not necessarily the most casual—see next section).

[4] Underlying hiatuses are often realized phonetically as a fused vowel in informal Canadian French (e.g. *le frère à Amable* [lɔ frɛr a:mab] 'Amable's brother') (Dumas 1974), which takes away from the number of possible hiatuses in surface structure.

TABLE 7.4. *Distribution of* à *and* de *according to phonetic class of following segment*

Following word begins:	à (N)	de (N)	Total	à (%)
With a vowel	0	13	13	0
With a consonant	21	96	117	18
TOTAL	21	109	130	16

TABLE 7.5. *Distribution of* à *and* de *according to type of possessive relationship*

Possessive relationship	à (N)	de (N)	Total	à (%)
Human relationship	10	54	64	16
Ownership	7	30	37	19
Human attribute	4	23	27	15
Inalienable possession	0	2	2	0
TOTAL	21	109	130	16

inalienable possession with human possessors (e.g. *les mains à mon père* 'my father's hands'). In fact, it is reasonable to expect that *à* is compatible with the expression of inalienable possession, since there is historical evidence that it was in Old French, at least with animal possessors. In this case the scarcity of data is due to the fact that inalienable possession is not a frequently expressed type of possession. Be that as it may, that the other types of possessive relationship do not have much of an influence on *à*'s frequency is consistent with the fact that, historically, it is not the reference of the possessee but that of the possessor which has had a bearing on *à*.

7.3.2. Social distribution

Our look at the linguistic distribution of possessive *à* and *de* revealed that it is only with specific human possessors that examples of both prepositions were recorded. We shall therefore restrict our attention to these contexts in this section. We shall be concerned with the social distribution of possessive *à* and *de* as a function of the speakers' social class, restriction in the use of French, locality of residence, and sex (see Table 7.6).

It is interesting to note that what is purportedly a stereotype of popular speech in France is not limited to the speech of working-class francophones in

TABLE 7.6. *Social distribution of* à *and* de

Factor groups	à (N)	de (N)	Total	à (%)
Social class				
Middle	0	14	14	0
Lower-middle	10	67	77	13
Working	11	28	39	28
French-language use				
Unrestricted	10	42	52	19
Semi-restricted	11	41	52	21
Restricted	0	26	26	0
Locality of residence				
Hawkesbury	9	21	30	30
Cornwall	2	24	26	8
North Bay	7	27	34	21
Pembroke	3	37	40	8
Sex				
Male	8	60	68	12
Female	13	49	62	21
TOTAL	21	109	130	16

Ontario, since the lower-middle-class speakers use it too (although it is completely avoided by the middle-class speakers). While this suggests that *à* might enjoy a similar wider social-class distribution in Paris, it also underscores the fact that by and large Canadian French has been significantly less standardized than its European counterpart. This is due to a variety of reasons, e.g. the disappearance of much of the local French élite after the English conquest, the recency of the standardizing efforts of the French grammarians and Academicians in relation to the beginning of colonization, the low levels of schooling among French Canadians up until relatively recently, etc. (see Chapter 8 for a more detailed examination of these reasons). That *à* was not used at all by the middle-class speakers could also be an indication that the interview situation was not informal enough to get them to use this variant (assuming that they do use it in their casual speech).

As Table 7.6 reveals, the restricted speakers also failed to use *à*. This absence underscores the fact that they do not receive much in the way of exposure to French at home. In fact, for a non-negligible number of these speakers, exposure to and use of French has been mostly confined to the school (see Chapter 4), a formal context in which we would not expect a variant showing sharp social stratification to be used conspicuously. Thus, in all likelihood, the restricted speakers' exposure to *à* must have been marginal at best. The fact that the French-language-use index value below which *à* failed to occur is as high as .48 suggests that rather substantial exposure to parental and peer-group speech is required before this non-standard vernacular feature can be internalized. This high cut-off point is perhaps not so surprising, given that possessive *de* remains much the more common of the two prepositions, even in working-class speech (see Table 7.6). Thus the transmission of possessive *à* from one Franco-Ontarian generation to the next would seem to be in jeopardy when the minority language is no longer spoken (and heard) often enough at home and in the neighbourhood by the members of the younger generation. In sum, the non-attestation of *à* in the speech of the restricted users of French constitutes a second bit of linguistic evidence (along with the similar absence of *sontaient*) that these speakers are indeed significantly cut off from the vernacular, with the result that their language fails to reproduce the normal social stratification of speech.

In order to explore further the phenomenon of sociolectal reduction, we present in Table 7.7 a cross-tabulation of the data on the use of *à* and *de* as a function of French-language-use restriction and social class. Table 7.7 provides a clearer illustration of this phenomenon. While the unrestricted and semi-restricted speakers reveal an obvious pattern of social stratification, chiefly characterized by the absence of *à* in middle-class speech and a relative concentration of this variant in lower-middle and working-class speech, the restricted users of French fail to reveal such a pattern, since their speech features categorical use of *de*. Admittedly, the restricted speakers as a group did not use the prepositional variable very often (this is especially true for those that are from middle- or working-class backgrounds). However, the absence of *à* in the speech of the lower-middle-class speakers—who used the variable a

TABLE 7.7. *Distribution of* à *and* de *according to language restriction and social class*

French-language use	Social class	*à* (N)	*de* (N)	Total	*à* (%)
Unrestricted	Middle	0	8	8	0
	Lower-middle	8	24	32	25
	Working	2	8	10	20
Semi-restricted	Middle	0	3	3	0
	Lower-middle	2	23	25	8
	Working	9	15	24	38
Restricted	Middle	0	3	3	0
	Lower-middle	0	20	20	0
	Working	0	5	5	0
TOTAL		21	109	130	16

significant number of times, i.e. twenty—can be taken as a solid enough bit of evidence that minority-language-use restriction tends significantly to reduce (if not erase) normal sociolectal variation. The above data suggest that minority-language-use restriction brings about stylistic reduction as well. As indicated in Chapter 4, we designed the interview questionnaire and carried out the interview with a view to elicit an informal variety of speech. That the working-class and lower-middle-class speakers who exhibit low or mid levels of French-language-use restriction did not abstain from using *à* during the interview confirms that we have not been unsuccessful in our attempt to reach that goal. Thus the absence of any *à* in the speech of the highly restricted users of French of working- and lower-middle-class background can also in turn be taken as evidence that these speakers' French tends to be stylistically reduced, i.e. to be lacking in the way of informal variants.

To the extent that the vitality of *à* depends on unrestricted—or at most semi-restricted—use of French, the results of Table 7.6 showing its distribution by locality of residence are very much as one would expect: *à* seems healthiest in Hawkesbury, the majority francophone community.

There only remains to examine the possible effect of the speakers' sex. Sexual differentiation of speech has been observed time and again (Labov 1972: 301–4). Table 7.6 shows another example of it. The female speakers used *à* almost twice as often, proportionally, as did the male speakers. This finding amounts to a reversal of the classic pattern of sexual differentiation of speech, whereby female speakers tend to favour standard variants more so than do male speakers, which is precisely the pattern which we found in the case of *sontaient*. Assuming that the difference is genuine, it might be said to augur well for the continued survival of possessive *à*. Indeed, while it is true that Weinreich, Labov, and Herzog (1968) spend some time arguing against the parent-to-child model of language transmission put forward in Halle's generative approach, Labov (1972: 302–3) is nevertheless prepared to concede that parents—and women more so than their husbands—influence children's early language.

7.4. Conclusion

It was quite intentionally that in the introduction to this chapter we chose to speak of the variation between *de* and *à* as a 'rivalry'. It seems to us that this is how most sociolinguists view variation, i.e. as pitting against one another two or more variants, one of which is expected to win out in the end (for a recent expression of this view in French linguistics, see Berrendonner, Le Guern, and Puech 1983). The end has certainly been long in coming in the case of possessive *à* and *de*, so long in fact (well over a millennium if we go back to the Vulgar Latin period), that it hardly makes sense any more to speak of a 'rivalry'. It would appear to be much more appropriate and accurate to speak instead of a harmony or peaceful coexistence between two prepositional exponents of possession, without there being any evidence of complementary distribution having set in. It follows that sociolinguistic theory needs to recognize variation as an inherent aspect of language, not only because it is the only way in which smooth, orderly change can come about, but also because, we would like to claim, along with Berrendonner, Le Guern, and Puech (1983: 31), 'speakers could not cope with a system which is too finely tuned' (our translation from the French original). In other words, there is fuzziness or play in language, and speakers know how to take advantage of it (with several choices the chances of being right are greater than with only one choice!). Hence the prediction is that variables which represent equally good ways of saying the same thing ('equally good' being defined in structural terms) should show considerable inertia, i.e. be very stable over time. Possessive *à* and *de* have already proven their longevity.

On the other hand, this study also explored the extralinguistic conditions under which long-term linguistic variation can be tipped in favour of one of the variants. Grammatical prescriptivism (which bears on the literary or formal styles of a language) is one such condition. We saw that impaired transmission of a minority language and concomitant restriction in its use is another extra-linguistic factor through which hitherto stable linguistic variation can become destabilized. To the extent that possessive *à* is a feature of popular speech, its loss in restricted-speaker performance amounts to what we like to call 'sociolectal' reduction.

This study also seems to have uncovered a discrepancy concerning the vigour of *à* in contemporary non-standard varieties of French. If we consider how well *à* is faring in the speech of the Franco-Ontarian speaker subgroup which is most likely to use this variant (i.e. working-class females who are unrestricted users of French), the rate obtained is still only 57 per cent. Even for these speakers, then, possessive *de* remains a frequent alternative to *à*. This is at variance with other linguists' observations on possessive *à* in popular Parisian French and in the French of L'Île-aux-Coudres, Quebec, where *à* is reportedly much more frequent than *de* with human possessors (even categorical according to one linguist). Before even trying to explain this discrepancy, we think it appropriate to make sure that it is genuine, and this is only possible by relying on quantitative sociolinguistic investigations of possessive *à* and *de* in these other non-standard varieties of French. All that is available at the moment are personal observations, which, as such, run the risk of being over-estimations of the true strength of possessive *à*, in view of the well-known problem of categorical perception of non-standard forms (Poplack 1982).

Finally, we would like to respond to a view recently expressed by Chaudenson, Véronique, and Valli (1986), namely that young children learning French as a mother tongue from parents who do not use possessive *à* (i.e.

middle-class children) could none the less produce this variant spontaneously, like *sontaient* or the levelled third person plural verb forms examined in
the two preceding chapters. According to these authors, possessive *à* would be
yet another example of the many points of convergence which can be shown to
exist between child speech, popular or regional varieties of French, older
stages of the language, and even in some cases the speech of learners of French
as a second language, and which illustrate the strong influence of the internal
systemic dynamics of French on language variation and change. In support of
their view these authors point out that, in a recent article on the acquisition of
Romance languages, Clark (1985) mentions that internominal possessive *à* has
been observed in child speech (e.g. *la conyé à bébé* 'baby's spoon'). While we do
not wish to deny the fact that possessive *à* has indeed been observed in child
speech, in the absence of information about the parental model of speech to
which the young children were exposed, we believe that it is too hasty to
conclude that possessive *à* is necessarily a spontaneously occurring feature of
child speech. Our own empirical study of the use of possessive *à* has shown that
this variant is not confined to working-class speech, but is also quite evident in
the speech of the lower-middle class—not to mention that even middle-class
speakers may sometimes resort to *à* in casual speech. Thus children who have
been observed to use possessive *à* might simply have picked it up from their
parents or from older adults around them. This is precisely the kind of
interpretation which Grégoire (1968: 150) offered by way of explanation, when
he observed instances of possessive *à* in the speech of one of his two infant
subjects: 'Charles seems to know another use of preposition *à*. He says towards
the end of his second year: *tasse à bébé* "baby's cup", meaning by this the cup
that belongs to him. He has thus made his an informal usage which his
entourage resorted to by way of a joke' (our translation from the French
original).

   As to the process which underlies the spontaneous production of possessive
à, Chaudenson, Véronique, and Valli (1986) simply see it as an analogical
extension of the pattern *être à quelqu'un* 'to be someone's', e.g. *c'est à moi* 'it's
mine'. They could have pointed to the existence of several other possessive
constructions (besides the *être à* pattern just mentioned) which involve the use
of *à*, witness the verb *appartenir* 'to belong' which takes a complement
introduced by *à* (e.g. *ça appartient à Paul* 'it belongs to Paul'), the informal
extraposed possessive construction (e.g. *sa voiture, à Paul* 'Paul's car'), or even
the resumptive benefactive/dative construction (e.g. *je lui coupe ses cheveux, à ma
mère* 'my mother, I cut her hair'). However, the existence of these constructions
does not in our mind necessarily constitute a sufficiently powerful analogical
complex to induce the child to extend possessive *à* to the internominal context.
For this to be the case at least two conditions would need to be met: (1) several
or all of these constructions would have to be very frequent, so as to be
acquired early by the child, i.e. before the prepositional expression of posses-

sion between nouns, and (2) there would have to be a lack of structural optimality on the part of possessive *de* (i.e. markedness). Unfortunately for the thesis of Chaudenson, Véronique, and Valli, only the first condition is partly fulfilled. Only the *être à* construction is truly basic and furthermore possessive *de* has a lot going for it, structurally speaking, as it is part of a large set of constructions whose function is to determine a head noun, i.e. head noun + *de* + complement noun (e.g. *le bouchon de la bouteille* 'the bottle cork'; *la maison de verre* 'the glass house'; etc.). Indeed, internominal possession may be rightly viewed as a form of noun determination. Finally, another reason, extra-linguistic this time, which militates against the thesis of Chaudenson, Véronique, and Valli is the absence of internominal possessive *à* in the speech of the restricted users of French and also, to our knowledge, in the inter-language of second-language learners of French in institutional settings (see, e.g., Spilka 1976). In Chapter 5 we saw that the restricted and semi-restricted users of French level the distinctive third person plural verb forms (just as young learners of French as a first language do) because of their markedness. In the case of the expression of internominal possession, no such problem exists; internominal possessive *de* is definitely unmarked and hence likely to be learned easily. That the restricted users of French do not 'tamper' with it is an interesting bit of extralinguistic evidence of its structural optimality.

8

Aborted Sociolectal Reduction

IN this chapter we shall examine another case of rather long-standing variation in Canadian French, with special reference once again to the French spoken in the province of Ontario. The variable belongs to the area of verbal morphology and involves the alternate forms of *aller* 'to go' and *s'en aller* 'to go, leave' in the isg. indicative present (*vais*, *vas*, and *m'as*), in both their main verb and auxiliary functions. The historical part of the study will show that a comparative examination of sociolinguistic data on contemporary Canadian French and other colonial varieties of French (including French-based creoles) can, owing to their conservative nature, provide insights into the popular French of the pre-colonial period (i.e. allow one to reconstruct unattested forms like *m'as*) about which still relatively little is known. The reason for this is that the sources which up until now have been exploited by language historians are either literary texts or the observations of prescriptive grammarians on the speech of the bourgeoisie or aristocracy, the latter containing, as we have seen in Chapter 7, only passing remarks on the speech of the common people (see Trudgill 1986 for a similar view on the value of colonial varieties of English).

The problem of reconstruction of ancestor forms in the pre-colonial 'language' (we are being deliberately vague at this point) is actually less straightforward than we have just depicted it. The source of the added complexity is the well-known fact that seventeenth-century France was a linguistic mosaic, with the immigrants to the New World usually hailing from all over the domain of *oïl*. Thus it is still a matter of much conjecture (see Barbaud's 1984 book on this topic) whether all of the immigrants would have been conversant in French, the patois or dialect which won out over the other Gallo-Roman speech forms. Barbaud advances much evidence to suggest that there were probably three linguistic categories of settlers in New France in the seventeenth century: (1) unilingual francophones, (2) unilingual dialecto-phones, and (3) bilinguals in French and one of the numerous imported dialects. Thus the widespread presence of a given non-standard form in today's colonial varieties of French which goes unattested in pre-colonial French (the case of *m'as* until just recently, as we shall see), while it does entitle us to

This chapter is based on a paper by the title '*Vais, vas, m'as* in Canadian French: A Socio-historical Study' which the authors presented at NWAV-XVI, University of Texas, Austin, 23–5 October 1987. It has since appeared in the proceedings edited by Kathleen Ferrara *et al.*, *Linguistic Change and Contact* (Texas Linguistics Forum, 30; Department of Linguistics, University of Texas, Austin, 1988), 250–60.

postulate the existence of a common ancestor predating colonial expansion, does not tell us precisely in which pre-colonial speech form we should reconstruct it (in popular French, or in some dialect, or in regional French, i.e. French as it was acquired in the 'provinces', e.g. Normandy, Picardy, etc.?). Since all the colonial speech forms are varieties of *French* (none of the patois ever survived abroad except in the form of substratal influences), the natural tendency is to reconstruct ancestor forms belonging to pre-colonial French (as opposed to some Gallo-Roman dialect). The case of *m'as* is there to remind us that it is also possible for pre-colonial French and one or several dialects to have exhibited common features, as we shall see.

Socio-historical explanations will be offered for the differential diachronic evolution of Canadian and European French with respect to the variable under study. This will be followed, as in the preceding chapter, with a synchronic part in which we shall enquire into the fate of *vas* and *m'as* in the speech of the restricted speakers of Ontarian French. We shall see that these two non-standard variants, unlike possessive *à*, are *not* the object of reduction (i.e. loss) and shall seek principled explanations for such aborted reduction.

8.1. The variable

Whether they function as main (i.e. motion) verbs or as auxiliaries of the periphrastic future,[1] *aller* and *s'en aller* present alternating forms (*vais* vs. *vas*) in the 1sg. indicative present, as shown in the examples below:

1a. *Ben j'vais souvent à Valleyfield* 'Well I often go to Valleyfield' (C12–503).
 b. *J'vas à l'église, oui, à chaque dimanche* 'I go to church, yes, every Sunday' (C18–063).
2a. *O.K. J'vais t'aider* 'OK. I'm going to help you ' (C25–049).
 b. *Ben j'vas y aller à l'université* 'Well I'm going to go to university' (N31–242).
3a. *C't'été j'm'en vais au collège* 'This summer I'm going to college' (C35–184).
 b. *J'm'en vas à Montréal l'année prochaine* 'I'm going to Montreal next year' (C36–269).
4a. *Pour le Jour de l'An, j'm'en vais aller garder chez ma sœur* 'On New Year's Day I'm going to go and baby-sit at my sister's' (N19–252).
 b. *J'ai pas hâte de partir pour l'université parce que j'm'en vas être séparée* 'I'm not looking forward to going to university because I'm going to be separated' (H01–8).

---

[1] The periphrastic future is sometimes referred to in semantic terms as the 'near' or 'proximate' or 'immediate' future, as opposed to the simple future, which is labelled 'distant'. As mentioned in Chapter 5, the former has all but supplanted the latter in everyday speech. The periphrastic future has therefore taken over the meaning of the declining simple future tense and neutralized the near vs. distant opposition.

It can be pointed out that *s'en aller* (but not *aller*) was used once (out of twenty times) without an overt subject pronoun. When so used, *s'en aller* was conjugated with the *vas* form:

5. *M'en vas l'année prochaine* 'I'm going next year' (C17–301).

In the auxiliary function there exists a third and quite unique variant, namely *m'as* or more rarely *j'm'as* (four tokens out of 126):

6a. *M'as le retourner* 'I'm going to bring it back' (C11–157).
  b. *Ben m'as le faire pour toé* 'Well I'm going to do it for you' (C32–045).
  c. *J'm'as retourner* 'I'm going to go back' (C30–164).

It is important to stress here that what we are interested in is the conjugation of *aller* and *s'en aller* with *vais* or *vas* in the 1sg., verb type and function being considered as possible linguistic constraints (see variable-rule analyses further). The variable, then, because of the strict morphological grounds on which we have defined it, obviates the problem of occasional lack of semantic equivalence between *aller* (which always means 'to go') and *s'en aller* (which sometimes means 'to leave'). The *m'as* variant, however, poses a problem of classification as it is not obviously a conjugated form of either *aller* or *s'en aller*. In the following historical section, we shall present evidence justifying its treatment as a separate variant.

8.2. History of the variants

The variation between *vas* and *vais* as conjugated forms of *aller* and *s'en aller* in the 1sg. dates back at least to the Middle French period (Fouché 1967). Both verbs were pressed into service as auxiliaries of the periphrastic future during this period and were used interchangeably (see Gougenheim 1971: 85–110 for a detailed account of this development). Fouché and others look upon *vas* as the result of a process of analogical regularization based on the 2sg. and 3sg. forms *vas* and *va* (phonetically identical).[2] *Vais* is also said to be rooted in a process of

---

[2] The analogical process which historically gave rise to 1sg. *vas* can still be observed today in child language (Clark 1985; Martinet 1969: 96) and in the interlanguage of second-language learners (Harley and Swain 1978: 55). But, as Deshaies, Martin, and Noël (1981: 416) point out, De la Chaussée (1977) has rightly wondered why, if 1sg. *vas* was formed by analogy with 2sg. *vas* and 3sg. *va*, 1sg. **as* was not formed from 2sg. *as* and 3sg. *a* in the case of *avoir* 'to have'? By the same token, we may ask, along with Frei (1971: 32), why 1sg. **es* is not attested for the 1sg. present indicative of *être* 'to be', given the possible analogy with 2sg. *es* and 3sg. *est*? Yet both these regularized forms are once again typical of first- and second-language acquisition. Following Martinet (1969), it may be that analogical regularizations are blocked from vernacularizing when the irregularity in question is highly recurrent (which is the case for *suis* and *ai*, *être* and *avoir* being the two most frequent French verbs, respectively four and three times more frequent than *aller*, judging, for example, by the frequency list of Beauchemin, Martel, and Théoret 1983). It may be mentioned here that *as* (for *ai*) is reported as a sporadic phenomenon in non-standard varieties of French, for instance in St Thomas French (Highfield 1979: 101, 124).

regularization, however, having operated across paradigms on the analogy of *avoir*: 1sg. *ai*, 2sg. *as*, and 3sg. *a* (Fouché 1967). It would seem then that both *vas* and *vais* were innovations, the historical form according to Fouché (1967) being *vois* (< VL *vao < *vado*).[3] The latter did not survive past the seventeenth century and its demise appears to have been accelerated by the prescriptive grammarians, who considered it archaic. The variation was henceforth reduced to *vas* vs. *vais*.[4]

Two well-known prescriptive grammarians commented on this case of variation. Vaugelas (1647/1981: 54) remarked:

Everybody who knows how to write and who has been educated says *je vais* and they are right according to the grammar, which conjugates this verb thus: *je vais, tu vas, il va*. When it comes to conjugation, it is better to have a different form for each person; it conveys richness and beauty to the language and lessens ambiguity (a characteristic of poor languages). However, everybody at the Royal Court says *je va* and cannot stand *je vais*, which is looked upon as a provincialism or a feature of the popular speech of Paris [our translation from the French original].

Less than three decades later, however, Ménage (1675–6/1972) had a quite different perception (quoted in Fouché 1967: 426):

Monsieur de Vaugelas wants us to say *je va* and pretends that this is the way they speak at the Royal Court; one must say *je vais* and this is how they speak at the Royal Court. *Je vais, tu vas* . . . that is the way this verb should be conjugated and not *je va, tu vas, il vat*, which is how the people of Burgundy conjugate it. . . . Those who are at Port Royal used to say *je va*, having been misled by Mr de Vaugelas' remark. But they have since corrected their speech and now say *je vais*. Although he would like us to say *je va*, Mr de Vaugelas himself has most often said *je vais* . . . [our translation from the French original].

The quotations above document an interesting case of change in progress involving the status of *je vas* in the course of the seventeenth century. Once used by both the common people and the aristocracy, it was now losing ground to *je vais* in the speech of the latter, maybe as a result of the promotional efforts of grammarians like Ménage. However, *je vas* was to prove difficult to eradicate

[3] There were in fact still other forms of *aller* in the 1sg. present indicative, but, according to Brunot (1909: 317), these were probably just orthographic variants of *vais* (e.g. *vay*), of *vois* (e.g. *voy*), and of *vas* (e.g. *va*). In any case, Brunot confirms Fouché's view that by the seventeenth century only two variants remained: *vais* and *vas*. However, Yves-Charles Morin (p.c.) does not find Fouché's analysis of the origins of *vois, vais*, and *vas* convincing. He wrote to us: 'Even *vois* has all the appearances of an analogical form. The expected regular phonetic form would be *vé* (tonic) [i.e. *vais*] and *va* (atonic) [i.e. *vas*]' (our additions and translation from the French original).

[4] While this account concerns literary or educated French, the popular language, as best as we can tell, seems to have evolved in essentially the same manner. The *vois* form has not survived in any non-standard variety of French of which we know. The attestation of *vais*, however, in some of these varieties poses a problem: conservatism or ulterior Standard French influence? It is clear that in varieties of New World French that have been completely sheltered from the Standard (e.g. St Thomas French), the attestation of *vais* argues for conservatism (see further in this section).

from 'distinguished' French, where it lingered more or less until the early nine-teenth century (Grevisse 1986: 1247). In 1835 the French Académie decreed that *vas* had become rare and colloquial. Nowadays, in France, *vas* is relegated to popular or rural speech (Grevisse 1986: 1247; Rey 1986: 259) and has acquired the status of a stereotype.

M'as, on the other hand, is nowhere to be found in the sources on literary or educated French or in the various sources on contemporary or former popular European French (including Steinmeyer's 1979 historical work); nor is it reported in the numerous dictionaries or other descriptive works on the regional varieties of European French or local patois of France consulted by the writers of the *Glossaire du parler français au Canada* (La Société du parler français au Canada 1968: 444). However, *m'as* is present in most of the French-based creoles of the Caribbean and Indian Ocean (Broussard 1942: 12; Goodman 1964: 87; Valdman 1979*b*: 197 n. 4), the only exception being those of the Lesser Antilles and French Guyana.[5] Here are some examples of the use of *m'as* from creoles in the Indian Ocean and Caribbean: *ma manzé* 'I shall eat' (Réunion creole; Chaudenson 1989*b*: 28); *ma prann lajann-an* 'I shall take the money' (Haitian creole; Valdman 1979*b*: 197 n. 4); *ma couri* 'I shall go' (Louisiana French creole; Broussard 1942: 19). Curiously enough, *m'as* is not attested in Acadian French or its offshoot Cajun French (Chaudenson 1989*b*: 100), but it is in St Thomas French, where, however, it cannot stand completely alone (e.g. **ma le fèr* vs. *ma ki (va) le fèr* 'I am going to do it'; Highfield 1979: 99–100). Old Mines, Missouri French also has *m'as*, but that is to be expected as it is an offshoot of Canadian French (Thogmartin 1979). So, given its wide geographical dispersion, it is improbable that *m'as* is an innovation of Canadian French or of any of the other varieties of colonial French in which it is attested. It is more plausible to suppose that it was already extant in France at the time of colonial expansion. There remains to try and locate *m'as* more precisely in the linguistic context of pre-colonial France. As discussed in Chapter 7, what we know of yesterday's popular French has to a very large extent come to us in the form of sociolinguistic observations of prescriptive grammarians concerned about correcting and standardizing educated speech. Very often their interventions provide a glimpse of the popular French of the seventeenth century by proscribing features deemed to belong to this sociolect, but none the less not entirely absent from the speech of the more educated (the case of possessive *à* examined in the preceding chapter). An hypothesis which immediately suggests itself, then, is that *m'as* must have had strictly popular

---

[5] These are known as the '*ka* creoles' (spoken in Martinique and Guadeloupe, but also French Guyana). Thus, in Martiniquan creole, one finds the following future options: *ké* + verb, indicating simple future (e.g. *Mwen ké chanté* 'I shall sing') and either *kay* or *ké* + verb, indicating the so-called near future (e.g. *Mwen kay/ké chanté* 'I am going to sing') (Crestor 1987: 25). *Ka*, more specifically, is used as a present and past progressive marker, e.g. *mwen ka chanté* 'I am singing'; *mwen té ka chanté* 'I was singing' (Crestor 1987: 24).

origins in order to have escaped detection by the prescriptive grammarians—or at least not deserved any special mention.

The etymology of *m'as* remains enigmatic as well. In fact, the most commonly held view—actually the only one proposed thus far, at least to our knowledge—is that it represents a morpho-phonemic reduction of *m'en vas* /mã va/ > **m'en 'as* /mã a/ (via disarticulation of intervocalic *v*) > *m'as* /ma/ (via vowel fusion), both phonological rules being independently motivated (Juneau 1976: 85).[6] It is clear, however, that we are dealing here with an historical process of reduction and that, in contemporary Canadian French, *m'as* must be analysed as an amalgam which has lost its ties with the full form *m'en vas* from which it is putatively derived. That the frequency of occurrence of *m'as* (122 tokens) by far outweighs that of *m'en vas* (one token only, and in the main verb function at that) also motivates ascribing it independent status. Finally, the above-mentioned fact that *m'as* is only sporadically encountered with an overt subject pronoun suggests that it is the base form and that *j'm'as* is to be accounted for by a rule of pro-insertion.

This account leaves a number of questions unresolved, however. First, the loss of nasalization in the reduction of **m'en 'as* /mã a/ to *m'as* /ma/ is rather unexpected. In Québécois French, which is noted for its many examples of radical morpho-phonemic reduction, vocalic fusion normally results in the retention of the nasal vowel, not the oral one (e.g. *dans la* /dã la/ 'in the' > *dans 'a* /dã a/—this intermediate stage does exist contrary to /mã a/—> *dans* /dã:/). Thus either *m'as* remains an unexplained exception, or the process of morpho-phonemic reduction postulated by Juneau for *m'as* is incorrect. In this connection, La Follette (1969: 71) reports an interesting variant of *j'm'en vas* in Québécois French, namely *j'm'a vas*, in which *m'a* appears to be a denasalized *m'en*. Could *j'm'a vas*, or rather the subjectless form *m'a vas* /ma va/, be the precursor of *m'as*? Even if it were, we would not really be further ahead, as an explanation for *m'en* /mã/ denasalizing to *m'a* /ma/ would have to be found.

Second, why did the contraction of *m'en vas* to *m'as* only take place in the auxiliary function (see examples 7*a*, *b*)? One could appeal to the oft-made observation that the syntactic function of main verb seems to be more conservative as regards linguistic change than is the auxiliary function (Cheshire 1982). In the case at hand, the fact that the auxiliary slot is unstressed could have favoured morpho-phonemic reduction, i.e. loss of intervocalic *v*.

7a. **M'as* à Montréal 'I'm going to Montreal'.
  b. **J'm'as* à la maison 'I'm going home'.

---

[6] Juneau provides several other interesting instances of the disarticulation of intervocalic *v* in Québécois French: *vous avez* /vu zave/ > /vzae/; *vous voulez* /vu vule/ > /vuule/; *avec* /avɛk/ > /aɛk/. According to Juneau, this phenomenon has been observed in popular European French (e.g. *s'i' 'ous plaît* for *s'il vous plaît* 'please') and, in certain linguistic contexts, goes as far back as Old French.

8a.　*(*Tu*) *t'as aller à Montréal* 'You're going to go to Montreal'.

　b.　*(*Il*) *s'a aller à la maison* 'He's going to go home'.

Third, why did it take place only in the 1sg. and not in the other person–number combinations (see examples 8*a*, *b*)?[7] An answer is suggested by Gougenheim's (1971) detailed study of the rise of the periphrastic future in French. The use of *(s'en) aller* + infinitive to indicate the near future originated in popular speech and gained currency during the fifteenth century. It also had strong expressive force, according to Gougenheim, as it was overwhelmingly concentrated in the 1sg. (e.g. *je m'en vois escripre ung mot à Laurencin* 'I am going to write Laurencin a line', an example from Rabelais's *Pantagruel* quoted by Gougenheim 1971: 99). This great preponderance of the 1sg. lasted well into the following century. The significant fact is that when periphrasis finally generalized to the other person–number combinations (apparently during the seventeenth century, when the construction was approved by the prescriptive grammarians and also extended to future in the past, e.g. *j'allais mourir* 'I was going to die'), only *aller* underwent generalization, the *s'en aller* + infinitive alternative remaining locked into the 1sg. The French of St Thomas to this day still reflects this uneven distribution of the two periphrastic constructions. Thus in St Thomas French the future is conjugated as follows (Highfield 1979: 99): 1sg. *je vas faire* or *m'en vais faire* 'I shall do'; 2sg. *tu vas faire* (**tu t'en vas faire*) 'you will do'; 3sg. *il va faire* (**il s'en va faire*) '(s)he will do'; 1pl. *on va faire* (**on s'en va faire*) 'we shall do'; 2pl. *vous-autres va faire* (**vous-autres s'en va faire*) 'you will do'; 3pl. *eux va faire* (**eux s'en va faire*) 'they will do'.[8]

Fourth, following Hull (1979: 175), how does one explain that *m'as* is practically never used with the subject pronoun *je* in view of the well-known fact that French is not a pro-drop language?[9] An answer could possibly be

---

[7]　*T'as* has been reported alongside *m'as* in the local French of Old Mines, Missouri. While this might mean that the parent dialect, Québécois French, once had *t'as*, a more plausible explanation is that of Louisiana French creole influence via the migration of Blacks up the Mississippi River (Thogmartin 1979). Many French-based creoles, including Louisiana French creole, have generalized the *m'as* pattern. Thus for instance in Lousiana French creole the future of a verb like *couri* 'to come' is as follows: *m'a couri* 'I shall come'; *t'a couri* 'you will come'; *l'a couri* '(s)he will come'; *n'a couri* 'we shall come'; *v'a couri* 'you will come'; *y'a couri* 'they will come' (Broussard 1942: 19).

[8]　It is becoming increasingly apparent to those like us interested in the linguistic reconstruction of popular pre-colonial French that, because of its very conservative nature, St Thomas French puts us in a position to verify what otherwise would remain mere hypotheses. In the particular case at hand, not only is the 1sg. connection of *s'en aller* + infinitive confirmed, but so is the subjectless use of this construction (as in *m'en vais faire*). Also, for a dialect which has been completely cut off from Standard French, the 'inertia' of the irregular *vais* form is quite intriguing. Either it argues for the continued psychological reality of the analogical process which is said to have given rise to *vais* (see historical section), or it merely shows once more how powerful a factor of conservation a high frequency of occurrence can be, *aller* being the third most frequent verb after *être* and *avoir* (but see n. 2).

[9]　However, when pro-dropping does occur it seems to be mostly in the 1sg. of reflexive verbs. For instance, Valli (n.d.) cites examples such as *m'en fous* 'I don't care' and *veux pas le savoir* 'I don't want to know' in popular European French. This was confirmed by a quick search conducted on

sought through a closer examination of the rise of obligatory subject pronouns in French. The great current preponderance of *m'as* over *j'm'as* suggests that *m'as* derives directly from *m'en vas* rather than *j'm'en vas*, a later rule of pro-insertion accounting for *j'm'as* as was postulated above. There is historical evidence that the periphrastic future dates back at least to the fourteenth century and perhaps earlier, thus to a time when the use of the subject pronoun was not yet compulsory. It is possible, then, that *m'en vas* would have been the rule and *j'm'en vas* the exception during the course of the evolution of the periphrastic future.[10] As we have just seen, the existence of the *m'en vais faire* construction in St Thomas French does indeed prove that, for this particular construction at least, the use of an obligatory subject pronoun did not develop until much later if at all, due in all probability to the reflexiveness of the verb, *me* (or *m'*) already signalling 1sg.[11]

To conclude the discussion concerning the origin of *m'as*, the etymological account just provided is basically the position defended in a recent article by Mougeon, Beniak, and Valli (1988). Since then, thanks to Yves-Charles Morin (p.c.), we have learnt of the attestation of *j'm'as* (but not *m'as*), as well as parallel forms like *j'm'on* differing only phonetically from *j'm'as*, in certain local varieties of the patois of Picardy spoken in northern France (Debrie 1982, 1988; Morin 1983). The fact that its geographic distribution is irregular suggests that it is currently a recessive form and that formerly it must have covered (without any holes in the pattern) the whole territory. The province of Picardy, however, was not very well represented among the immigrants to New France in the seventeenth century (only ninety-six out of the 4,894 immigrants—or 2 per cent—were Picards according to the detailed statistics provided in Barbaud 1984: 20–1). Hence it does not appear likely that substratum interference is a sufficient explanation of the existence of (*j'*)*m'as* in Canadian French. Only if further research were to detect (*j'*)*m'as* in the provincial patois of Normandy, Poitou, etc. (regions which contributed much more heavily to the colonization of New France) might the substratum explanation then suffice. For the

our own speech corpus, which revealed further examples of pro-dropping confined to the 1sg. of reflexive verbs, such as *me souviens* 'I remember', *m'en prive pas* 'I don't deprive myself', *m'en rapelle* 'I remember', etc. However, the search also confirmed the infrequency of pro-dropping in this context, thus making it an implausible explanation of the numerical superiority of *m'as* over *j'm'as*.

[10] If we are to go by the copious examples cited by Gougenheim (1971), *je* was categorically present in the very earliest popular literary texts. However, Alexander Hull (p.c.) has indicated to us his suspicion that *m'as* or *m'en vas* may be disguised under the full written form *je m'en vas*. An analogous case in contemporary French would be *il y a* 'there is', which is pronounced *ya* in speech but not represented as such in writing (except in the works of a few writers like Queneau in France and Tremblay in Canada, who have made it a point to render the flavour of popular speech). The ideal historical sources (if they exist) would not be literary representations of popular speech (since these will always show more or less important adaptations to standard orthography), but actual samples of French written by individuals with little or no formal education.

[11] Regarding the phenomenon of subject incorporation into morphologically complex verbs like *aller* in the 1sg. indicative present, see Morin (1985: 809 n. 29).

moment, it is necessary to continue to postulate the existence of *m'as* in pre-colonial popular French. Hopefully, it will turn up sooner or later in some as yet undiscovered and/or unexplored historical source.

8.3. Synchrony of the variants

We shall now examine the sociolinguistic status of *vais*, *vas*, and *m'as* in contemporary Canadian French and then discuss the results in the light of the historical facts just presented. The only other quantitative study of this variable seems to be that of Deshaies, Martin, and Noël (1981), which was centred on the informal speech of Quebec City adolescents resident in two neighbour-hoods, one lower class, the other middle class. Restricting their observations to the auxiliary context, where all three variants alternate (see section 8.1), and not differentiating between *aller* and *s'en aller*, they found the following order of frequency: *vas* (75 per cent), *m'as* (20 per cent), and *vais* (5 per cent). They concluded from the extreme infrequency of *vais* that this variant is in all likelihood a marker of more formal style. Furthermore, as far as they could tell without doing a formal statistical analysis of their data, *vas* and *m'as* were evenly distributed between the two neighbourhoods. In other words, neither form seemed to have particular social connotations. Their status was simply that of informal stylistic variants.

Let us see to what extent these findings are corroborated by our quantitative examination of the social distribution of *vais*, *vas*, and *m'as* in Ontarian French. The analysis proceeded in two stages: first we examined the alternation between *vais* and *vas* as main verbs, then *vais*, *vas*, and *m'as* as auxiliaries. In both cases we used the VARBRUL programme in its microcomputer-adapted version. The results of the two analyses are presented below in Tables 8.1 and 8.2.

Table 8.1 shows the very high degree to which *vas* is present in the informal speech of Franco-Ontarian adolescents in the function of main verb (as reflected in the input term of .91). Moreover, it shows that *vas* is statistically evenly distributed between the two verbs *aller* and *s'en aller* and between the various speaker categories, excepting the two genders and the three social classes. The higher the class, the lower the probability of using *vas*, with females showing a tendency to avoid *vas* to a certain extent. However, the low effects (.32 and .29) assigned to the factors female gender and middle class should not conceal the fact that these two categories of speakers used *vas* no less than 80 per cent and 77 per cent of the time respectively! It should be noted finally that, strictly speaking, the results in Table 8.1 cannot be compared with those of Deshaies, Martin, and Noël, as theirs were based on the auxiliary context, to which we now turn.

The results displayed in Table 8.2 were generated by a multinomial version

TABLE 8.1. *Variable-rule analysis of* vas *vs.* vais, *main-verb function*

Factor groups	vas (N)	vais (N)	Total	vas (%)	Factor effects
Sex					
Male	106	8	114	93	.64
Female	71	18	89	80	.32
Social class					
Middle	23	7	30	77	.29
Lower-middle	87	15	102	85	.41
Working	67	4	71	94	.71
Locality of residence					
Hawkesbury	34	4	38	89	
Cornwall	44	3	47	94	not
North Bay	42	8	50	84	sig.
Pembroke	57	11	68	84	
French-language use					
Unrestricted	70	7	77	91	not
Semi-restricted	70	13	83	84	sig.
Restricted	37	6	43	86	
Verb					
Aller	162	25	187	87	not
S'en aller	15	1	16	94	sig.
TOTAL	177	26	203	87	.91

of the VARBRUL programme.[12] The reader should bear in mind that, in the case of a trinomial analysis, .333 (not .5) is the neutral factor-effect value.

Looking at the factor effects in Table 8.2, we note that *vas* appears to be evenly distributed across the various speaker groups, as indicated by the smallness of the spread between the effects within each factor group, with the probable exception of the factor group locality of residence. The effect of residence in Hawkesbury on probability of use of *vas* is quite favourable (.504), whereas residence in either Cornwall or North Bay is disfavourable (effects of only .143 and .156). A subsequent binomial analysis of *vas* vs. the other two variants combined (*vais* and *m'as*) confirmed the lack of contribution of all the factor groups excepting locality of residence (see Table 8.3).

If we now go back to Table 8.2 and look at the effects associated with *vais* and *m'as*, it can be seen that the spread between the factor effects is of considerable magnitude as regards locality of residence and of lesser but still sizeable

---

[12] We are indebted to Susan Pintzuk for kindly making the IBM PC version of the VARBRUL programmes available to us and for providing helpful advice on more than one occasion.

TABLE 8.2. *Variable-rule analysis of* vas *vs.* vais *vs.* m'as, *auxiliary function*

Factor groups	vas		vais		m'as		Total	Factor effects		
	N	%	N	%	N	%		vas	vais	m'as
Social class										
Middle	53	59	11	12	26	29	90	.287	.406	.307
Lower-middle	106	61	19	11	50	29	175	.359	.269	.372
Working	107	60	22	12	50	28	179	.351	.332	.317
Locality of residence										
Hawkesbury	84	78	3	3	21	19	108	.504	.057	.438
Cornwall	49	37	9	7	75	56	133	.143	.198	.659
North Bay	43	57	27	36	5	7	75	.156	.792	.053
Pembroke	90	70	13	10	25	20	128	.334	.418	.247
Sex										
Male	131	56	18	8	85	36	234	.344	.213	.433
Female	135	64	34	16	41	20	210	.295	.476	.229
French-language use										
Unrestricted	119	64	11	6	56	30	186	.278	.405	.317
Semi-restricted	98	56	30	17	48	27	176	.335	.229	.436
Restricted	49	60	11	13	22	27	82	.374	.375	.251
TOTAL	266	60	52	12	126	28	444	.690	.105	.204

TABLE 8.3. *Variable-rule analysis of* vas *vs.* vais *and* m'as, *auxiliary function*

Factor groups	vas (N)	vais and m'as (N)	Total	vas (%)	Factor effects
Locality of residence					
Hawkesbury	84	24	108	78	.69
Cornwall	49	84	133	37	.27
North Bay	43	32	75	57	.46
Pembroke	90	38	128	70	.60
Sex					
Male	131	103	234	56	not
Female	135	75	210	64	sig.
Social class					
Middle	53	37	90	59	
Lower-middle	106	69	175	61	not sig.
Working	107	72	179	60	
French-language use					
Unrestricted	119	67	186	64	
Semi-restricted	98	78	176	56	not sig.
Restricted	49	33	82	60	
TOTAL	266	178	444	60	.61

magnitude for the factor group sex. The results of a subsequent binomial analysis of *vais* vs. the other two variants combined (*vas* and *m'as*) confirmed that there is a strong correlation between *vais* use and locality of residence. Also selected was the factor group sex, female speakers using *vais* significantly more often than male speakers (see Table 8.4).

The binomial analysis of *m'as* vs. *vais* and *vas* combined yielded analogous results (see Table 8.5). Only two factor groups were selected as significant, namely locality of residence and sex once again, male and especially Cornwall speakers showing a greater proclivity to use *m'as*.

TABLE 8.4. *Variable-rule analysis of* vais *vs.* vas *and* m'as, *auxiliary function*

Factor groups	*vais* (N)	*vas* and *m'as* (N)	Total	*vais* (%)	Factor effects
Locality of residence					
Hawkesbury	3	105	108	3	.19
Cornwall	9	124	133	7	.47
North Bay	27	48	75	36	.84
Pembroke	13	115	128	10	.59
Sex					
Male	18	216	234	8	.39
Female	34	176	210	16	.62
Social class					
Middle	11	79	90	12	
Lower-middle	19	156	175	11	not sig.
Working	22	157	179	12	
French-language use					
Unrestricted	11	175	186	6	
Semi-restricted	30	146	176	17	not sig.
Restricted	11	71	82	13	
TOTAL	52	392	444	12	.09

8.4. Discussion

Anyone familiar with French as it is spoken in France will probably have been startled by the findings concerning the variable under study. It will be recalled (see historical section) that *vas* is a stereotype of lower-class or rural speech in France. Even when adopting a casual style of speech, no educated Frenchman

TABLE 8.5. *Variable-rule analysis of* m'as *vs.* vas *and* vais, *auxiliary function*

Factor groups	m'as (N)	vas and vais (N)	Total	m'as (%)	Factor effects
Locality of residence					
Hawkesbury	21	87	108	19	.47
Cornwall	75	58	133	56	.79
North Bay	5	70	75	7	.19
Pembroke	25	103	128	20	.40
Sex					
Male	85	149	234	36	.57
Female	41	169	210	20	.43
Social class					
Middle	26	64	90	29	not sig.
Lower-middle	50	125	175	29	
Working	50	129	179	28	
French-language use					
Unrestricted	56	130	186	30	not sig.
Semi-restricted	48	128	176	27	
Restricted	22	60	82	27	
TOTAL	126	318	444	28	.25

would ever use *vas* instead of *vais* (as main or auxiliary verb).[13] In Ontarian French, on the contrary, *vas* is in widespread use, showing only gradient correlations with social class and sex when it functions as a motion verb, and none at all, apart from a curious and hard to explain geographical correlation, when it functions as an auxiliary. Thus the social distribution of *vas* in the French of the Franco-Ontarian adolescents is rather reminiscent of its distribution in the French of the Quebec City adolescents, where it was basically even according to Deshaies, Martin, and Noël (1981).

The marginal status of *vais* in Canadian French in both main-verb and auxiliary functions represents another marked difference with European French. Indeed, it is striking that a form which is considered standard usage should be used so infrequently (only 23 per cent and 12 per cent of the time in the main-verb and auxiliary functions respectively) by the adolescent middle-class speakers of Ontarian French. This finding would seem to lend support to

[13] We are unfortunately not familiar with any quantitative study that could back this claim. We are relying here on our intuitions as educated native speakers of European French and on the repeated allusions in the literature to *vas* as a feature of popular or rural speech in France (Frei 1971: 32, 163; Martinet 1969: 96; Rey 1986: 259; etc.).

the claim of Deshaies, Martin, and Noël that in Canadian French *vais* is probably relegated to formal styles. Nothing more need be said concerning the expected association of *vais* (whether motion verb or auxiliary) with female speakers, except that it is quite in keeping with the formal status of this variant. We find the geographical correlation of *vais* (in the auxiliary function) rather puzzling. The only plausible explanation we can offer is that the speakers from Pembroke, North Bay, and Cornwall are proportionally more exposed to *vais* than the Hawkesbury speakers, because the school tends to be the chief locus of French-language use for many of the minority locality speakers (see Chapter 4). However, the absence of a similar correlation with locality when *vais* functions as a motion verb would seem to lessen the validity of our explanation.

M'as stands in even sharper contrast to European French usage than *vas* or *vais*, since it has not survived in the popular or rural French of France (assuming it was there in the first place—see historical section). We saw that *m'as* does not show any sharp social stratification (it is the geographical variation which stands out again). As such, it is somewhat surprising that the female speakers were found to use non-standard *m'as* significantly less often than the male speakers. Sexual differentiation of speech often goes hand in hand with social stratification, which is absent here. In any case, the sex effect is not a very strong one. These findings are thus once again consistent with those of Deshaies, Martin, and Noël, which, it will be remembered, did not suggest any obvious social stratification for *m'as*. It can be pointed out, however, that such findings differ from what Mougeon, Beniak, and Valli (1988) found when they examined the social distribution of *m'as* in the spoken French of a sample of *adult* Franco-Ontarians. In that study, *m'as* was found to be used significantly more often by speakers from the working and lower-middle class than by speakers from the middle class. In fact, these latter speakers hardly used *m'as* at all. This difference may be an illustration of the fact first established by Labov (1964) that social speech differentiation tends to diminish considerably during adolescence due to the homogenizing effect of peer-group pressure.

There is often a tendency in quantitative sociolinguistics to consider only significant factor groups as somehow worthy of discussion. Understandable though this may be—after all, the purpose of statistical analysis is precisely to determine whether linguistic variation is correlated or not with linguistic and/ or social factors—we would maintain that there are cases where absence of statistical significance can be just as if not more important or revealing! Tables 8.1, 8.3, and 8.5 provide just such an example with regard to the factor group French-language use. In Chapters 6 and 7 we saw that traditional features of Canadian French (i.e. non-standard features inherited from earlier stages of the language, coincident with or predating the exportation of French to the New World) undergo reduction in the speech of the restricted users of French. The next chapter will document another old non-standard feature (*sur* or *su'* meaning *chez*, e.g. *aller su' quelqu'un* 'to go to someone's house') for which we could only search in vain in restricted speaker performance. Against this background, that the latter speakers use *vas* (motion verb), *vas* (auxiliary), and *m'as* statistically no less frequently than the unrestricted and semi-restricted speakers is certainly in sharp contrast, to say the least. Two explanations may be offered. The first follows from the observation that *vas* and *m'as*, though non-standard, show no or at best gradient social stratification, whereas possessive *à* and *sontaient* were very sharply stratified. In other words, there is a pertinent distinction to be made between non-standard variants which exhibit mere stylistic variation (*vas* and *m'as*) and others which exhibit socio-stylistic variation. Restricted users of French would stand a greater chance of being exposed to the former, because of their wider social distribution in informal speech, not to mention that *vas* and *m'as* are highly recurrent forms (much more so than possessive *à* or *sontaient* or *su(r)* meaning *chez*). The second explanation goes for *vas*. As discussed previously (see historical section), *vas* was and still is underlain by a process of analogical regularization. We suspect that the restricted speakers have simply succumbed to this analogy, either initially as children (insufficiently exposed to French at home) or later as what we have called 'school' or 'second-language learners' of French. The analogical status of *vas* might then also explain why this feature is not simply used by the restricted speakers of French, but used with the same high frequency as the other speakers use it.

In sum, we suspect that the presence of *vas* in the speech of the restricted users of French is due in part to the same linguistic and extralinguistic factors which were argued to trigger the levelling of the distinctive 3pl. verb forms examined in Chapter 5, and that, even if the restricted speakers were only exposed to *vais*, *vas* might still end up being present in their speech as a fossilized language-learning error.

The key to explaining the above cross-dialectal differences between Canadian and European French lies, we think, in a consideration of the sociolinguistic status of *vas*, *vais*, and *m'as* in pre-colonial French and of the differential status and spread of the educated norm here and there. The reader will recall that in seventeenth-century French society *vas* was still largely socially unmarked, used as it was by the common people as well as by the aristocracy, *vais* had started to make some inroads in educated speech, and *m'as* was as best as we can tell a typical feature of popular speech. Since colonization of New France took place precisely during that century, New World French simply inherited this particular sociolinguistic situation. The local élite (e.g. nobility, colonial administrators, army officers), who could have played a role in the diffusion of the standard of the time and hence of the incipient normative variant *vais* at the expense of *vas* and *m'as* and in its transmission to future generations by providing models of speech which featured *vais*, for the most part returned to France shortly after the British Conquest of

1760. Relations between the colony and France were severed and the settlers (for the most part of rural or popular backgrounds) were largely left on their own. If we add to this reduction in social stratification, that formal education remained up until very recently underdeveloped in Quebec (Corbeil 1976), we can understand better why *m'as* did not get eradicated from the speech of the lower classes as it must have done in France and why *vas* still has a strong foothold in the informal speech of the educated class here, including school teachers. Indeed, it has been observed by several authors quoted in Gagné (1980) that there is still a significant discrepancy between what French-Canadian teachers prescribe according to the standard norm (e.g. *vais*) and what they actually variably practise themselves (e.g. *vas*), a behaviour which is not out of line with the absence of sharp social stratification found with respect to *vas*.

The socio-historical explanations just offered for *vas* also apply, we believe, to a number of other cases of differential evolution between European French and its Canadian descendant. For instance, the use of auxiliary *avoir* instead of *être* in the compound past (e.g. *j'ai venu* 'I came'), the use of temporal *à* instead of zero (e.g. *à tous les jours* 'every day'), the double conditional (e.g. *si j'aurais su j'aurais pas venu* 'if I would have known I wouldn't have come'), etc., are all features which in the seventeenth century were socio-stylistically unmarked or had just started to be targeted for eradication by the grammarians. Like *vas*, they still enjoy a wide social distribution in Canadian French, whereas in France they have been relegated to popular or regional varieties.

8.5. Conclusion

The present study has illustrated the fact that, if an examination of seventeenth-century European French can indeed shed some light on the starting-point of New World French, it has obvious limitations, since, as has been pointed out by Valli (n.d.), the historical sources that have been exploited by language historians bear only indirectly on the popular language. The value of colonial varieties of French—including Canadian French—is that they constitute a potentially rich and still underused source of information on pre-colonial popular French, given their high degree of conservatism (see the pioneering works of Chaudenson 1973 and Poirier 1979 in this respect). Colonial varieties of French, then, are called upon to play an important role in the development of what Valli (n.d.) has termed a 'sociolinguistic history' of French in which the popular language would be given its rightful place. That Romaine (1982b) has made a similar call in relation to the history of English is perhaps symptomatic of a more general dissatisfaction which sociolinguists experience when they want to delve into the history of the contemporary varieties of spoken language that they are studying, only to find that the work of language historians deals essentially with the literary language or with educated speech.

Another important finding to emerge from the synchronic part of this study is the realization that the phenomenon of loss of non-standard variants in restricted speaker performance may be constrained by the socio-stylistic status of the variants. Non-standard variants which evidence sharp social stratification (e.g. *sontaient*, possessive *à*) are much more likely to undergo reduction than variants exhibiting only stylistic variation (e.g. *vas*, *m'as*). Other properties of the variants may also be relevant, such as their frequency of occurrence and their structural status. In fact, there is a generalization to be captured here, which is that the more a non-standard vernacular form is 'visible' to the restricted speaker, on account of its frequency of occurrence and/or social distribution, the less likely s/he will be to 'miss' it. And, should it be overlooked, it still has a good chance of escaping reduction at the hands of the restricted speakers if it stands as an unmarked alternative to the standard counterpart (e.g. *vas*), since it may then fossilize as a developmental feature during primary- or secondary-language acquisition.

9

Covert Interference

THE present chapter is, as it were, transitional between the previous ones—all of which were concerned with system-internal developments—and the following ones—all of which will be concerned with interference-related developments in the speech of Franco-Ontarian adolescents. We examine here a rather complex case of variability in the prepositional subsystem of this regional variety of Canadian French. The variable expresses the basic notions of movement to/location at a person's dwelling and is realized by two types of variants: the simple prepositions *chez*, *sur*, and *à* (e.g. *je suis chez moi* 'I'm at home') and prepositional phrases involving the noun *maison* (e.g. *je vais à la maison* 'I'm going home'). Its interest lies in the fact that through its variants may be seen operating the different effects that bilingualism and restriction in language use have been observed to have on linguistic form, both in our own research and in that of others: (1) simplification (Dorian 1981: Chapter 4; Giacalone Ramat 1979; Trudgill 1983: Chapters 5 and 6; Chapter 5 in this volume), (2) loss of ability to shift styles (Gal 1984; King 1985) and even total loss of sociolectal features (Chapter 7 in this volume), and (3) interlingual influence, which may be subdivided into overt vs. covert interference (see Chapter 1 and below for definitions). It will be seen that interlingual influence is far from easy to prove when there are (and there usually are) competing internal explanations for the suspected cases of transfer, a fact which has inclined Andersen (1982: 108) to opine, as regards morphosyntactic transfer, that it is '*only possible* in those cases where both forces internal to the language and forces traceable to transfer co-exist' (his emphasis).

In this connection, special attention will be paid to trying to prove a case of covert interference within the prepositional variable under study. Covert interference is probably one of the least-well-documented effects of language contact, undoubtedly because it is so difficult to prove (Poplack 1983). Linguists have traditionally gone about searching for already completed cases of covert interference (Gumperz and Wilson 1971). It is said that covert interference has been isolated when the loss of a form cannot be imputed to internal causes but only to contact with another language in which no equivalent form is

This chapter is mostly based on an article by Mougeon, Beniak, and Valois entitled 'A Sociolinguistic Study of Language Contact, Shift, and Change', which appeared in *Linguistics*, 23 (1985), 455–87. It also draws to some extent on an article by Beniak, Mougeon, and Valois entitled 'Sociolinguistic Evidence of a Possible Case of Syntactic Convergence in Ontarian French', published in the *Journal of the Atlantic Provinces Linguistic Association*, 6–7 (1984–5), 73–88.

attested. It can be appreciated, then, that in the historical approach the only possible evidence for covert interference rests on structural linguistic arguments. In this study, however, we take a synchronic approach to the problem and try to prove a case of covert interference in progress. Unlike overt interference and borrowing, covert interference does not entail a qualitative deviation from the monolingual norm, only a statistical one, i.e. it is manifested by the *decline* of a form which has no counterpart in the superordinate language. Therefore quantitative sociolinguistic methodology is required in order to be able to show that the language under investigation is (or is not) drawing closer to the other language with which it is in contact. More specifically, with quantitative sociolinguistic methodology it is possible to examine the frequency of the form with no counterpart in the superordinate language as a function of subgroups within the speech community. The expectation is that speakers of the subordinate language who know the superordinate language well should be the instigators and therefore be further along the covert-interference path than speakers who remain dominant in the subordinate language. None the less, it should be borne in mind that quantitative sociolinguistic methodology does not make it possible to go beyond the mere isolation of potential cases of covert interference. The burden of proof, as in the historical approach, still rests on the linguist, who must argue that the candidates for covert interference cannot be explained away as internal changes.

It will also be seen that, whereas Puerto Rican Spanish has purportedly maintained its structural integrity by resisting grammatical influence from English despite intensive contact with this language, the same cannot be said of Ontarian French, suggesting that the distinction between stable and unstable bilingualism is crucial when it comes to predicting the likelihood of grammatical influence of superordinate on subordinate languages.

In a different vein, synchronic variation is usually not studied within a historical perspective and so we are very often left in the dark concerning when and how the variants arose in the course of the language's history.[1] In this chapter as in the earlier ones we shall trace back the different variants within the recorded history of the French language. It will be seen that two of the variants (*chez* and *sur*) admit alternative explanations to those that have traditionally been proposed to account for their origins. Another interesting finding to emerge from the historical examination will be that two other variants (*à* and *à la maison de*), both of which are attested during the earliest stages of the language, are actually not the result of uninterrupted transmission from Old French to the present but innovations due to the instability of the

---

[1] As Dorian has rightly pointed out to us (p.c.), 'Often enough a historical perspective isn't even available for use in the study of synchronic variation; the number of languages well and long enough studied to provide that kind of perspective is too small relative to the number of languages showing synchronic variation today.' Though in agreement with her statement, we would still maintain that the investigation of synchronic variation, even in languages whose history has been well studied (e.g. the Romance languages), is often not approached from a historical perspective.

bilingual situation. Their synchronic social distribution will be shown to confirm their discontinuous history.

9.1. The variable

As indicated, the variable under investigation is composed of an assortment of prepositions and prepositional phrases through which the idea of location at/ movement to a person's dwelling may be expressed in Ontarian French. For the moment let us say that we found four (later we shall see that it is really five) different manifestations of the variable in the computerized alphabetical concordance of the interview transcripts: the prepositions *chez*, *sur*, and *à*, and the prepositional phrase *à la maison de*.[2]

The first step in any variation study should be to examine the linguistic distribution of the variants in order to make sure that they are indeed substitutable and not in complementary distribution (Thibault 1979: 3). At the same time this exercise will serve to familiarize the reader with the different variants, all of which will be illustrated by a series of examples drawn from our corpus. The ideal situation would be one where the speakers actually produced minimal pairs but as a rule such evidence is not available when dealing with non-phonological variables. We shall examine the distribution of the variants with respect to two features of the linguistic context which immediately suggest themselves as potential conditioning factors: the verb (static vs. motion) and the complement (noun vs. pronoun). Let us begin with the variant *chez*:

1 a. *Pis on est allé heu . . . chez ma grand-mère* 'And we went uh . . . to my grandmother's' (P25–136).
   b. *J'étais chez mon cousin* 'I was at my cousin's' (C23–139).
   c. *Tout le monde vient chez nous* 'Everyone comes to our house' (N33–295).
   d. *Y'étaient pas chez eux* 'They weren't at home' (N19–335).

Chez is a variant which corresponds to standard usage and whose frequency of occurrence was highest of all the variants (166 tokens). As the above examples show, *chez* is both directional and locative and can introduce either a nominal or a pronominal complement referring to a person. Other pronouns besides personal ones are possible (e.g. indefinite pronouns such as *quelqu'un*

---

[2] It goes without saying that there are other types of location and direction besides simply being at or going to a person's home. Thus we also found expressions of direction away from or location other than at a person's dwelling (e.g. *un gars pis une fille qui ont parti de chez eux* 'a guy and a girl who left their house' P31–051; *j'aimerais ça être plus libre, sortir de la maison* 'I would like to be freer, to leave the house' P02–085; *j'en connais pas parce que alentour de chez moi y'en a pas assez de Français* 'I don't know any because around my home there aren't enough French people' P18–468; *ben y'en a vers la maison* 'well there are some near my house' N31–443; etc.). We decided against extending the scope of the variable to include these other examples because of the unmanageable complexity this would have created, not to mention the fact that it is not clear whether such an extension would be legitimate in the first place.

'someone') but are far less frequent and in any case they too (notwithstanding their name) refer to a person.

Sur, on the other hand, is a non-standard variant and it occurred only infrequently in our corpus (eight tokens):

  2*a.* *On été sur heu . . . ma tante* 'We went to uh . . . my aunt's' (C31–093).
  b. *Moi j'restais su(r) ma cousine* 'I was staying at my cousin's' (C03–136).
  c. **Quand qu'on va su(r) eux* 'When we go to their house'.
  d. **Moi j'restais su(r) elle* 'I was staying at her house'.[3]

Examples 2*a* and 2*b* are in every respect analogous to 1*a* and 1*b*. They show that *sur*, like *chez*, can indicate direction to and location at a person's home. But we failed to note any occurrence of *sur* with a personal pronoun (2*c*, *d*). We do not think that this is simply an artefact due to the low frequency of *sur*, because Seutin (1975: 345–6) also reports that *sur* never co-occurs with personal pronouns in the spoken French of L'Île-aux-Coudres, where it is a much more common variant of *chez*.[4] Be that as it may, *chez* is not confined to pronominal complements and so the two prepositional usages cannot be said to be in complementary distribution.

À, also a non-standard and infrequent variant (only eight tokens), is distributed just like *sur*:

  3*a.* *J'été à mon grand-père* 'I went to my grandfather's' (N20–055).
  b. *J'ai resté pour une coup'e de journées à mon grand-père* 'I stayed for a couple of days at my grandfather's' (N20–058).
  c. **J'été à lui* 'I went to his house'.
  d. **J'ai resté pour une coup'e de journées à lui* 'I stayed for a couple of days at his house'.

It may be seen that *à* can co-occur with a motion verb or with a static verb and that it was never found introducing a personal pronoun. The literature is not of help this time in weighing the plausibility of such a categorical constraint, since none of the works on contemporary or past varieties of Canadian French attests *à* as a variant of *chez*.[5] This in itself is a significant observation to which we shall return in the historical section. The historical section (etymology of *chez*) leads one to believe, however, that the non-

---

[3] Among the eight occurrences of *sur*, three were pronounced without the final *r* (this is indicated by its enclosure in parentheses). We shall have more to say about this point when we consider *sur* from a historical perspective.

[4] The same pattern seems to hold for *sur* in Prince Edward Island Acadian French, although there *sur* + NP and *chez* + pronoun appear to be in complementary distribution (Ruth King, p.c.). Thus, the cross-dialectal evidence points to the ungrammaticality of *sur* + pronoun.

[5] In contrast, there is frequent mention of the use of *à* instead of *chez* in the related sense of 'at/ to someone's place of work' (e.g. *aller au docteur* 'to go to the doctor's'), both in popular Canadian French (Dionne 1974: 1; La Société du parler français au Canada 1968: 1) and in popular European French (Frei 1971: 150; Guiraud 1973: 73). It is a very old usage according to Grevisse (1975: 978). There are many examples of it in our own corpus.

occurrence of *à* + personal pronoun, like that of *su(r)* + personal pronoun, is well founded and categorical (hence the asterisks preceding examples 3*c* and 3*d*). Indeed, the only reason *chez* can co-occur with a personal pronoun is that it was etymologically a noun (< Latin *casa* 'house') and could be used in constructions like *a ches nos* 'at our house'.

Matters are a bit more complex when it comes to the prepositional phrase *à la maison de*. Indeed, it hides a certain amount of complementary distribution as well as 'free' variation. *À la maison de* remains as is before a noun (as in examples 4*a* and 4*b*) but surfaces as *à* + determiner + *maison* when the complement (in deep structure) is a personal pronoun (as in examples 4*c–h*). We might wish to call *à la maison de* and *à* + determiner + *maison* 'allophrases' because of their complementary distribution. However, and this is where the complication arises, *à* + determiner + *maison* is realized equivalently as *à* + possessive adjective + *maison* or as *à la maison* when the underlying personal pronoun is coreferential with an intrasentential antecedent (practically always the sentential subject, as in examples 4*c* and 4*e*) or has as its referent the speaker (as in examples 4*d* and 4*f*). The absence of a possessive marker in *à la maison* corresponds to the well-known tendency in French not to mark overtly inalienable possession, of which a person's dwelling must be presumed to be an instance. When the underlying pronoun has an extrasentential antecedent or when it does not refer to the speaker, possession must then be overtly marked, as illustrated in examples 4*g* and 4*h*:

4*a*. *On se rencontre à ('a) maison de son... mon ami* 'We get together at his . . . my friend's house' (C37–272).

   b. * *On est allé à la maison de mon ami*[6] 'We went to my friend's house'.

   c. *Une fois arrivé à sa maison y'a...* 'Once he arrived home he . . .' (N35–413).

   d. *Elle voulait rester à notre maison* 'She wanted to stay at our house' (P27–280).

   e. *Elle travaille à la maison* 'She works at home' (C01–002).

   f. *I' viennent à la maison* 'They're coming to our house' (P30–209).

   g. *Quand j'vas à leur maison* 'When I go to their house' (P24–596).

   h. *À ('a) place de moi aller à sa maison* '. . . Instead of my going to his house' (C04–310).

In view of the above, having initially distinguished nominal from pronominal complements, we must now distinguish the latter (personal pronouns) according to the (co)reference relations into which they enter: those that refer to the speaker or are used coreferentially with an intrasentential antecedent (PROi) and those for which neither is true (PRO), remembering that the pronouns are present only at a deeper level of structure. On the grounds that *à*

---

[6] Our failure to come across any occurrence of *à la maison de* in the context of a motion verb is surely an artefact of the very low frequency of occurrence of this variant (only two tokens in the entire corpus).

la maison (1) alternates with *à* + possessive adjective + *maison* in the context of PROi, (2) is the only one of the three prepositional phrases which is considered correct usage here in Canada (Bélisle 1974: 733) as well as in France (Larousse 1966: 699; Robert 1972: 1026), and (3) displayed a frequency of occurrence in our corpus (69 tokens) far outweighing that of the other prepositional phrases (only 6 tokens of *à* + possessive adjective + *maison* and 2 of *à la maison de*), we decided, in the final analysis, to set up *à la maison* as a variant separate from *à la maison de*, the latter having the allophrase *à* + possessive adjective + *maison*.

In ending this section, we wish to reiterate that all we have done to this point is consider the possibility of categorical constraints bearing on the use of the different variants. This was necessary in order to make sure that we were dealing with genuine variation and not complementary distribution. Although we did find evidence of complementary distribution, it was purely internal to the prepositional phrase *à la maison de* and in no way called into question *à la maison de*'s status as a true variant of the simple prepositions *chez*, *sur*, and *à*. In a later section, when we analyse the data quantitatively, we shall be able to see whether any weaker constraints or tendencies obtain. It will probably help the reader visualize the variable better if we represent it as in Figure 9.1.

9.2. History of the variants

Without disagreeing with Saussure (1974: 114–50) that diachrony and synchrony are best kept completely separate, by which we mean, as Kiparsky (1980: 411) has written, that 'the role of an element in the linguistic system is something in principle absolutely independent of its historical origin', we shall try to show that historical information may be suggestive of synchronic explanations that the linguist would (and could) otherwise never have considered. Moreover, our intention here is not merely to report facts concerning the variants' historical origins and evolution but to question some of the interpretations that have been made of these facts.

9.2.1. Chez

This preposition is attested for the first time in the twelfth century in examples like *chies un hoste* 'at a host's' or *ches son hoste* 'at his host's' (Littré 1968a: 264; Wartburg 1940: 450). *Chies* (or *ches*) was the atonic form of the noun *chiese* (or *chese*) 'house' (< Vulgar Latin *casa* 'house') (Greimas 1968). It was normal for word-final *a* to reduce to schwa as in *casa* > *chiese* (or *chese*). That the vowel was dropped altogether in *chies* (or *ches*) is probably due to the atonic position of the word (Nyrop 1899: 209). According to Wartburg (1940: 452), *casa* was replaced very early by *mansio* 'house' (> *maison*) in Gallo-Romance, especially in the north. But traces of *casa* in Old French are said to be seen in examples like *en*

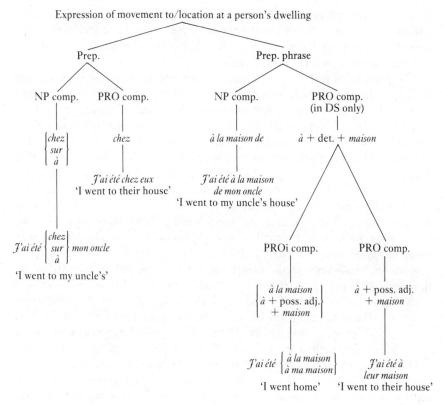

FIG. 9.1. *Graphical display of the variable*

Source: adapted from Mougeon, Beniak, and Valois (1985: 465)

chies son hoste 'at his host's house' or *a ches nos* 'at our house' (Nyrop 1899: 95). In fact, Nyrop suggests that the preposition *chies* (or *ches*) emerged as a result of *en* and *a* 'dropping' and goes on to note that in Danish the preposition *hos* meaning *chez* must have extracted itself in the same way from prepositional phrases involving the noun *hus* 'house'. Nyrop's view of *chez*'s formation is echoed by Bloch and Wartburg (1950: 123), who note a parallel development in Picard and Wallon where the preposition *mon* meaning *chez* is said to have formed out of the dialectal equivalents of prepositional phrases like *à notre maison* 'at our house'. Picard and Wallon are in fact dialects in which no trace of Latin *casa* remains (Wartburg 1969: 248). It is instructive to consider what Wartburg had to write about the precise mechanism or stages of preposition *mon*'s formation in Picard and Wallon: 'In the extreme northern part of Roman Gaule, in Picardy-Wallonia, *mansio* was able to displace its oldest adversary *casa* even in its prepositional usage; the composed forms *en meson, à meson*, etc. gave birth to the prepositions *émon, amon*, etc. These prepositions with *en* and *à* in turn gave rise to the elliptical form *mon* 'chez'. It is the proclitic use of the prepositions *émon* and *amon* that explains the phonetic fusion' (our translation and adaptation from the German original).

The question is whether this account is convincing. It seems to us a rather roundabout way to explain *mon*'s formation and by extrapolation that of *chies* (or *ches*). Indeed, while the fusion or coalescence of the initial prepositions *en* and *a* with the following nouns *meson* and *chies* (or *ches*) is a natural development, the dropping of the initial prepositions or their merging with the noun to the point of leaving absolutely no trace is not. An alternative hypothesis is that *chez* or more precisely *chies* (or *ches*) is a direct descendant of the Vulgar Latin noun *casa*, used without a preposition to signal location at or motion to a person's dwelling. Though we lack information on Vulgar Latin, this view derives support from the fact that the Classical Latin noun *domus* 'house' (which *casa* replaced in Vulgar Latin) could be used in exactly this way (e.g. *domum Pompenii venire* 'to come to Pomponius' house') (Gaffiot 1934: 555). Of course, the breakdown of the case system must have led quite early to the introduction of the prepositions *in* and *ad* before *casa* (Bloch and Wartburg 1950: 123) and this is precisely what is reflected in the Old French forms *en chies* and *a ches*. But since *maison* had become the common word for 'house' in Old French, *chies* (or *ches*) could hardly still have had nominal status in *en chies* and *a ches*. Despite the spelling, *en chies* and *a chies* were probably already fused forms in Old French and in this respect it may be noted that Wartburg (1940: 451) and Toblers and Lommatzsch (1954: 203–4) cite the Old French preposition *enchies* represented graphemically as a single lexical unit. We may suppose that the fused form *aches* existed as well, especially since there are reflexes of it (e.g. *assi* or *assié*) in certain dialects of France (Wartburg 1940: 450). We would contend, then, that, instead of depicting *chies* (or *ches*) as having somehow extracted itself from the analytic forms *en chies* and *a ches* (via an as yet unexplained dropping of the initial prepositions) or from the fused forms *enchies* and *aches* (via an as yet unexplained phonetic reduction of *en* and *a*), the coexistence of three prepositional options should be posited in Old French: *chies* (or *ches*), *enchies*, and *aches*. It turns out that *chies* (or *ches*) is the option which won out in French to give *chez*, but in other dialects it is the fused forms which survived (see the above-mentioned examples of *assi* and *assié*). In other dialects still, none of these prepositions survived if they were ever formed (see the above-mentioned examples of *mon* in Picard and Wallon).[7]

---

[7] A question to consider is why *mansio* did not take *casa*'s place as a preposition as well. We know that in Picard and Wallon *mansio* took over both functions. The answer might be that the atonic form *chies* (or *ches*)—the one that gave rise to the preposition *chez*—grew to be so phonetically distant from the tonic form *chiese* (or *chese*)—the one that was replaced by *mansio*—that speakers no longer perceived them as related to each other. In effect this would have curtailed the generalization of *mansio* to the prepositional context.

9.2.2. Sur

The preposition *sur* (< Latin *super* 'on, above'), used in the sense of *chez*, is attested by both Wartburg (1966: 432) and Littré (1968*b*: 595) in the late fourteenth or early fifteenth centuries (e.g. *Je descendis à l'hostel de la Lune sur un escuyer du comte, lequel* . . . 'I stayed at the Hotel de la Lune at a gentleman of the count's, who . . .'). The same usage is attested again by Huguet (1967: 135) in the sixteenth century (e.g. *Le bon chevalier* . . . *la mena* . . . *coucher sur une gentil-femme sa parente* 'The good knight . . . took her . . . to sleep at a gentlelady's, a relative of his'). Haase (1969: 351–3), however, does not report this usage in the next century. While this may be taken as an indication that *sur* meaning *chez* had probably disappeared from the standard language in the seventeenth century, it must be assumed to have survived in the popular language and/or in some of the dialects and then been brought over to Canada by the French settlers. Indeed, *sur* meaning *chez* is attested in Québécois French at the turn of this century by La Société du parler français au Canada (1968: 647) and is reported again more recently by La Follette (1969: 152–3), Barbeau (1970: 263–5), Seutin (1975: 345–6), and in Acadian French (see n. 4).

It so happens, however, that there was another preposition, *sus* (< Latin *sursum* 'at the top, towards the top'), which is attested in the sense of *chez* roughly at the same time as *sur* (Wartburg 1966: 463). And we learn from Juneau (1972: 200) that there was already a strong tendency not to pronounce word-final *s* in sixteenth-century French. This suggests that the weakening of word-final *s* started much earlier (Morin 1981: 35–47). Now we learn from Straka (1965: 591–4, reported in Juneau 1972: 164) that word-final *r* was also not pronounced between the thirteenth and seventeenth centuries. As a result of these two rules of final-consonant deletion, the prepositions *sur* and *sus* must have merged very early in the history of French. Hence it is not possible to tell whether the form we have attested in our speech corpus and transcribed as *su(r)*, pronounced [sy], descends from *sus* (< Latin *sursum*) via final-*s* deletion, or whether it comes from *sur* (< Latin *super*) via final-*r* deletion. Juneau (1972: 170 n. 36) opts for the former etymology, although he provides no convincing argument in support of his choice.

Apart from this etymological problem, what remains puzzling (and only serves to add to the etymological dilemma as we shall see) is how *sur* (and *sus* for that matter) managed to acquire the meaning of *chez*. The reader will no doubt agree with us that this novel meaning appears far removed from the original meanings of *sur* 'on, above' and *sus* 'at the top, towards the top'. It is conceivable, therefore, that *sur* and *sus* did not acquire the meaning of *chez* via a natural semantic evolution. An alternative explanation is the following. In many dialects of France the initial consonant of *chies* changed to /s/ and its vowel to /y/, wherein Bloch (1917: 116) sees an influence of the preposition *sus*; but Wartburg (1940: 452) cautions that the phonetic changes that *chies* underwent may have taken place naturally, given the atonic position of the word. If Wartburg is correct, *sur* and *sus* may have acquired the meaning of *chez* due to their homophony with *su* (< *chies*). We already know that *chies* is attested several centuries before either *sur* or *sus* acquired the additional meaning of *chez*. This would have given *chies* more than enough time to undergo its presumed natural phonetic evolution to *su*. Should this scenario prove accurate, it would mean that there is yet a third possible etymological source for synchronic *su(r)* meaning *chez* (i.e. < *su* < *chies*).

How, then, do our speakers of Ontarian French interpret *su(r)*? As our orthographic transcription has intimated all along, there is reason to think that, synchronically speaking, *su(r)* must be analysed as a phonetic variant of the full form *sur*. First of all, it will be remembered that *sur* occurred more often (5 tokens) than did *su(r)* (3 tokens) with the meaning of *chez*. Thus, if the two forms are to be related lexically, as we think, it follows that *sur* should be taken as the base form. Secondly, the rule of final-*r* deletion is still operant synchronically in linguistic contexts where *sur* has the primitive meaning of 'on, above', as illustrated in examples 5*a* and 5*b*:

5*a*. *Il va (y) avoir un homme su' la lune* 'There is going to be a man on the moon' (C23–275).
  b. *Si t'avais toujours de l'argent su' toé* 'If you always had money on you' (P35–479).

Given these two observations, the optimal grammar must be one in which *su(r)* meaning *chez* is also interpreted as an *r*-less pronunciation of *sur*. Of course, another possibility would be to claim that *su(r)* meaning *chez* is really a separate preposition and that our speakers are hypercorrecting by inserting a final *r* on the analogy of *sur* > *su(r)* 'on, above'. But this is tantamount to saying that our speakers do indeed perceive a lexical relationship between *sur* and *su(r)* meaning *chez*. Whichever way one chooses to look at the problem, then, it appears that the simplest solution is to argue that *su(r)* is an *r*-less pronunciation of *sur*. We still maintain, however, that, had we not had the benefit of historical information, we would probably never have considered the possibility that *su(r)* could be anything else but a phonetic variant of *sur*.

In light of the fact that the use of the preposition *sur* in the sense of *chez* disappeared from the standard language in the seventeenth century, it will be interesting to see just how well this archaism has managed to survive in Ontarian French. As we shall see, we should not be misled into thinking that it is on the brink of extinction just because we found only eight occurrences representing merely 3 per cent of the total number of actualizations of the variable.

9.2.3. À

The use of the preposition *à* in the sense of *chez* most probably predates the emergence of the preposition *chez* itself, since in Classical Latin *ad* > *à* was already used in this way (e.g. *fuit ad me sane diu* 'he stayed at my house a very long time') (Gaffiot 1934: 28). Yet there is no explicit reference to any such use of the preposition *à* in the etymological dictionaries that we consulted. However, Toblers and Lommatzsch (1925: 3) do list, under the preposition *à*, several Old French examples where *à* appears to translate the meaning of *chez* (e.g. *se hierbegoient as boines gens que il trovoient* 'they stayed with the good people that they found'; *hebergier en boine vile au plus haut oste, au plus nobile* 'to stay in a good city with the highest host, with the noblest'). Still, it should probably be assumed that *à* was used in the sense of *chez* in Old French at best only occasionally for this usage to have escaped the attention of historical linguists. Could it be that the creation of the preposition *chez* in Old French curtailed the need to maintain another preposition? It is interesting to note that in Occitan, a southern Gallo-Roman dialect in which *chez* is not attested, it is precisely the preposition *à* which is found instead (e.g. *à M. tal* 'at Mr so and so's') (Piat 1970). In accord with the lack of explicit reference to *à* meaning *chez* in Old French, Huguet (1925: 1–4) does not report this usage in the sixteenth century, nor does Haase (1969: 314) in the seventeenth century. This is also quite in keeping with the fact that none of the works on past or contemporary varieties of Canadian French that we consulted makes note of the use of *à* in the sense of *chez*. By all appearances, the *à* we have attested in Ontarian French in the sense of 'at/to someone's home' is not a historical preservation like *sur*, since it goes unattested after the Old French period. Though it could have survived unnoticed in certain dialects and/or in the popular language and made its way to Canada at the time of colonization, we shall see that there is synchronic evidence that *à* is indeed not an archaism but an innovation (admittedly resembling a previously attested usage in the history of French).

9.2.4. À la maison and à la maison de

The prepositional phrase *à la maison* does not seem to be attested until the sixteenth century, in other words several centuries after *chez* (Wartburg 1969: 241). This is not to say, however, that from the twelfth century (period of *chez*'s first attestation) to the sixteenth there were no prepositional phrases with *maison* serving as alternatives to *chez*. Littré (1967: 1862) cites examples of *à la maison de* and *en la maison de* dating back to the eleventh and twelfth centuries (e.g. *Si le pere truvet sa file en avulterie en sa maison* 'If the father found his daughter committing adultery in his house'). This is an indication that, at the same time as the old prepositional phrases *en chies* and *a ches* were becoming opaque, due to the replacement of *chiese* (or *chese*) by *maison* and/or to the divergent phonetic evolution of *chiese* (or *chese*) in tonic vs. atonic position (see n. 7), the language wasted no time in creating new transparent phrases around the noun *maison*. But why *à la maison* was apparently created some considerable time later than *à la maison de* is a question that we cannot answer at this moment. What little is known about the evolution of *à la maison* and *à la maison de* after the Old French period (Wartburg 1969: 241) seems to indicate that the only one of these two variants which survived beyond the Middle French period to the present day is *à la maison*. It would be interesting to find out whether the other variant fell by the wayside naturally or whether on the contrary the prescriptive grammarians intervened in some way or other. Assuming that *à la maison de* really does have a discontinuous history (i.e. did not linger on unnoticed in some dialects and/or popular French), then its presence in Ontarian French seems to be another instance of 're-emergence' of a previously attested usage, like the variant *à*. In the following section synchronic evidence will again be adduced in favour of the hypothesis that we are indeed dealing with an innovation.

9.3. Synchrony of the variants

Judging from the cases which have been reported in the literature, linguistic variation is usually binary (see Sankoff and Labov 1979: 194 for a similar impression). As a result, the statistical analysis of linguistic variation normally requires an ordinary two-variant variable-rule analysis (Sankoff and Rousseau 1989). Sankoff and Rousseau have demonstrated that the statistical analysis of linguistic variables that are realized by more than two variants—what might be termed 'multivariables'—poses the problem of token classification (see Chapter 4). However, Table 9.1 provides a general picture of the variants' distribution as a function of the linguistic and social factor groups under consideration, from which it can be seen that the only variants deserving of a more sophisticated statistical analysis are the standard options *chez* and *à la maison*, the other variants being just too infrequent. We shall nevertheless discuss the infrequent variants' distribution, especially as it sheds light on their synchronic status (i.e. archaism vs. innovation).

Among other things, the examination of the variants' synchronic social distribution will not only provide proof of the status of *à* and *à la maison de* as innovations, it will also play up the existence of a tendency on the part of some speakers to overuse the variant *à la maison*. In attempting to account for these qualitative and quantitative developments, we shall systematically adopt a contrastive vs. internal approach. By contrasting the English and French prepositional systems we shall weigh the plausibility of interlingual transfer; yet, remembering the axiom of historical linguistics that change proceeds first and foremost from system-internal causes, we shall give equal consideration to the possibility of an autonomous origin of these developments. By proceeding

TABLE 9.1. *Social and linguistic distribution of* chez, sur, à, à la maison, *and* à la maison de

Factor groups	chez		sur		à		à la maison		à la maison de		Total
	N	%	N	%	N	%	N	%	N	%	
Locality of residence											
Hawkesbury	40	83	1	2	0	0	7	15	0	0	48
Cornwall	51	65	5	6	1	1	17	22	4	5	78
North Bay	35	52	2	3	3	4	25	37	2	3	67
Pembroke	40	61	0	0	4	6	20	30	2	3	66
French-language use											
Unrestricted	69	77	2	2	0	0	18	20	1	1	90
Semi-restricted	53	54	6	6	3	3	33	34	3	3	98
Restricted	44	62	0	0	5	7	18	25	4	6	71
Social class											
Middle	29	71	1	2	0	0	11	27	0	0	41
Lower-middle	71	59	1	1	3	2	40	33	6	5	121
Working	66	68	6	6	5	5	18	19	2	2	97
Sex											
Male	74	61	2	2	5	4	36	30	5	4	122
Female	92	67	6	4	3	2	33	24	3	2	137
Verb											
Motion	73	74	6	6	5	5	11	11	3	3	98
Static	93	58	2	1	3	2	58	36	5	3	161
Complement											
PROi	126	64	0	0	0	0	69	35	1	1	198
PRO	6	67	0	0	0	0	NA†	NA	3	33	9
NP	34	65	8	15	8	15	NA	NA	2	4	52
TOTAL	166	64	8	3	8	3	69	27	8	3	259

† NA = not applicable.

in this fashion, we shall illustrate one of the pitfalls of language-contact research, namely that developments which are claimed to be due to inter-lingual transfer are often just as easily explained intralingually as simplifications (see Muysken 1984: 53, who makes the same point).

9.3.1. The main variants

We performed a variable-rule analysis of the variation between *chez* and *à la maison* in the context of a following PROi. To this end we disregarded the three occurrences of *à la maison de* (or more precisely its allophrase *à* + possessive adjective + *maison*) that occurred in the same context. The results of the VARBRUL 2S analysis of *chez* vs. *à la maison* appear in Table 9.2. Although not all of the factor groups have a bearing on the issue of primary concern to us (i.e. what are the effects of bilingualism and language restriction on linguistic structure?), we shall consider them all the same because of their own particular interest. However, the germane factor groups will be considered first.

9.3.1.1. Locality of residence

Table 9.2 reveals that the speakers residing in the predominantly francophone locality of Hawkesbury show a much higher

TABLE 9.2. *Variable-rule analysis of* chez *vs.* à la maison

Factor groups	*chez* (N)	*à la maison* (N)	Total	*chez* (%)	Factor effects
Verb					
Motion	50	11	61	82	.669
Static	76	58	134	57	.331
Locality of residence					
Hawkesbury	36	7	43	84	.745
Cornwall	37	17	54	69	.532
North Bay	24	25	49	49	.342
Pembroke	29	20	49	59	.366
French-language use					
Unrestricted	56	18	74	76	not
Semi-restricted	42	33	75	56	sig.
Restricted	28	18	46	61	
Social class					
Middle	22	11	33	67	not
Lower-middle	55	39	94	59	sig.
Working	49	19	68	72	
Sex					
Male	56	37	93	60	not
Female	70	32	102	69	sig.
TOTAL	126	69	195	65	.375

propensity to use *chez* (.745) than the speakers residing in the minority francophone localities of Cornwall (.532), Pembroke (.366), and North Bay (.342). One interpretation of these results is suggested by contrasting the English and French prepositional systems. The variant *à la maison* corresponds to the English equivalent structure '(at) home' and therefore we might suppose that those among our speakers who know English well (i.e. the minority-locality speakers) identify *à la maison* with '(at) home', resulting in a tendency on their part to overuse this variant at the expense of *chez* + PROi, a construction which has no similar English equivalent. This interlingual identification and resultant covert interference would be to the bilingual, as Weinreich (1968: 8) aptly put it, 'a reduction of his linguistic burden'. It needs to be recognized, however, that the minority-locality speakers' proclivity to use *à la maison* only constitutes necessary, not sufficient empirical evidence in support of the covert-interference hypothesis. The hypothesis must be taken one step further in order to see whether there are not any plausible internal explanations for the minority-locality speakers' greater inclination towards *à la maison*. Beforehand, however, it will be helpful to consider the results pertaining to the factor group French-language-use restriction.

9.3.1.2. French-language-use restriction   This factor group was not selected as a significant predictor of variant choice despite what would appear to be a substantially higher frequency of use of *chez* by the unrestricted speakers (76 per cent) than by the restricted and semi-restricted users of French (61 per cent and 56 per cent respectively). This is, it turns out, because locality of residence is a confounding factor group when it comes to assessing the effect of frequency of use of French. The Hawkesbury speakers, all of whom except one (see Chapter 4) reported unrestricted French-language use, used *chez* 84 per cent of the time. It is this very high percentage that elevates the frequency of use of *chez* by the unrestricted speakers as a whole (i.e. irrespective of their locality of residence) to 76 per cent. If we were to disregard the Hawkesbury speakers' occurrences of the variable, the percentage of use of *chez* by the minority-locality speakers who exhibit unrestricted French-language use (i.e. twenty out of thirty-one, or 65 per cent) would no longer be very different from the percentages that obtain for the speakers who display restricted or semi-restricted French-language use.[8]

---

[8] That locality of residence is a confounding factor group is also mathematically illustrated by the various steps of the regression analysis. When French-language-use restriction was considered by itself in the first step of the regression analysis, it was found to be significant at the .05 level. Even at the next step, when it was considered in combination with the previously selected factor group (i.e. verb), it still contributed significantly to predicting variant selection ($p < .05$), but locality of residence was chosen instead because of its higher level of significance ($p < .01$). But then, when French-language-use restriction was considered jointly with the two previously selected factor groups (i.e. verb and locality), it no longer contributed significantly to predicting variant choice ($p < .80$ only).

The reader will recall that our original motivation for controlling language restriction was the expectation not only that restricted users of French would experience influence from English, but also that they would simplify the language (where it presents less than optimal structure, e.g. irregularities, infrequent forms, etc.). In this connection, we discovered a significant tendency on the part of the restricted and semi-restricted users of French to level the distinctive third person plural verb forms via the unmarked third person ones (see Chapter 5). Returning to the case at hand, could not the minority-locality speakers' greater inclination towards *à la maison* also be the result of a move towards simpler structure? There are certainly grounds to argue that *à la maison* is more transparent than *chez* + PROi. First of all, *à* is the general locative and directional preposition in French; also, *maison* denotes the notion of 'dwelling'. In contrast, *chez* is a highly specialized preposition of location and direction, added to which its pronominal complement obviously does not designate a person's home. Assuming for the sake of argument that there is a difference in semantic transparency, then, all else being equal, in cases of restricted exposure to and use of French the bilingual's speech might be expected to show a higher than normal frequency of use of *à la maison* in comparison to the less transparent *chez* + PROi. Our assumption is analogous to Andersen's (1982: 99) hypothesis regarding syntactic reduction in the speech of learners undergoing language attrition (LAs): 'The LA will preserve and overuse syntactic constructions that more transparently reflect the underlying semantic and syntactic relations.'

This internal scenario, however, contradicts the fact that the unrestricted users of French residing in the minority-francophone localities were found to use *à la maison* no less frequently than the restricted and semi-restricted users of French (i.e. those who have been shown in Chapter 5 to speak a simplified form of French). If all of the minority-locality speakers, irrespective of degree of French-language-use restriction, overuse *à la maison* in comparison to the majority-locality speakers, then it seems obvious that more or less restricted use of French cannot be the sociological stimulus. This may be due to the fact that, in reality, not all else is equal between the two prepositional variants. *Chez* enjoys a much wider linguistic distribution (see section 9.1) and is much more frequent in the specific context of PROi (almost twice as frequent, in fact, judging by the complement results in Table 9.1). Thus it would seem that Andersen's prediction regarding the overuse of transparent constructions as a result of language restriction (or 'attrition' in his terminology) may not hold in the situation where the alternative construction possesses properties which militate in favour of its maintenance.

In sum, in light of the quantitative sociolinguistic evidence of a greater tendency to use *à la maison*, the English-like variant, in localities where contact with English is intensive (i.e. where there are many bilingual francophones) and considering the implausibility of ascribing this cross-linguistic rapprochement to internal factors, the conclusion seems warranted that covert interference is responsible.[9]

9.3.1.3. Sex and social class   Not only is linguistic variation usually binary, but one of the variants usually corresponds to standard usage while the other does not (see Thibault 1983: 55 for a similar opinion). The two variants are thus expected to show an uneven distribution between the two sexes and across the social classes, or a related measure such as degree of insertion in the linguistic market (Sankoff and Laberge 1978). However, since the two principal variants *chez* and *à la maison* correspond to standard usage, the expectation is that they should be *evenly* distributed across the social classes and between the two sexes. As indicated by the results in Table 9.2, the variable-rule analysis confirmed this hypothesis, since neither sex nor social class was selected as a significant predictor of choice of *chez* vs. *à la maison*. So, contrary to what Bourdieu (1982: 20) has written, there do seem to be words that are 'neutral' if we interpret neutral to mean 'spread equally throughout the various social classes and between the two sexes'. As Table 9.2 reveals, however, this does not mean that each variant is used half of the time. All the social classes and both sexes show a distinct preference for *chez* over *à la maison*. *Chez*'s wider linguistic distribution (see section 9.1) may be the reason.

9.3.1.4. Verb   Selection of *chez* vs. *à la maison* turned out to be predicted best by a feature of the linguistic context, namely the type of verb (i.e. motion vs. static) with which these variants co-occurred. Table 9.2 shows that *chez* co-occurred with a motion verb significantly more often than did *à la maison* (.669 vs. .331). This is the sort of weaker constraint or tendency we said we might find when examining the data quantitatively, though we admit we are at a loss to explain it.

9.3.2. The secondary variants

Let us now return to Table 9.1 in order to discuss the less frequent variants' distribution. Because no statistical tests were performed, we shall selectively discuss only those factor-group results which have a bearing on the question of the archaic vs. innovative status of the infrequent variants.

9.3.2.1. Sur   *Sur*'s concentration in working-class speech is consonant with its non-standard status. Furthermore, its absence in the speech of the restricted

---

[9] It would be interesting to try to ascertain whether the variation between *chez* and *à la maison* is stable or moving in the direction of greater use of one of the variants to the detriment of the other. If the covert-interference hypothesis is correct, as we think, then Ontarian French should be evolving towards ever-increasing use of *à la maison* in localities where francophones are a minority (i.e. where bilingualism and language-use restriction are likely to become even more widespread), but may be stable or evolving in the opposite direction where they are a strong majority. A cross-dialectal comparison with Québécois French could prove illuminating in this regard, since one would expect Québécois and Hawkesbury French to evolve in tandem.

users of French is reminiscent of the similar fate of another non-standard prepositional usage we studied in Chapter 7: possessive *à* . In other words, we are dealing with yet another case of sociolectal reduction. That we failed to find any instances of *sur* in the speech of the restricted users of French is consistent with our earlier argument (see Chapter 8) that the non-standard feature has (1) to display sharp social stratification, and (2) to be of low frequency, factors which have the effect of reducing considerably the probability of exposure to the non-standard variant.

From the fact that *sur* was not used at all by the restricted users of French we can also deduce that there is no intra- and/or intersystemic process underlying this variant and hence that it relies solely on intergenerational transmission for its survival. The question arises, then, as to how well (or poorly) it is faring. In order to answer this question, we must limit ourselves to the context of a following nominal complement, since this is the only context which seems to allow *sur*. In so doing *sur*'s frequency jumps from 3 per cent overall to 15 per cent. In other words, the variable is actualized as *sur* 15 per cent of the time when the following complement is a noun. But, in order to gain an even more accurate measure of *sur*'s vitality, we should also restrict ourselves to working-class speech, since this is the sociolect in which *sur* is mainly concentrated. When this is done, its frequency reaches 22 per cent.[10]

9.3.2.2. À   Does Table 9.1 also enable us to be more definite about *à*'s synchronic status if we look at this variant's distribution? It will be recalled that *à*'s discontinuous history suggested it was not a preservation of an analogous usage previously attested in Old French but an innovation of Ontarian French. Were *à* an archaism, its distribution as a function of level of French-language-use restriction should resemble *sur*'s, but what we observe instead is almost the opposite distribution: the unrestricted speakers never use *à* while those with the most restricted use of French use *à* the most. Such a distribution suggests strongly that the variant *à* cannot be a typical trait of the vernacular, otherwise it would have been handed down first and foremost to the speakers who do not experience restriction in the use of French. It has, then, to be the case that the restricted and semi-restricted users of French acquire *à* in some way other than through exposure to it. The contrastive approach again offers one possible explanation, namely that *à* is the result of interference from English, a language that all of the restricted and semi-restricted users of French know well and by definition use actively. English uses the prepositions 'at' or 'to', the equivalents of French *à*, to express the notion of location at/motion to a person's home (see glosses of examples in section 9.1). The interference hypothesis is plausible to the extent that anglophone second-language learners of French have been

---

[10] This percentage cannot be calculated directly from Table 9.1, since it is based on a cross-tabulation of working-class and NP complement. The cross-tabulated results were six out of twenty-seven, or 22 per cent.

observed to have the same feature in their interlanguage (Spilka 1976). However, the investigation of the learning of French as a second language should be extended to other groups whose mother tongue is not English (more generally whose mother tongue does not allow prediction of the use of *à* in the sense of *chez* from a contrastive analysis). Absence of *à* in their interlanguage would constitute strong evidence in favour of English interference as at least one—but not necessarily the only—cause of the occurrence of this variant in restricted-speaker French. A counter-explanation, however, is that the variant *à* is an instance of overgeneralization, due to incomplete learning of the rule restricting the use of the general locative and directional preposition *à* to inanimate nouns referring to places. This internal-simplification hypothesis is also plausible in view of the fact that young francophones learning their mother tongue overgeneralize *à* in precisely this way (based on the first author's informal observation of his children's linguistic development). We are thus confronted with a structural development admitting competing inter- and intralingual explanations.

The social-class results reveal that *à* is an innovation of the lower-middle and working classes, especially the latter. This ties in well with the results of our examination of the effect of social class on the levelling of the distinctive third person plural verb forms (see Chapter 5). While levelling was almost exclusively concentrated in the speech of the restricted and semi-restricted users of French, it was also socially stratified, i.e. working-class speakers levelled more often than lower-middle-class speakers, who in turn levelled more often than middle-class speakers. It would seem, then, that we have adduced a second bit of evidence for the hypothesis advanced in connection with levelling, according to which the restricted users of French exhibit a differential capacity, depending on their social background, to tease linguistic innovations out of their speech (probably through monitoring).

9.3.2.3. À la maison de   The interrupted history of *à la maison de* (and its allophrase *à* + possessive adjective + *maison*) suggests that it too is an innovation of Ontarian French as opposed to a surviving usage first attested in Old French. This suggestion is further supported by the results in Table 9.1, to the extent that the variant's distribution by social class and French-language-use restriction is quite similar to that of *à*. The same two types of explanation that were proposed in the case of *à* can be offered here as well. On the one hand, it is possible that *à la maison de* is the product of the influence of the corresponding English construction 'at/to someone's house' (see glosses of examples in section 9.1). In this connection, the second author has informally observed examples of *à la maison de* in the spoken French of anglophone early French immersion students in Montreal. On the other hand, it is possible that *à la maison de* is a natural analogical extension of the standard and frequent variant *à la maison* to contexts involving nominal complements and pronominal complements whose antecedent lies outside the sentence or which do not refer to the speaker (i.e. PRO). In support of the latter explanation we can once again rely on the first author's informal observation of numerous tokens of *à la maison de* (also *dans la maison de*) in the spoken French of his two young monolingual children (the very constructions that are attested in Old French and that preceded the emergence of *à la maison*). So there is ambiguity surrounding the exact structural cause of this innovation, just as there was in the case of *à*.

9.4. Conclusion

Through the multiplicity and diversity of its variants, the variable examined in this chapter 'encapsulates' as it were three distinct consequences of bilingualism, and accompanying language-use restriction, on linguistic structure: (1) covert interference, (2) ambiguous change (i.e. overt interference vs. simplification), and (3) sociolectal reduction.

Bilingualism makes an impact on linguistic structure through interlingual influence, which famous scholars such as Weinreich (1968) and Haugen (1969) have claimed to be an inevitable by-product of language contact. In this regard, the principal finding was that, due to covert interference, there is a tendency for Ontarian French to converge with English in localities where francophones are outnumbered by anglophones. Covert interference is a subtle effect of language contact that can only be isolated through quantitative investigation, since it does not entail any qualitative deviation from the conservative norm, only a statistical one, as we have seen. We would like to see other sociolinguists working in bilingual settings take an interest in the problem of covert interference and of how to go about adducing convincing proof of it, especially when it is still in progress as opposed to already completed. It was demonstrated here that careful examination of the available sociolinguistic evidence makes it possible to establish the origin of quantitative structural tendencies in a minority language which are such as to increase the degree of overlap with the superordinate language. As Silva-Corvalán (1983: 8) has written, 'the influence of one language on another may be evident only through differences in the frequency of use of a certain structure, rather than in the development of ungrammatical constructions'. Therein lies the originality and interest of covert interference.

In retrospect, however, it seems we need to qualify our original equation between the speech of those of our subjects who exhibit unrestricted French-language use and the conservative norm (a qualification already alluded to in Chapter 1). In localities where Franco-Ontarians form only a minority of the population, there is in fact no guarantee that the speech of the unrestricted users of French will be a valid base-line for gauging the speech of those who do not maintain the minority-language to the same degree. The problem is that the same developments that are observable in the speech of the latter might well also be observable in the speech of the former. When this is the case, it becomes necessary to have a control group of even higher retainers of French, i.e. ones residing in a locality where francophones are in the majority. Thus it appears that minority-language disuse need not be very pronounced before certain linguistic consequences begin to manifest themselves (here covert interference, but see also Chapter 10 for a case of overt interference). In fact, we may rightly wonder whether language restriction *per se* plays a part at all in the observed case of covert interference. Knowledge of English (i.e. bilingualism) on its own seems to be sufficient, as was argued above. Thus the issue at stake is this: does a bilingual's proficiency in that one of his two languages which is in a subordinate position sociologically have to become weakened through restriction before his other (i.e. the superordinate) language can begin to exert interlingual influence? The linguistic behaviour of the unrestricted users of French residing in the minority-francophone localities suggests that the answer is no.

A more salient manifestation of interlingual influence is overt interference, which differs from covert interference in that it produces a new usage or qualitative change in the minority language. Despite their differences, covert and overt interference are really two manifestations of the same underlying process of reduction or levelling of structural dissimilarities between languages in contact. In this connection, we saw that two innovative variants (i.e. *à* and *à la maison de*) were arguably possibly due to overt interference from English. Alternatively, it seemed just as plausible to view *à* and *à la maison de* as simplifications due to relative-to-severe restriction in French-language use. Interestingly enough, both were once used in the early stages of the language's history. Though a lack of conclusive data meant we were compelled to remain uncertain concerning these variants' structural origins (interlingual and/or intralingual?), it was indicated how indirect evidence to settle the issue might be adduced through further research on the learning of French, but by non-anglophones.

As we pointed out in Chapter 1, the ability to adapt the style of language to the level of formality of the speech situation is another aspect of the competence of fluent speakers that poses problems for speakers experiencing language restriction, who have been shown to display a relative incapacity (Gal 1984) to switch from informal to formal phonological styles. In a related vein, we have played up here and in preceding chapters a failure to acquire sociolectal variants (i.e. non-standard features typical of the working class) on the part of speakers whose use of French is restricted to the school, where presumably the standard variety predominates. Andersen's (1982: 91) assumption (quoted in Chapter 4) could easily be expanded to encompass socio-stylistic distinctions as well. However, it was discovered that sociolectal reduction is rather tied to language disuse in specific contexts (what others

have called restriction in language *function*), whereas grammatical simplification is tied to general restriction in language use.

We would like to end the discussion on a sensitive issue raised by the
findings of this study: the question of the structural integrity of minority
languages. The present findings (as well as those of the next chapter) suggest
that not even a high level of retention of French in Ontario is a safeguard
against grammatical influence from English. In contrast, Poplack's (1982)
results seemed to suggest that, as long as Spanish is spoken as often as English
by New York's Puerto Rican community, its grammar will not be adversely
affected by influence from English. Perhaps most forcefully in Poplack (1984),
an attempt is made at demonstrating that Spanish–English bilingualism in
New York City is stable, even if English-language use is advancing among the
young Puerto Ricans. There is no question, on the other hand, that French–
English bilingualism is unstable in all except one of the Franco-Ontarian
communities examined here. (In fact there is some doubt whether we can speak
of the exceptional Franco-Ontarian community—Hawkesbury—as being
bilingual; see Chapter 4). We would then tentatively advance that it is perhaps
only in a situation of unstable bilingualism that the structure of a minority
language becomes prone to grammatical influence, despite being used more
often than the superordinate language by individual bilingual speakers. One
difference between the two types of societal bilingualism is that, when unstable
bilingualism obtains, semi-restricted minority-language use may be merely a
transitory stage towards shift to the majority language for some speakers. They
might therefore be less motivated to preserve the integrity of their mother
tongue. Another feature of unstable bilingualism is that speakers who are
unrestricted users of the minority language are very often outnumbered by
restricted or semi-restricted users of that language. This is the case among the
adolescent generation in each one of the three minority communities we
investigated. It is possible that, in these French-speaking communities, some
of the transfer-induced innovations which arise in the speech of the restricted
and semi-restricted users of French then spread to the speech of the speakers
who experience no significant French-langage-use restriction, or at least
reinforce the latter's tendency to produce them. This question will be
examined at greater length in the following chapter.

10

Overt Interference

ANY discipline which purports to be scientific practises self-criticism. Linguistics is no exception. One particular theoretical concept which has attracted more than its share of criticism in this field is *interference*. In our view, the generally bad press which it has received is due not to a flaw in the theory that languages in contact may influence one another—no serious linguist would deny this fact— but rather to shoddy methodology (and, to some extent also, ideological bias). The literature literally abounds in studies hastily and erroneously attributing language change to foreign influence due to lack of a proper methodology. This exaggerated appeal to interference will be illustrated with examples drawn from various subfields (e.g. historical linguistics, minority languages, pidgins and creoles, second-language learning), with particular reference to French. As a result of these errors of 'gross negligence', interference has predictably been pooh-poohed by many linguists. Clearly, this is an overreaction. In our opinion, interference needs to be rehabilitated. Since the chief reason for its misfortune seems to be the lack of a proper methodology, we shall reillustrate the one already largely exposed in the preceding chapter by applying it this time to a case of overt rather than covert English interference in Ontarian French. The methodology consists, as was seen, in confronting the linguistic arguments for and against interference (or more accurately perhaps, the contrastive and non-contrastive arguments) with the sociolinguistic evidence. In this study the methodology will feature in addition a cross-dialectal comparison with Québécois and European French and profitably borrow a guideline from the work of Thomason (1985, 1986) on the demonstration of interference in a language's history.

10.1 Exaggerated claims of interference

Although the present study belongs resolutely to synchronic linguistics, a preliminary consideration of the status of interference in historical linguistics will be a useful and interesting starting-point. Not being historical linguists

This chapter is a much revised version of a paper first presented at NWAV-X, University of Pennsylvania, Philadelphia, 23–5 October 1981, under the title 'The Problem of Ambiguous Change in a Contact Language'. It has not previously appeared in print. We have benefited at various stages from the comments of several colleagues, especially Daniel Valois, Shana Poplack, Yves-Charles Morin, and Suzanne Romaine, all of whom we would like to thank here.

ourselves (despite appearances to the contrary!), we were rather intrigued by the discovery of a striking parallelism between the fluctuating fortune of interference in synchronic linguistics and its up-and-down status in historical linguistics. It seems that historical linguists have traditionally worked on the basis of the assumption that language change proceeds first and foremost from system-internal causes, an appeal to system-external causes (i.e. foreign influence) being justified only failing a plausible intrasystemic explanation (see e.g. Thomason 1985, 1986; Thomason and Kaufman 1988). A theory known as 'substratum' interference (and the associated notions of 'superstratum' and 'adstratum' influence) was advanced to explain refractory language change, that is, change resisting an internal account (see, e.g., Anderson 1973: 89–95). Briefly, substratum theory basically started out as an attempt to explain language divergence, and especially the ramification of Latin into the various Romance languages. It was held that the indigenous populations, in shifting to the language of their Roman conquerors, retained some features of their original languages and especially their articulatory habits.[1] However—and somewhat paradoxically—, today's historical linguists freely recognize that substratum interference was often invoked rather unreflectingly, with the result that the theory has lost much of the popularity it first enjoyed and is currently considered controversial at best. Anderson (1973: 90) writes, for instance, that 'nasalized vowels in French have been credited to Celtic influence, but they appear in other Romance languages such as Portuguese—in an area where Celts were rather scarce. The front rounded vowels in French, /ü/ and /ö/, are often attributed to the Celts in Gaul but they appeared also in early Latin', and he goes on to conclude that, 'if no substantial structural reason is readily observable for a modification, the change is too often attributed to "something" in the substratum'.

Nevertheless, there are those who would argue that the baby should not be thrown out with the bath water, that the theory of substratum interference is not globally invalid just because our predecessors were prone to oversimplifications. This is the position defended by Thomason (1985, 1986) and Thomason and Kaufman (1988). The rehabilitation of interference in historical linguistics, according to them, depends crucially on the fact that 'there are at present no widely accepted ground rules for establishing that a particular structural change was caused by interference from some other language', such

---

[1] As Dorian (1981: 4) aptly put it, 'language shift frequently leaves a dying language in its wake'. This is the other side of the coin, the 'dark' one, one might say, since not much is known about the linguistic aspects of language extinction in historical linguistics. If substratum theory is an attempt at explaining the changes undergone by the target languages in a shift situation (e.g. Latin in Gaul), curiosity if nothing else leads us to wonder about the kinds of changes which the source languages (e.g. Celtic in Gaul), the ones being shifted from, underwent as they receded and finally died. The many threatened minority languages spoken around the world today all provide synchronic windows so to speak on the types of linguistic consequences of language attrition and extinction which in all probability also took place in diachrony.

that what is required are 'methodological guidelines for claims of foreign interference in a language's history' (Thomason 1986: 243). One of the purposes of this study will be to show that one of these methodological guidelines in particular—having to do with whether change brings about simplification or complication of the language—can be profitably transposed to synchronic linguistics to help clinch the case for majority-language interference in a minority language.

The trials and tribulations of interference in historical linguistics are not without parallels in synchronic linguistics. Here the evidence of a contact situation is so directly observable, as are the structures of the languages in contact, that there has been an almost natural tendency to exaggerate the role of interference as a source of change in minority languages (see, e.g., Poplack's 1982 and 1983 critical examinations of claims of English interference in the Spanish spoken in the United States) as well as in pidgins and creoles (see, e.g., Bickerton 1981; Chaudenson 1979; Romaine 1988*b*; Wittmann and Fournier 1983). Ontarian French is a good example of a minority language concerning which exaggerated claims of English-language interference have been made. For instance, Cassano (1977) offered a convincing refutation of the supposed intersystemic origin of several aspects of Windsor French studied by Hull (1956). Orkin (1971: 30), referring to the same study by Hull (1956), reports that 'the French dialect of Windsor has become completely hybridized, to the point where speakers can no longer understand French Canadians from Quebec'. And in a reply to a paper by Mougeon and Canale (1982, see discussion at the end of the article, pp. 84–5), Bernard St-Jacques (professor at University of British Columbia) goes as far as to claim that 'the most important linguistic difference between Ontarian French and Standard French is to be sought in the considerable influence of the English language on this variety of French' (our translation from the French original).

Québécois French has not been spared either, even though its contact with English has been much less intensive. Poirier (1979: 412), a specialist in Québécois French etymology, had this to say about some of the studies in his specific field: 'The authors of dictionaries or even linguistic studies of Québécois French are too often prone to ascribe to English interference features of Gallo-Roman origin which have an equivalent in English. A rudimentary search through the history of French or of its western dialects is often sufficient to refute the thesis of an English origin for these features' (our translation from the French original).

The above quotation is doubly interesting in that it states explicitly the reason for the unwarranted claims of English influence on Québécois French, namely the failure to take even the most elementary methodological precautions. In the introduction to his book on anglicisms in Québécois French, a study which contains many instances of older Gallo-Roman features which were wrongly attributed to English interference, Colpron (1973: 19) confides that he would have liked to extend his inventory of anglicisms to the whole of French Canada, had such a task not been so vast. Nevertheless, Colpron proceeds to provide—as if to whet our appetite—a long series of examples of anglicisms that he noted in the language of the 'diaspora' (*sic*) but failed to observe in Quebec, among which figure *sur la radio* 'on the radio' and *sur la télévision* 'on television' (two of the constructions to be studied in this chapter). Colpron's book is a classic example of another serious methodological flaw typical of so many studies of interference: absence of quantification. Poplack (1983) has argued that such lists of 'deviant' phenomena, instructive and even entertaining though they may be, break Labov's famous principle of 'accountable reporting', according to which it is incumbent upon the linguist to report the number of times a form appeared out of the total number of times it could have appeared. Observing this principle is all the more imperative when dealing with interference, since failure to do so may leave behind the negative impression that interference is pervasive or categorical. Thus, though it cannot be denied that Canadian French has undergone influence from English, it is no excuse for not undertaking a careful measurement of this influence in the hope of putting interference in a proper perspective.

In research on minority languages, unfortunately, the tendency has also lately been to overreact and neglect interference. As Flora Klein-Andreu sees it (p.c.)—a viewpoint which we share as well—a stigma is attached to interference (see also Klein-Andreu 1985): 'It seems to me that the reason for this neglect is a kind of covert purism: the results of transfer are considered undesirable or "bad"; therefore they are ignored or seriously downplayed, as a kind of courtesy to the population under study.'

We touch here on the problem of ideological bias alluded to in the introduction. Klein-Andreu is perfectly correct to intimate that there are linguists who purposefully ignore or seriously downplay interference in their research on minority languages. Suffice it to say that scientific objectivity should always take precedence over personal convictions, no matter how noble or well intentioned.

Creole studies is another area where unwarranted claims of interference have been made. For example, African substratum influence has been overplayed with respect to the formation of French-based creoles, according to Chaudenson (1979: 76–7). Apparently the linguistic competence of the investigators is at fault here, rather than their methodology! Chaudenson provides convincing evidence that French-based creoles are imperfectly learnt varieties of seventeenth-century popular or dialectal French, from which they derive most of their structures, a fact which would have escaped his predecessors, most of whom were foreigners acquainted only with Standard French. Chaudenson writes (1979: 76–7):

One may wonder if what appears to be a minor fact didn't play a significant role in the evolution of creole studies. One knows . . . that almost all the linguists who have done serious work in the area were foreigners. Granted they could all speak French but they were probably much better acquainted with the educated variety of this language than with its everyday popular guise. As a result, many of the shared features of the creoles which, according to these authors, could not be related to French usages had to be ascribed to a common origin which was not French [our translation from the French original].

Another area of linguistics which comes to mind is that of contrastive analysis and its popularization of transfer theory in the 1950s and 1960s. Predictably, it did not take too long before the pendulum started swinging towards the other theoretical extreme, and so it was that in the 1970s second-language learning began to be likened to first-language acquisition, as studies revealed a developmental-learning sequence holding across learners irrespective of their first language (Romaine 1988*b*: 206–9).

In concluding this section, we are reminded of a comment heard one day on the radio and which is worth airing here because of its wisdom and pertinence to the present situation. The comment was to the effect that 'simple solutions to complex problems are simply wrong'. The assignment of language change (or learner errors) to systemic causes is one such complex problem and there is no *a priori* reason to expect that the causes will always turn out to be internal or external. The complexity of the problem is epitomized when both internal and external structural causes are seemingly involved in a particular instance of change. Only through an appeal to extralinguistic evidence is it then possible to settle such cases of causally ambiguous change. We were successful in the preceding chapter in proving a case of covert interference in just this way: neither the geographical distribution of *à la maison* nor its distribution according to French-language-use restriction were compatible with the argument of system-internal change. Very much the same kind of distributional evidence will be provided in this study in favour of a case of overt interference.

10.2. The variable

The development under study involves the use of the preposition *sur* instead of *à*—we say 'instead of' because the substitution is a departure from Standard Canadian French—to introduce nominal complements expressing the idea of location on the broadcasting media, i.e. radio, television, TV channels, and radio stations, as in the following examples:

1 *a.* *Ah ben! S'a télévision y'en a [des films] des fois* 'Well! On television there are [films] sometimes' (C22–033).
   b. *C'est toute de la musique su' la radio* 'There's nothing but music on the radio' (C03–522).
   c. *Je regarde [le hockey] su' le canal neuf* 'I watch [hockey] on channel nine' (P29–510).

    d. Quand Montréal joue c'est toujours su' le poste français 'When Montreal plays it's always on the French station' (N22–490).

2*a. Comme Jaws, j'me dis ça va passer à la télévision* 'Like Jaws, I tell myself, it'll be on television' (No6–046).

    b. Y'a pas de programmes à la radio on va dire, t'sais 'There are no programmes on the radio let's say, you know' (C30–469).

    c. Ben si le meilleur joue en français au canal neuf 'Well if the best one is playing in French on channel nine' (P21–288).

    d. J'tournerais tou' suite au poste français 'I would switch right away to the French station' (N36–353).

Let us now examine the issue of the structural origin of this usage from the viewpoints of contrastive analysis and intrasystemic analysis.

10.3. Linguistic evidence

One obvious explanation of the change from *à* to *sur* was proposed in an initial study by Mougeon, Bélanger, Canale, and Ituen (1977), i.e. English interference. English uses the preposition 'on' to express location on the broadcasting media (see earlier glosses). And *sur* is the translation equivalent of 'on' when the latter is used in its basic sense to indicate contact with a surface (e.g. *le beurre est sur la table* 'the butter is on the table'). The extension of *sur* in Ontarian French to express location on the broadcasting media certainly gives the appearance of being modelled on the distribution of 'on' in English. This would make it a case of overt interference considering that there has been a qualitative change in the distribution of the preposition *sur*. The impression that *sur* might be modelled on English 'on' is reinforced by the finding that the determiner, which is obligatory in French, was dropped on several occasions, as in example 3*a*:

    3*a. Les choses qu'ils met sur (la) télévision* 'The things they show on television' (Po1–75).

In popular Canadian French the sequence *sur* + *la* can undergo successive morpho-phonemic reductions to *s'a* /sa/ (< /sy a/ < /sy la/ < /syr la/), but the article cannot be dropped entirely.

However, in the initial study by Mougeon, Bélanger, Canale, and Ituen (1977) it was not considered whether *sur*'s extension, albeit unusual in terms of the previous prepositional changes we had examined (see below), might not all the same show internal motivation. By pursuing a non-contrastive approach, Mougeon, Bélanger, and Canale (1978) discovered that *sur* already has a certain proclivity to signal location on the broadcasting media in Canadian French, in linguistic contexts which are semantically related to the ones in which the change is taking place (e.g. *ce programme va passer sur les ondes de CJBC* 'this programme will be aired on CJBC'; *diffusé sur le réseau CTV* 'broadcast on the CTV network'; *sur le petit écran* 'on the small screen'; etc.). An internal explanation of the change, then, would be that *sur* is being extended via analogy (including ellipsis) from the above contexts, in which it is perfectly standard in Canadian French, to the ones under investigation here. We may anticipate here on the later presentation of cross-dialectal evidence to say that undeniable proof of *sur*'s internal proclivity to signal location on the broadcasting media comes from European French, where *sur* is the only standard option with names of TV channels (e.g. *sur Antenne 2* 'on Antenne 2') and radio stations (e.g. *sur Radio-Luxembourg* 'on Radio-Luxemburg').[2] Thus it was no longer all that obvious that interference from English was at the root of *sur*'s expanded distribution in Ontarian French. The change had become ambiguous. We would like to push the linguistic analysis of *sur*'s origins a little further here by considering this usage within the broader context of the substantial research we have carried out on variability in the prepositional system of Ontarian French (see in particular Mougeon, Bélanger, and Canale 1978).

If there is one generalization that we can make based on this research, it is that general prepositions tend to be overgeneralized at the expense of semantically related but less general ones in this variety of French. In other words, the prepositional system of Ontarian French tends towards greater consistency by eliminating exceptions. Now the change from *à* to *sur* runs counter to this generalization, since the standard variant *à* is the general locative preposition in French and *sur* a rather more specialized one. From a purely internal point of view, then, the expectation is that the preposition *à* should be very stable as a marker of location on the broadcasting media; its unexpected replacement by *sur* can in this regard be looked upon as a case of complication of the preposition system.

Bearing this in mind, it is instructive to consider what Thomason (1986: 246) has to say to historical linguists concerning the explanation of linguistic changes in former contact situations which 'make the changing language more similar to the proposed source language and also seem relatively unlikely to arise through internally-motivated language change'. She claims that, 'if a change seems to increase the overall markedness of the grammar, most skeptics

---

[2] This observation on Standard European French is based on a consultation of issues of *Télé 7 jours* (a weekly TV and radio guide), *Le Monde* (a daily newspaper), *L'Express*, and *Le Nouvel Observateur* (two weekly news magazines) going back to the creation of the first television network in France in the 1950s. The categorical use of *sur* with names of TV channels and radio stations in Standard European French must be assumed to have come about via the sort of analogical or elliptical processes just mentioned (e.g. *sur la deuxième chaîne* 'on the second network' > *sur Antenne 2* 'on Antenne 2' via analogy; *sur les ondes de Radio-Luxembourg* 'on the air waves of Radio-Luxemburg' > *sur Radio-Luxembourg* 'on Radio-Luxemburg' via ellipsis). But we are at present without an explanation for the fact that Standard European French features categorical use of *à* with *radio* and *télévision*, even though *sur* would seem to be compatible with these two nouns as well.

will agree that the external explanation is reasonable'. This description fits the change from *à* to *sur* under study: (1) we have a situation of intensive language contact; (2) the change to *sur* makes Ontarian French more similar to English; (3) it increases the markedness of this variety of French; and (4) the internal explanations we have just proposed for the change, though they are theoretically possible, are none the less 'relatively unlikely', given that the change in question is attested in a situation of intensive language contact, i.e. a setting not normally associated with internally motivated linguistic *complication* (see Trudgill 1983: Chapters 5 and 6, where he defends the view that language contact is associated with simplificatory linguistic change). Does this settle the issue of the linguistic origins of *sur* in favour of interference, then? At this stage the only thing that prevents us from giving an affirmative answer is the possibility that, after all, the change under study might be located primarily in the French of the unrestricted speakers, in which case there would no longer be a contradiction with the internal complication scenario. In any case, the ambiguity surrounding *sur*'s structural origins does not appear to be as unsurmountable as was the ambiguity surrounding the origins of *à* or *à la maison de* examined in the preceding chapter, which were both plausibly interpretable as instances of internal simplification in addition to being reasonably ascribable to interference. Even for such changes Thomason is not prepared to favour internal causation. As she explains (1986: 250)—a point of view which contrasts with Trudgill's (see above):

It has often been claimed that one should not even consider external explanations for such 'natural' changes, because we don't need to—the internal explanation will do. . . . However, there is certainly no reason to expect all contact-induced change to complicate the grammar, or in general to be less 'natural' than internally motivated change: the same factors that make simplifying changes (or changes from more marked to less marked structure) natural as internal changes make them natural as externally motivated changes too—ease of perception, ease of production, and overall ease of learning.

10.4. Sociolinguistic evidence

10.4.1. Cross-dialectal comparison

The discovery that certain changes in Ontarian French are predictable both intra- and intersystemically was first made by Mougeon and Carroll (1976a, b). These studies already contained, implicitly if not explicitly, a methodology for solving the problem of internal vs. external causation, i.e. for establishing if there is a sole or at least primary cause of an ambiguous change. The methodology involved a cross-dialectal comparison of the speech of bilingual Franco-Ontarians with that of similarly-aged but monolingual Québécois. The rationale behind this, as opposed to some other cross-dialectal comparison (e.g. with European French), was that Ontarian French and Québécois French could be looked upon as sister dialects, given that the Franco-Ontarian population is very chiefly the product of a more or less continuous immigration of Québécois (see Chapter 2). This ensured that the two dialects were indeed comparable. It was reasoned that, if there was also evidence of the change in the monolinguals' speech, its origin had to be internal (with English interference perhaps still acting as secondary reinforcement), and that, if there was not, its origin had to be external.[3]

It was later realized, however, that the non-attestation of the change in the speech of the monolingual Québécois was a necessary but still not sufficient proof of English interference. The problem was that the change might be latent (i.e. only observable in child speech) in a non- or at best weak contact variety of French like Québécois French. In other words, it might be an acquisition error which is overcome in due course by the monolingual child but not by the bilingual child who is a restricted speaker of French. As we saw in Chapter 5, errors may persist beyond the language-acquisition phase *per se* and into adolescent and eventually adult speech when certain speakers are insufficiently exposed to the minority language to acquire it completely. In the case at hand, however, it is almost certain that *sur* is not such an acquisition error. The semantically related expressions on the analogy of which the error could be made are rather sophisticated (see section 10.3), implying knowledge both of French and of the physical world that seems well beyond the grasp of children. Nevertheless, there does seem to be an error which children commit en route to acquiring the use of *à* to express location on broadcasting media, which is to replace it by *dans* with the nouns *radio* and *télévision* (e.g. *C'est la collègue de maman qui parle dans la radio?* 'Is it mummy's colleague who is talking in the radio?').[4]

All in all, then, it is very unlikely that monolingual (and for that matter bilingual) children could come to produce *sur* via analogical extension, although this does not preclude the possibility that older monolingual speakers could, a possibility we are now going to investigate.

10.4.1.1. Québécois French The corpus of monolingual adolescent Québécois speech that we examined was gathered in 1976 by the Centre for Franco-Ontarian Studies. It is composed of taped interviews carried out with grades 9 and 12 students enrolled in a Quebec City high school. A total of 15 students were interviewed following a schedule similar to the one used for the Franco-Ontarian interviews, that is, designed to tap a spontaneous style of speech

---

[3] Evidence that the internal change is more advanced in the contact variety would at least lend some credibility to the interlinguistic reinforcement hypothesis.

[4] This and other examples were observed in the speech of the first author's two- and four-year-old children. We may suppose that it is the three-dimensional shape of radio and TV sets which is the factor responsible.

approaching the students' vernacular. No occurrences of *sur* were found in the speech of the Quebec City monolinguals, in contrast to 11 occurrences of *à*, 8 with the nouns *radio* and *télévision* and 3 with names of TV channels or radio stations. With a view to verifying that *sur*'s absence in the speech of the Quebec City monolinguals was not just an artefact of the small number of times that location on broadcasting media was expressed, but a true indication of the absence of this innovative non-standard feature in Québécois French, we also consulted the Montreal-French corpus (D. Sankoff, G. Sankoff, Laberge, and Topham 1976).[5] The Montreal-French corpus yielded a total of 157 occurrences of the 'variable' (if we may call it thus), all *à*'s with the exception of 3 *sur*'s (two of which were produced by a speaker whose father happened to be Franco-Ontarian!). These results are all the more conclusive, as there are valid grounds to argue that, in Montreal, French is to a certain extent in contact with English. By all appearances, then, even older monolingual French-Canadian speakers do not seem to extend the use of *sur* to nouns referring to broadcasting media, in spite, no doubt, of knowing the related technical expressions that could serve as an analogical source for such an extension. This would seem to us to be sufficient proof that the use of *sur* is due to the influence of English on Ontarian French. The fact remains, none the less, that this novel, contact-induced use of *sur* is apparently not in violation of the semantics of the preposition *sur* in French (recall the situation in European French). We have studied other interference-based uses in the speech of adolescent Franco-Ontarians which are far from faring as well as *sur*, e.g. *dessus* in expressions of the type *la télévision est dessus* 'the TV set is on' (Mougeon, Bélanger, Canale, and Ituen 1977; Mougeon, Bélanger, and Canale 1978). We argued that this use of *dessus* is totally foreign to the normal semantics of this adverb. This suggests that the recipient language has its say in determining just how well an interference-induced form will fare.

10.4.1.2. European French Interestingly enough, while contact with and resultant interference from English seem to have been both necessary and sufficient to trigger the use of *sur* to convey location on broadcasting media in Ontarian French, the same change is observable in European French, despite this variety of French's lack of contact with English. Indeed, we have some evidence that European French probably started out with categorical *à*, like Québécois French. The evidence comes from the Nuffield Foundation's (1966 and 1968) survey on the spoken language of French children in France. The children (nine- and ten-year-olds) were found to be categorical users of *à* with *radio* and *télévision* (in keeping with Standard European French), but also almost categorical users of *à* with names of TV channels and radio stations (in departing from the Standard which, as mentioned in n. 2, seems always to have

---

[5] We wish to thank Henrietta Cedergren for kindly granting us the permission to consult the Montreal-French corpus.

featured *sur* in this context). Unless we are willing to entertain the hypothesis that this departure is nothing more than an acquisition error which has not yet been overcome—improbable, since, as mentioned, the child-language variant is *dans* before *radio* and *télévision* and since, after all, we are dealing with monolinguals who are no longer very young—, we are forced to admit that the children's speech reflects what adult usage must have been like in the mid-1960s in France, i.e. near categorical use of *à* with names of TV channels and radio stations. This in turn suggests that everyday European French initially developed the simplest or most natural prepositional option for expressing location on the broadcasting media. This stands in sharp contrast to more recent observations by the authors of the speech of adults in France, which indicate that they now show a next to exclusive preference for *sur* with names of TV channels and radio stations. In fact, now and then *sur* is even heard with *télévision* and *radio*![6] All of this suggests that a change from *à* to *sur* with names of TV channels and radio stations has been unfolding in European French, no doubt under the influence of the standard variety, which, as we said, displays categorical use of *sur* in this context.[7] Curiously enough, then, Ontarian French and European French both exhibit the same change, but for what would appear to be quite different reasons. The reasons do share this in common, however, that both are so to speak 'external' (in one case influence from another language, in the other influence from a prestige variety of the same language). This suggests—and Québécois French provides the proof—that the use of *sur* to signal location on broadcasting media is not a change which could develop internally on its own (i.e. without external stimulus) in the speech of the average speaker.

10.4.2. Intradialectal comparison

The Franco-Ontarian interview transcripts were gone over for all instances of *à* and *sur* expressing location on the broadcasting media.[8] Each recorded instance was coded for the social characteristics of the speaker and for the

[6] The second author could not believe his ears when he heard *sur la télévision* in the part played by one of the actors in Claude Lelouch's film titled *Les uns et les autres* 'Bolero'. The scene in which the example occurs features a man who sees his daughter again after a long absence (she is a TV hostess). He says something like this to her: *Je t'ai vue hier soir sur la télévision* 'I saw you last night on television'.

[7] The question is begged as to how Standard European French got *sur* in the first place. The technical nature of the prepositional phrases which we argued to have given rise to *sur* via analogy or ellipsis smacks of the scientific register. Our hypothesis is that the standard language was influenced by the latter.

[8] We recorded one instance of the adverb *dessus* used as a preposition in place of *sur* (e.g. *y'a pas trop dessus cette canal* 'there's not too much on that channel' P13–505). We simply coded it as a token of *sur*. The prepositional use of adverbs is a feature of non-standard French which goes back to an earlier stage of the language when adverbs and prepositions were interchangeable, even in literary French (Grevisse 1975: 961). It is yet another example of a feature whose social distribution got restricted following the intervention of the prescriptive grammarians.

nominal complement (i.e. *télévision* vs. *radio* and names of TV channels or radio stations).

Table 10.1 shows that only one of the five factor groups under study (i.e. French-language-use restriction) was found to be significantly correlated with the probability of use of *sur*. The results reveal a very sharp distribution: the restricted and semi-restricted users of French have much higher probabilities of use of *sur* (.763 and .665 respectively) than the unrestricted users of French (.135). This is precisely the relationship one would *not* expect to hold between the frequency of an innovation which complicates the grammar,[9] and the level of French-language-use restriction. As argued above, in order for the examination of *sur*'s distribution according to language-use restriction to substantiate the internal complication scenario, use of *sur* would have had to be primarily

TABLE 10.1. *Variable-rule analysis of* sur *vs.* à

Factor groups	sur (N)	à (N)	Total	sur (%)	Factor effects
French-language use					
Unrestricted	5	14	19	26	.135
Semi-restricted	41	9	50	82	.665
Restricted	37	5	42	88	.763
Locality of residence†					
Cornwall	23	5	32	72	
North Bay	22	8	30	73	not
Pembroke	38	11	49	78	sig.
Complement noun					
Télévision	41	18	59	69	not
Other	42	10	52	81	sig.
Social class					
Middle	11	10	21	52	
Lower-middle	50	11	61	82	not
Working	22	7	29	76	sig.
Sex					
Male	52	21	73	71	not
Female	31	7	38	82	sig.
TOTAL	83	28	111	75	.696

† Hawkesbury was a knockout factor (zero *sur* out of sixteen) and so had to be excluded from the variable-rule analysis (see Rousseau and Sankoff 1978: 66 for more information on the problem of knockout factors).

[9] Obviously, structural complexity is a relative notion. The change from *à* to *sur* is only a complication if considered from a purely intrasystemic viewpoint. When considered from a contrastive viewpoint, it ceases to be a complication because it gets rid of a cross-linguistic difference and thus eases the bilingual's 'linguistic burden', as Weinreich would put it.

concentrated in the spoken French of the unrestricted users of the minority language. That it is not constitutes further confirmatory evidence of the intersystemic origin of *sur*.

What might seem surprising, however, is that the unrestricted speakers resorted to *sur* no less than 26 per cent of the time. Upon closer examination, it was discovered that only two such speakers (one from Cornwall, the other from North Bay) used *sur* and that they were both balanced (not French-dominant) bilinguals. In spite of the fact that these two speakers do not display any significant level of French-language-use restriction, it is possible that their high level of bilingualism makes them prone to interference from English as far as the particular usage under study is concerned.

Another way of looking at things might be that *sur*'s presence in their speech is due not to direct interference, but to 'transference' (Weinreich, Labov, and Herzog 1968: 155), the process whereby a linguistic innovation spreads from one speaker to another. Under this hypothesis, *sur* would have originated in the speech of the restricted and semi-restricted users of French (via interference from English) and then spread or transferred to the speech of the more bilingual of the unrestricted users of French (in fact, had we had a bigger data base at our disposal, we might have found that *sur* can even transfer to French-dominant unrestricted speakers). The hypothesis of transference derives apparent support from the fact that *sur* was never used by the students who reside in Hawkesbury, a locality where francophones far outnumber anglophones and where, therefore, linguistic assimilation of the French population is at a minimum, as we saw in Chapter 2. It follows that the number of potential agents of interference must be quite small in such a staunchly francophone locality. In other words, transference of interference-based forms can probably take place only if the restricted or semi-restricted users of French constitute a group to be reckoned with in the community. The preponderant model of French in, say, Pembroke most probably exhibits more interference from English (and more system-internal restructuring) than the preponderant model of French in, say, Hawkesbury. According to the assumption of transference, speakers will tend to conform to the preponderant model in their locality, such that their speech will contain more or less interference (and system-internal restructuring) than would be expected on the basis of their level of French-language restriction alone. We saw in Chapter 5 that Poplack (1989) provides convincing sociolinguistic evidence of just such a community effect in her recent research on code-switches and lexical borrowings from English in Ottawa–Hull French.

A further assumption which can be made is that the degree of transference will depend on just how widespread the preponderant model is in a given locality. This is the locality effect we are after. The results in Table 10.1 pertaining to the factor group locality of residence do not, however, provide further confirmation of a locality effect *within* the minority localities. In sum, although the transference hypothesis makes much intuitive sense, it needs to be more strongly buttressed by sociolinguistic evidence before it can be adopted as a better alternative to the view that unrestricted users of French who are balanced bilinguals may get *sur* directly via interference from English.

The complement noun results show that the frequency of use of *sur* is lower with *télévision* than with the other complements (i.e. *radio* and names of TV channels or radio stations). Although the difference is less than significant, the results are none the less interesting because they cannot be explained contrastively. Indeed, 'on' is categorical in English before both types of complement nouns. Other factor(s) of an internal nature must be at work in controlling *sur*'s diffusion. Linguists have often observed that infrequent elements tend to be subject to change more easily than frequent ones, other factors being equal (Hooper 1976; Martinet 1969; Chapters 5 and 6 in this volume). As the results show, *télévision* recurred more often than did *radio* and the names of TV channels and radio stations taken together. It could be that *à*'s greater reinforcement with *télévision* is the reason why this complement is less susceptible of being introduced by *sur* than are *radio* and the names of TV channels and radio stations.[10]

That *sur* is not significantly correlated with social class is at first sight surprising in view of (1) its appreciably lower frequency of use by the middle-class speakers, and (2) the differential monitoring capacity that restricted and semi-restricted speakers seem to exhibit, depending on their social class (see Chapters 5 and 9). Two explanations can be offered. The first one hinges on the premiss that our findings really do reflect an absence of social-class stratification in the wider community. The infrequency of the variable (see n. 10) and the interference-based origin of *sur* would have the effect of lessening the probability that *sur* will be monitored out of our subject's French. An infrequent form will be harder to spot than a frequent one and a form which has arisen via overt interference may also be harder to spot by bilingual speakers than a form which has surfaced via simplification (see Chapter 5) or via lexical borrowing (see next chapter). The second explanation—which we would tend to favour—is purely technical and rests on the premiss that, in the wider community, the restricted and semi-restricted users of French do indeed exhibit a differential capacity to monitor *sur* out of their speech depending on their social background, but that the statistical programme concluded otherwise due to the variable's infrequency (see raw data in Table 10.1).

[10] In fact, the low frequency of the locative expressions under study as a whole (only 127 occurrences or slightly more than one per speaker on the average) may explain why the change from *à* to *sur* is so advanced and even this figure is probably an overestimation of the locative expressions' true frequency in Ontarian French, since the interview schedule specifically included questions on the interviewees' viewing and listening habits. Ideally, we would have wanted to consider each nominal complement separately (i.e. *télévision*, *radio*, *station*, *poste* 'station', and *canal* 'channel') in the variable-rule analysis, but the very low frequency of some of these complements precluded this possibility.

Similar explanations can be offered for the absence of a sex effect. It can be pointed out, however, that, should social class have a real effect on the use of *sur* in the wider community, and should we have been able to capture it in our statistical analysis, it would not necessarily follow that we should also find the expected sex effect (i.e. females using the standard variant more often than males), because, when variation is found to be correlated with sex in the expected way, the correlation is usually weaker than that found with social class (see Chapters 5 and 6 and the wider sociolinguistic literature).

10.5. Discussion

The results presented in this chapter invite discussion of at least two main issues. The first one is already familiar (see Chapter 9): it is the question of the precise point—measured either in terms of degree of language-use restriction or degree of bilingualism—at which majority-language interference in a minority language begins to manifest itself. The second one—which was broached in Chapter 1—concerns the fact that, in a minority language which is in intensive contact with its majority counterpart, linguistic innovations, and hence language variation, can arise in a massive way in the speech of restricted, semi-restricted, or even unrestricted but fluent bilingual speakers of a minority language, and thus bypass the regular processes of emergence and gradual social diffusion of innovations identified by Labov in his research on variation in monolingual settings.

The discussion here will be restricted to changes that are ascribable to interference from the majority language. In the conclusion to this book (Chapter 12) we shall again raise the issue of the thresholds of minority-language-use restriction and their associated types of linguistic change to encompass all the different types of linguistic change we have identified in our research. In the preceding chapter we saw that the case of covert interference under study was observable not only in the speech of the restricted users of French, but also in that of the semi-restricted users of French, and, surprisingly, in that of the unrestricted speakers of French from the minority francophone communities. This led us to posit that it is not necessary that the speakers of French exhibit any significant measure of restriction in the use of this language for this type of interference to manifest itself, but simply that they be bilingual in English—a condition met by all the subjects residing in the three francophone minority communities. In short, the case of covert interference we examined turned out to be most pervasive, in that it failed to appear only under a low threshold of bilingualism.

In the present chapter we have found a similar situation, since, as far as the case of overt interference we have examined is concerned, again the unrestricted speakers from the minority communities are not immune to it. The difference between the two cases of interference-induced change is one of degree: the latter seems to be less widespread in the speech of the unrestricted speakers from the minority francophone communities than the former; more specifically, it was found only in the speech of two of our unrestricted users of French, both of whom were balanced bilinguals. Two facts follow from our examination of the distribution of *sur* according to degree of French-language-use restriction. The first is that our findings contradict once more those of Poplack (1982). In her study of the verbal system of Puerto Rican Spanish, she found that there was no evidence at all of grammatical interference from English in the speech of those of her subjects who used Spanish about as frequently as English (the equivalent of our semi-restricted users of French). The second is that the findings of this chapter constitute a refutation of Andersen's (1982) general hypothesis regarding transfer-induced change and degree of bilingualism (see Chapter 4) and of the particular hypothesis we formulated based on his, namely that various forms of morpho-syntactic and lexical transfer from English would manifest themselves first and foremost in the French of those of our subjects who exhibit clear cases of English-language dominance and concomitant French-language-use restriction.

We believe that the findings presented in this chapter also constitute the best type of evidence for our contention that minority-language-use restriction and/or advanced bilingualism can bring about rapid and massive linguistic change, a situation which contrasts sharply with the way linguistic change comes about in a monolingual community, i.e. through a process of gradual diffusion of an innovation usually mediated by social class. We have seen that (1) the innovation under study is indeed quite pervasive, as it is used no less than 82 per cent of the time by the semi-restricted speakers and 88 per cent of the time by the restricted speakers, (2) it seems even to show signs of being actively produced by the unrestricted speakers in the minority francophone communities, and (3) there is little evidence that its production is constrained by social class. Finally, it is possible to surmise that it has arisen quite rapidly in the speech of the adolescents from Cornwall, North Bay, and Pembroke, since it is only lately that bilingualism and language shift have been sharply on the rise among the younger Franco-Ontarian generations, including in these three communities (see Chapter 2).

10.6. Conclusion

Our research on Ontarian French has unearthed many changes which at first sight look like interference, but which, after due non-contrastive analysis, may be shown not to be lacking as regards internal motivation. It may well be that the reason we have found so many of these ambiguous changes is that French and English are typologically related languages showing a high degree of structural overlap. Thus, whenever a variety of French which is in contact with English evolves in such a way as to make the overlap between the two languages more complete at some level of structure, it is often not possible to tell (on the basis of strictly linguistic evidence) whether the change took place on its own (i.e. internally) or under the external stimulus of contact with English. Reflexive-pronoun deletion (e.g. *j'aime (me) baigner* 'I like to swim') (Beniak, Mougeon, and Côté 1980), levelling of the auxiliary *être* with *avoir* (e.g. *il a venu* 'he came') (Canale, Mougeon, and Bélanger 1978), substitution of *à* for *chez* (e.g. *je vais aller à ma tante* 'I'll go to my aunt's') (see Chapter 9 in this volume), etc. are all examples of ambiguous change in Ontarian French, in that they may be seen as the outcome of regularization/simplification or interference from English. Unfortunately, the fact that these changes have been found to be mostly concentrated in the spoken French of the restricted and semi-restricted users of French cannot be taken as sufficient evidence to settle the question of their origin in favour of interference, since these Franco-Ontarian speakers have been shown to be prone to regularize or simplify various aspects of French. It seems to us that linguists ought to avoid forcing an interpretation for the structural origin of these changes and openly acknowledge the possibility of multiple causation (see Thomason and Kaufman 1988 for a similar opinion).

In this chapter we demonstrated that the use of *sur* to express location on the broadcasting media is another instance of ambiguous change in Ontarian French. However, we showed that (1) the ambiguity concerning *sur*'s origin involved not an opposition between internal simplification and interference, but one between internal complication and interference, and (2) the ambiguity could be definitely resolved via a cross-dialectal comparison with a basically non-contact variety of French. Following Thomason (1986), we viewed the fact that *sur*'s putative internal origin involved complication as a valid reason to suspect that it had to have an intersystemic origin. When the cross-dialectal comparison was done, it was seen that *sur* was to all intents and purposes non-existent in Québécois French. The conclusion seemed warranted, therefore, that *sur* is in all likelihood the result of interference from the English preposition 'on'.

The comparison with European French served primarily two purposes. The first one was to provide a concrete illustration of the general validity of the hypothesis that *sur* might conceivably have an internal origin. The second purpose was to show that, if internal complication is very unlikely in a situation of intensive language contact, it is quite possible in a monolingual setting, as is shown by the way the use of *sur* before the names of radio and TV stations has arisen in that non-contact variety of French.

Finally, we hope to have convinced the reader that the idea is not to avoid the study of interference, but to approach it in a scientific and socially responsible way. As a general rule (inspired from the axiom of historical linguistics), we ought to seek internal explanations for change in a minority language even if it is strongly suspected that interference is responsible, and we ought further-more to measure the extent of the change especially if it is indeed due to interference. Heeding this advice should constitute a guarantee against repeating the errors that have been made in the past: (1) falsely attributing a change in a minority language to the (sole) influence of the majority language, and/or (2) exaggerating the extent of this influence. Needless to say, Franco-Ontarians and all other minority language groups could do without further linguistic prejudice.

11

Core Lexical Borrowing

In his by now classic survey of the linguistic consequences of language contact, Weinreich (1968: 56–61) proposed several reasons for lexical borrowing, the most universal, according to him, being the need to designate cultural novelties, that is, items peculiar to another culture and therefore for which the recipient language lacks lexical designations. Twenty years later Scotton and Okeju (1973), in a study devoted to lexical borrowings in Ateso, an East African Nilotic language, would remark—indeed complain—that lexical borrowings serving as designations for cultural borrowings have so attracted the attention of linguists as to obscure the existence of lexical borrowings infringing on the 'core' or common vocabulary of the recipient language. Among the examples of the latter kind of borrowing provided by Scotton and Okeju were the function words *alakini* 'but' (from Swahili), *tena* 'again' (also from Swahili), and *kada* 'even if' (from Dhopadhola). Scotton and Okeju also made a plea for research on lexical borrowing as a process, that is, on its sociological correlates, as opposed to study only of its product or the loanwords themselves. Their call was of course understandable at the time, given the still incipient state of socio-linguistics. But, with the coming of age of this discipline, a number of *socio-linguistic* studies of lexical borrowing have appeared in the literature, one of the best and most recent being that by Poplack, Sankoff, and Miller (1988) on English loanword integration in Ottawa–Hull French. Yet core lexical borrow-ing *per se* has remained relatively little studied. The present study pursues the line of work of Scotton and Okeju by reporting on a case of core lexical borrowing in Ontarian French. Among the core vocabulary that has been borrowed from English is the consecutive conjunction *so*. We shall restrict our attention to this specific core borrowing, for it is one of the few borrowings whose frequency of occurrence in our corpus is great enough to justify a statistical analysis.

11.1. Why investigate core lexical borrowing?

The interest of core lexical borrowing lies in its 'gratuitous' nature; by definition, the recipient language always has viable equivalents. As such, core

This chapter is a revised version of a paper by the same title published in the proceedings of NWAV-XV, edited by Keith Denning *et al.*, *Variation in Language: NWAV-XV at Stanford* (Department of Linguistics, Stanford University, 1987), 337–47.

lexical borrowing is the ultimate proof of the accuracy of Haugen's (1969: 373) contention that borrowing 'always goes beyond the actual "needs" of language'. If the reason behind lexical borrowings for cultural novelties is immediately apparent, core borrowings challenge the linguist's resourcefulness. Although many of the core borrowings reported in the literature have the status of function words, they are by no means confined to this category. Interjections, greetings, interaction markers, common nouns and adjectives, etc. also appear in lists of core borrowings. What could possibly lead speakers to make such 'unnecessary' borrowings?

While Scotton's and Okeju's study had the merit of putting core vocabulary back on the map of lexical borrowing, they cannot be given credit for 'discovering' core lexical borrowing. Weinreich was certainly not ignorant of it. In fact, he not only recognized its existence but 'ventured' an explanation for its occurrence (1968: 59–60):

If one language is endowed with prestige, the bilingual is likely to use what are identifiable loanwords from it as a means of displaying the social status which its knowledge symbolizes. This can be observed ... in the intimate, 'unnecessary' borrowing of everyday designations for things which have excellent names in the language which is being spoken ... Those American immigrants who borrow as heavily as possible to show their advanced state of acculturation, act upon a similar motive.

In this he was echoed by Haugen (1969: 372ff.), who ascribed the borrowing of core lexical items from English by American Norwegians to the lack of social status of this immigrant group. That core lexical borrowing is a feature of linguistic groups who enjoy little social status receives additional support not only from studies conducted on other immigrant languages, e.g. American Finnish (Karttunen 1977), Chicano Spanish (Gumperz and Hernández-Chavez 1972), but also from studies of language death (J. Hill and K. Hill 1977) and of minority (i.e. indigenous) varieties that are socio-economically diversified. Scotton and Okeju themselves, for instance, discovered that core lexical borrowings were much more frequent and varied in the recorded speech of non-standard speakers of Ateso than in that of standard speakers. In their study of francophones in Welland, Ontario, Mougeon and Hébrard (1975) likewise noted that borrowed core items such as *anyway*, *well*, *you know*, etc. were associated mainly with working-class speech. The present study will examine whether *so* in Ontarian French lends further support to the working-class connection of core lexical borrowing.

11.2. Language contact

A factor which has been linked to core borrowing is degree of contact. It has been claimed that sufficient cultural contact (Scotton and Okeju 1973) or intensive linguistic contact (Hudson 1980) are necessary conditions for core borrowings to occur. However, these authors did not provide quantitative evidence in support of their claim. *So*'s distribution in geographical dialects of Canadian French is in line with these statements, as it is confined to varieties that are in close contact with English, such as the local French of Moncton, New Brunswick (Roy 1979) or local varieties of French in Ontario (see section 11.4). Dessureault-Dober (1975), who studied the expression of consequence in Montreal French, which is in far less intensive contact with English, failed to note the borrowing of *so*. Does the general relationship that holds between core lexical borrowing and sufficiently intensive cultural and/or linguistic contact mean that all speakers belonging to low prestige linguistic groups satisfying this condition are equally prone to borrow into the core lexicon of their mother tongue? Roy's study is particularly interesting in this regard, all the more as it is focused on the same borrowing under study here. She distinguished her informants according to whether they spoke only French at home or both French and English. Results showed the latter speakers to be the prime users of *so*. Roy's findings therefore suggest that the link between core lexical borrowing and intensive linguistic contact can also be established within a community at the individual level. However, Roy's measure of language use was restrictive, as it was centred on the home (admittedly the most important domain for minority and/or subordinate languages) and, more importantly, was imprecise, as it was based only on a two-level distinction of frequency of French-language use.

11.3. The variable

The English consecutive conjunction *so* (e.g. *y'a dit 'j'étais trop tanné', so y'a pris l'auto pis y'a sacré le camp avec* 'he said "I was too fed up", so he took the car and got the hell out of there' Co8–081) finds itself in alternation with no fewer than three native equivalents, namely *ça fait que* (e.g. *à ('a) maison on parle tout le temps français, ça fait que on va, tout' suite on va le mettre en français* 'at home we always speak French, so we'll, right away we'll put it on the French station' P30–685), *alors* (e.g. *j'sais pas les mots en anglais, alors i' faut qu'j'utilise mon français, comme* 'I don't know the words in English, so I have to use my French, like' P01–400), and *donc* (e.g. *y'était plus vieux quand y'a appris l'anglais, donc y'a de la difficulté en anglais* 'he was older when he learnt English, so he has trouble in English' P18–332). In addition to occurring in their 'normal' intersentential position, all four variants also occurred in sentence-final position followed by a pause, where they may be interpreted as turn-yielding signals (e.g. *j'ai eu la religion toute ma vie, ça fait que* ... 'I have had religion all my life, so ...' N28–065)[1] or in

---

[1] The variant *ça fait que* may undergo various degrees of reduction due to phonetic and/or syntactic factors, the extreme form being *(ça) fait (que)*, i.e. *fait* alone.

sentence-initial position at the start of a new turn, where they may be said to function as shifters (e.g. *so c'est décourageant! J'ai rien fait* 'so it's discouraging! I didn't do anything' C12–105).[2]

In her study Roy found only binary variation (*alors* and *donc* were unattested). However, this may simply be due to the fact that her speaker sample was gathered exclusively among the working class, *alors* and *donc* being two variants which are more typical of middle-class speech (see next section). All three French variants were reported by Dessureault-Dober (1975) in Montreal French, a variety of French which does not include *so*, as mentioned. She found the working-class speakers (old and young) make exclusive use of *ça fait que*, a popular variant which seems to be spreading very rapidly to the young middle-class speakers (most of whom, in fact, prefer *ça fait que* to *alors*!), while the old continue to use *alors* exclusively or almost exclusively. She also found *donc* to be a very marginal variant, which she ascribed to its strong association with the written language. In short, the study of *so* and its native variants in Ontarian French offers the possibility of useful comparisons with previous research and of arriving at firmer conclusions about the sociological correlates of this particular core borrowing and hopefully of core lexical borrowing in general.

11.4. Results and discussion

Of the several different ways in which this case of quaternary variation could be analysed, we chose two that represented the most natural ways of combining and contrasting the different variants (see Chapter 4), given what we wanted to find out or already knew about them. First of all, it was decided to exclude *donc* from the analysis due to its very low frequency of occurrence.[3] Of the two analyses that we chose to perform, one features a contrast of *so* against *ça fait que* and *alors*, and the other pits *ça fait que* against *alors*. The first type of analysis consists of focusing on the core borrowing under study, with a view to finding out which of the extralinguistic parameters we examined are associated with it. The second type of analysis is one which leaves the problem of *so* usage aside to focus on the two traditional French variants. This analysis involves a regular sociolinguistic contrast between a non-standard vernacular variant, i.e. *ça fait que*, and a standard one, i.e. *alors*, and is expected to reveal a sociolinguistic pattern that we have grown accustomed to by now, namely a tendency for the non-standard vernacular variant to be used more frequently by working-class

---

[2] Roy (1979) found *so* occurring more frequently at the end of a sentence (as a turn-yielding signal) than in the other two positions. Although this suggests that there is an influence of the syntactic context on the probability of use of *so*, we chose not to pursue this question in the present study.

[3] *Donc*'s marginality in our corpus lends support to Dessureault-Dober's (1975) contention that this variant is a highly formal element essentially restricted to writing.

speakers than by speakers from the higher classes (the regular pattern of social stratification). There should also be a concomitant tendency for the non-standard variant to be used least frequently by the restricted users of French (i.e. the phenomenon of sociolectal reduction).

11.4.1. So

All of the extralinguistic factor groups considered were found to predict the use of *so*, with French-language-use restriction selected as the best predictor (see Table 11.1). As can be seen, the relationship between language restriction and probability of use of *so* is not a linear one. Indeed, the semi-restricted speakers are by far the most frequent users of *so* (effect of .763), the restricted speakers come in second place (effect of .437), and the unrestricted speakers use it least frequently (effect of only .285). This pattern is a nice illustration of the predicted effect of intensity of language contact. It may be useful to recall here Weinreich's (1968: 1) definition of 'contact': 'two or more languages will be said to be *in contact* [his emphasis] if they are used alternately by the same persons'. According to this definition, the semi-restricted speakers of French would be the locus of most intensive contact in view of their roughly equal use of the two

TABLE 11.1. *Variable-rule analysis of* so *vs.* ça fait que *and* alors

Factor groups	*so* (N)	*ça fait que* and *alors* (N)	Total	*so* (%)	Factor effects
French-language use					
Unrestricted	22	237	259	8	.285
Semi-restricted	217	197	414	52	.763
Restricted	30	130	160	19	.437
Locality of residence					
Hawkesbury	4	135	139	3	.160
Cornwall	120	75	195	62	.856
North Bay	66	170	236	28	.449
Pembroke	79	184	263	30	.521
Social class					
Middle	21	128	149	14	.243
Lower-middle	125	302	427	29	.441
Working	123	134	257	48	.798
Sex					
Male	155	255	410	38	.591
Female	114	309	423	27	.409
TOTAL	269	564	833	32	.155

languages. In contrast, the speakers belonging to the two other categories of French-language use would represent less intensive contact. Furthermore, of these two groups of speakers, the unrestricted would exhibit the lowest amount of contact, since they include many subjects who make categorical use of French in the private domain, whereas none of the restricted speakers makes categorical use of English in this domain (although many use English pre-dominantly).

The very infrequent use of *so* by the unrestricted speakers deserves further comment, since this category (the Hawkesbury students excepted) includes individuals who are proficient bilinguals (some going as far as reporting balanced bilingualism). Even if we calculate a separate score for the unrestricted speakers resident in the minority-francophone communities, we only get 15 per cent use of *so*. This suggests that bilingualism alone, i.e. without intensive language contact (in the Weinreichian sense, that is, regular use of both languages), is not sufficient to bring about a significant importation of *so*. With a view to exploring further the role of bilingualism in the use of *so*, we decided to correlate this parameter with the frequency of use of *so*.

On the basis of the subjects' self-report answers to the questions on knowledge of French and of English, three levels of bilingualism were distinguished: more proficient in French than in English (French-dominant), equally proficient in both languages (balanced), and more proficient in English than in French (English-dominant). In order to assess the effect of level of bilingualism on the use of *so*, we examined the distribution of *so* against the other two variants, first according to level of bilingualism on its own (see Table 11.2) and second according to level of bilingualism and French-language-use restriction (see Table 11.3).

Table 11.2 provides a second indication that bilingualism is not as good a predictor of variation in *so* usage as is degree of French-language-use restriction. Indeed, the differences in frequency of use of *so* according to level of bilingualism are clearly not as sizeable as those associated with level of French-language-use restriction (compare Table 11.1). Table 11.3 provides

TABLE 11.2. *Distribution of* so *by degree of bilingualism*

Degree of bilingualism	*so* (N)	*ça fait que* and *alors* (N)	Total	*so* (%)
French-dominant	72	221	293	25
Balanced	98	132	230	43
English-dominant	99	211	310	32
TOTAL	269	564	833	32

TABLE 11.3. *Distribution of* so *by language restriction and degree of bilingualism*

French-language use	Degree of bilingualism	so (N)	ça fait que and alors (N)	Total	so (%)
Unrestricted	French-dominant	17	182	199	9
	Balanced	5	31	36	14
	English-dominant	0	24	24	0
Semi-restricted	French-dominant	55	39	94	59
	Balanced	93	56	149	62
	English-dominant	69	102	171	40
Restricted	French-dominant	NA†	NA	NA	NA
	Balanced	0	45	45	0
	English-dominant	30	85	115	26
TOTAL		269	564	833	32

† NA = not applicable; there were no speakers who were both restricted users of French and French-dominant.

further confirmation of the fact that degree of bilingualism is a poor predictor of variation in *so* usage. As concerns the prime users of *so*, i.e. the semi-restricted speakers, the frequency differences in the use of *so* according to level of bilingualism are such that the balanced bilinguals stand out even less than when level of bilingualism was considered on its own (compare Table 11.2). Furthermore, it can be seen that the frequency of *so* usage by the balanced bilinguals (speakers who, on the basis of Table 11.2, might be suspected of favouring the use of *so*) differs dramatically according to frequency of French-language use: 14 per cent for the unrestricted balanced bilinguals vs. 62 per cent for the semi-restricted vs. 0 per cent for the restricted.

To sum up, the results on the effects of level of bilingualism and level of French-language use are interesting because they suggest (1) that differential patterns of language use, i.e. the extent to which English is actively used along with French by the bilinguals (i.e. Weinreich's notion of language contact), are a much better predictor of *so* usage than differential patterns of language dominance, and (2) that, as far as bilingualism is concerned, the only safe thing we can assert is that speakers who are not proficient bilinguals (e.g. the Hawkesbury adolescents) are unlikely to borrow *so*, or, put differently, that proficient bilingualism is a necessary but not a sufficient condition for the importation of *so* to take place.

Still on the issue of the relationship between variation in the use of *so*, level of bilingualism, and level of language restriction, in their study of English lexical borrowings in Ottawa–Hull French Poplack, Sankoff, and Miller (1988) quoted an earlier paper by Mougeon, Beniak, and Valois (1985*a*) in which these authors reported (among other things) on the use of *so* by their Franco-Ontarian adolescent subjects. According to Poplack, Sankoff, and Miller (1988: 84), the finding of Mougeon, Beniak, and Valois (1985*a*) that use of *so* was preferred by the mid-level users of French (in this volume the semi-restricted speakers) ran counter to their own finding that in the Ottawa–Hull French-speaking communities 'it is precisely the less bilingual speakers who favor widespread loanwords; that is, those that are transmitted along with the French lexicon and require no prior knowledge of English to use'.

We disagree with their interpretation of our findings for several reasons. First of all, it is clear that the category of widespread loanwords examined by Poplack, Sankoff, and Miller is mostly made up of what might be appropriately referred to as old established English borrowings in Canadian French, i.e. words like *le fun*, *la job*, *le truck*, *le hot dog*, etc., which indeed require no prior knowledge of English to be used. In other words, such loanwords have the status of bona fide French lexical items. The correlation with level of bilingualism which they have found concerning widespread loanwords is therefore understandable and, indeed, we have also found individual estab-lished loanwords to be correlated with level of bilingualism in exactly the same fashion in previous research of ours (see, e.g., Mougeon, Heller, Beniak, and Canale 1984).

In spite of its being widespread, *so* does not, however, belong to the set of old established borrowings of Canadian French but to the set of what we have referred to elsewhere (Mougeon, Beniak, and Valois 1985*b*) as 'Franco-Ontarian' borrowings, and, more specifically, within this latter category, to those showing signs of entering the French lexicon, e.g. words like *boyfriend*, *high school*, *TV*, *watcher* (< 'to watch'), etc. This new generation of English lexical borrowings is to a large extent the result of the intensification of contact with English after the emigration of French Quebecers to Ontario. Now it is precisely because *so* (1) belongs to the set of *Franco-Ontarian* borrowings, (2) is still in the process of getting into the local variety of French, and, of course, (3) is a borrowing from the 'core', that we thought it to be a prime candidate for an examination of the extralinguistic correlates of its importation into Ontarian French. In their research Poplack, Sankoff, and Miller did not consider Franco-Ontarian borrowings as a separate category. To them, the fact that *so* is relatively widespread in our corpus was enough of a reason to equate it to a widespread borrowing. What we have found in the way of correlations with levels of French-language use and bilingualism is in fact a good indication that *so* does not belong yet to the set of established borrowings. So it would seem that our findings concerning the effect of French-language-use restriction and degree of bilingualism on the use of *so* do not, after all, contradict those of Poplack, Sankoff, and Miller (1988), but indeed point to interesting avenues for further research on the connection between core lexical borrowings, language-use restriction, and bilingualism.

Locality of residence was the second-best predictor of the probability of use of *so* according to the variable-rule analysis. *So*'s extreme infrequency in the Hawkesbury speech sample (effect .160) provides a further illustration of the link which we seem to have found between core lexical borrowing and intensive language contact. In Hawkesbury, French is at best only in weak contact with English and all the subjects who reside in that locality make categorical use of French in the private domain. In other words, the case of *so* does not seem to be different from those of covert and overt interference which we examined in the preceding chapters; when French ceases to be in intensive contact with English, these different types of interference simply do not manifest themselves.

As concerns social class (the third-best predictor), we note that working-class speakers are more likely to use *so* (.798) than lower-middle-class speakers (.441) and far more likely than those of the middle class (.243), a finding quite in keeping with the previous reports in the literature (Mougeon and Hébrard 1975; Scotton and Okeju 1973) concerning the socio-economic stratification of core lexical borrowings. It is not obvious, however, at which end of the social-class hierarchy we should attempt to provide an explanation. On the one hand, it may be that the middle-class bilinguals, like those belonging to the other social strata, are inclined to borrow into the core vocabulary and/or make use of already integrated core borrowings, but tend to suppress this inclination because the 'unnecessary' nature of this kind of borrowing makes it particularly objectionable. The Franco-Ontarian middle class exhibits strong favourable attitudes towards French and its maintenance (Mougeon and Beniak 1989*a*) and presumably feels equally strongly about preserving its structural and lexical integrity. This view of things is echoed by Poplack, Sankoff, and Miller (1988: 87): 'unskilled workers and the chronically unemployed use far fewer nouns (55 %), with concomitantly more loanwords distributed across the more innovative parts of speech, than do members of the other occupational classes (66 % to 77 % nouns), suggesting that not only borrowing, but particularly borrowing into any other than the most common category, is stigmatized by the latter groups'.

On the other hand, it could be—in fact we know (Mougeon and Beniak 1989*a*)—that Franco-Ontarian working-class speakers have less positive attitudes towards French and its preservation, because of its lack of importance for socio-economic promotion in Ontario. Borrowing core lexical items from English may be for them a way to display 'the social status which its knowledge symbolizes', as Weinreich (1968: 60) supposed. In fact, the two explanations are probably not mutually exclusive. Both have in common the implication that core lexical borrowing lies above the level of linguistic awareness. In this it would differ from (c)overt interference, which would appear to be a more 'insidious' form of interlingual influence (the reader will recall that we failed to note any social stratification for the interference-induced changes studied in Chapters 9 and 10, i.e. the replacement of *chez* by *à la maison* and *à* by *sur*).

The selection of sex (i.e. the favouring effect of male sex) goes hand in hand with the previous finding that *so* is primarily a working-class variant and furthermore it is in line with what we have already found in preceding chapters and what is usually reported in the literature regarding the effect of sex on linguistic variation.

11.4.2. Ça fait que and alors

Let us now turn briefly to the results of the second variable-rule analysis, which, it will be remembered, concerned the opposition of the two French variants *ça fait que* and *alors* (see Table 11.4).

The first factor group selected, locality of residence, reveals a sharp polarization of the two variants: whereas *alors* is practically unattested in the Hawkesbury speech sample, the opposite is true in North Bay and, generally speaking, *alors* is favoured by the minority-locality speakers. The quasi-absence of *alors* in Hawkesbury French suggests that *ça fait que*'s status has changed from social-class marker to style marker, similarly to what is taking

TABLE 11.4. *Variable-rule analysis of* ça fait que *vs.* alors

Factor groups	*ça fait que* (N)	*alors* (N)	Total	*ça fait que* (%)	Factor effects
Locality of residence					
Hawkesbury	133	2	135	99	.986
Cornwall	30	45	75	40	.308
North Bay	23	147	170	14	.044
Pembroke	76	108	184	41	.406
French-language use					
Unrestricted	180	57	237	76	.649
Semi-restricted	75	122	197	38	.806
Restricted	7	123	130	5	.142
Sex					
Male	126	129	255	49	.678
Female	136	173	309	44	.322
Social class					
Middle	52	76	128	41	.322
Lower-middle	125	177	302	41	.596
Working	85	49	134	63	.588
TOTAL	262	302	564	46	.450

place in Montreal French according to Dessureault-Dober (1975). Thus *ça fait que* is apparently well on its way to displacing *alors* in informal varieties of Canadian French which are not in intensive contact with English (i.e. whose speakers remain essentially monolingual). Where contact is intensive, however, as in the Franco-Ontarian minority communities of Cornwall and Pembroke, *ça fait que* is in serious competition against *alors* and indeed the former may give signs of disappearing, as in North Bay French. The results pertaining to French-language-use restriction (the second-best predictor) throw light on the geographical distribution of *ça fait que* and *alors*. Indeed, we see that the restricted speakers (all of whom reside in the minority francophone localities) have a much lesser tendency to use *ça fait que* than the semi-restricted or unrestricted speakers. In other words, we seem to have found yet another instance of the phenomenon of sociolectal reduction whereby the restricted speakers are losing (or rather have not acquired) yet another typical feature of vernacular Canadian French.

The third-best predictor was speaker gender, females being associated with a much lower probability of use of *ça fait que* than males, just as they were found to show a lesser inclination to use *so*, an understandable finding considering that *ça fait que*, like *so*, is mainly a feature of working-class speech. As regards the effect of this latter parameter, if we cross-tabulate social class with level of French-language use (see Table 11.5), we can observe an interesting and complex picture.

As concerns the unrestricted speakers, we can see that the locus of variation is essentially centred on the *ça fait que* vs. *alors* contrast, *so* having the status of a secondary non-standard variant. As far as the semi-restricted speakers are concerned, we can see that the locus of variation seems to have shifted to the contrast between *so* and *alors* and that *ça fait que* no longer has the status of an informal variant, that is, if we go by the way it patterns with social class. If anything, it seems to be in the process of acquiring the opposite status! Finally, as far as the restricted speakers are concerned, we see no firm pattern of social stratification in their speech. By virtue of its quasi-absence, *ça fait que* can obviously no longer function as a marker of sociolectal variation. *Alors* and *so* seem to correlate in the expected way with social class (if we except the middle-class speakers' scores due to paucity of data). However, this does not alter the fact that, in comparison to the spoken French of the unrestricted speakers, the spoken French of the restricted speakers is 'abnormally' standardized, as shown by the astonishingly frequent use of *alors* by the lower-middle and working-class restricted speakers.

TABLE 11.5. *Distribution of* so, *ça fait que, and* alors *by social class and language restriction*

Social class	French-language use																	
	Unrestricted						Semi-restricted						Restricted					
	so		*ça fait que*		*alors*		*so*		*ça fait que*		*alors*		*so*		*ça fait que*		*alors*	
	N	%	N	%	N	%	N	%	N	%	N	%	N	%	N	%	N	%
Middle	1	2	28	52	25	46	14	6	24	28	48	56	6	67	0	0	3	33
Lower-middle	6	5	80	70	28	25	106	55	38	20	49	25	13	11	7	6	100	83
Working	15	17	72	79	4	4	97	72	13	10	25	18	11	35	0	0	20	65
TOTAL	22	8	180	70	57	22	217	52	75	18	122	30	30	19	7	4	123	77

11.5. Conclusion

Our examination of *so* vs. *ça fait que* vs. *alors* has revealed an interesting case of two-pronged linguistic change: one which seems mostly instigated by the semi-restricted speakers (i.e. those subjects who exhibit the highest level of contact with English) and which involves massive borrowing of *so,* and another which is essentially confined to the speech of the restricted speakers and involves the demise of *ça fait que,* a variant which shows absolutely no sign of weakening in the speech of the unrestricted speakers or in non-contact varieties of Canadian French. At the risk of repeating ourselves, these results add further support to our contention that minority-language-use restriction and intensive language contact can bring about sweeping and sudden linguistic change.

Has the sociolinguistic approach adopted in the present study made for a better understanding of *so* and perhaps core lexical borrowing in general? The cross-dialectal comparisons certainly lend support to the commonly held view that core lexical borrowing arises in settings of intensive language contact. We saw that *so* is restricted to contact varieties of Canadian French. An original contribution of this study has been to provide preliminary empirical evidence of a link between core lexical borrowing and intensive language contact at the individual level. Results showed that speakers who use English and French more or less equally in the private domain are the prime users of *so.* The gratuitous nature of core lexical borrowing is reminiscent of the phenomenon of code-switching, which is also especially characteristic of speakers who exhibit unpatterned bilingualism (see Amastae and Elías-Olivares 1982 as concerns Spanish in the United States and Heller 1988 as regards French in Ontario). In fact, that sentence connectors and other kinds of discourse organizers like *so* are so often reported in lists of core lexical borrowings may not be a coincidence, since these items all occur at prime switch points. We would tentatively advance the hypothesis that core lexical borrowings like *so* or other sentence connectors may start out as code-switches (either as single words or as part of switched sentences) which by dint of repetition become loanwords.

The following interchange contains an instance of *so* in a code-switch to English:

Enquêteur: Est-ce que tu t'intéresses à la politique?
Informateur: Heu j'sus t'un peu au courant qu'est-ce qui se passe mais, j'veux dire, l'année passée c'était pas mal intéressant, on avait Monsieur Bissonnette et puis i' nous forçait à lire le papier . . . et puis à chaque semaine ben on discutait pour les nouvelles internationales, provinciales puis . . .
Enquêteur: Heum.

| Informateur: | . . . municipales, 'so I was getting into it, anyway', j'es lisais pis j'discutais. |

Interviewer:	Are you interested in politics?
Informant:	Uh, I know a little bit what's happening but, I mean, last year it was pretty interesting, Mr Bissonnette was our teacher and he made us read the paper . . . and every week well we would talk about the international news, provincial and . . .
Interviewer:	Mhm.
Informant:	. . . municipal, so I was getting into it, anyway, I was reading the news and talking about it.

If this view of things is correct, then core lexical borrowing (or at least some of its manifestations) would simply be a by-product of code-switching. Perhaps a more natural and comprehensive explanation (applying to all core borrowings, not just link words) is the one proposed by Weinreich and Haugen, namely that gratuitous borrowings like *so* serve to symbolize the advanced state of acculturation of bilingual speakers who experience high levels of contact with a superordinate language.

12

Conclusion

THE primary purpose of this final chapter is to provide the reader with an overview of (1) the main types of linguistic change which were examined in Chapters 5–11, (2) the extralinguistic parameters which were found to be associated with these changes, and (3) the particular effects these parameters have on the changes. With this purpose in mind, we have summarized the results of our investigation of the effects of the four extralinguistic parameters French-language-use restriction, locality of residence, social class, and sex on the various cases of change under study (see Table 12.1). This table provides information on the percentages associated with the different extralinguistic factors under study and, when a VARBRUL analysis was performed, on the effects of the different factors and on the predictive power (or rank) of the different factor groups. This table does not provide the raw numbers associated with the percentages and factor effects, nor does it provide the results of the special cross-tabulations of French-language-use restriction with other extralinguistic parameters (e.g. social class) which were performed in a number of studies. The reader can refer to the individual chapters for such detailed information. Here and there in our overview we shall attempt to link up our findings on the effects of the four extralinguistic parameters mentioned above with similar or related findings in the wider literature.

Let us first review briefly the four types of linguistic change we have identified in this volume, change being defined as a departure from the non-contact conservative norm spoken by the adolescent subjects resident in Hawkesbury.

The first type of change is morpho-syntactic simplification, which can be defined as the emergence of innovations which are simpler (i.e. more regular, more transparent, etc.) alternatives to complex (i.e. irregular, opaque, etc.) morpho-syntactic elements. The case of morpho-syntactic change examined in this volume (Chapter 5) is the levelling of the distinctive 3pl. verb forms via substitution of the unmarked 3sg. forms. Another such case which we examined (Mougeon 1982) is the levelling of the distinction between pronominal and non-pronominal verbs via deletion of the reflexive pronouns.

The second type is interference-induced change, which can be defined as the emergence of innovations due to various types of transfer from the majority language. The different subtypes of interference-induced change examined in this volume are covert interference (the rise of *à la maison* at the expense of *chez*) (Chapter 9), overt interference (the rise of *sur* at the expense of *à* before *radio*,

TABLE 12.1. *Summary of the effects of four extralinguistic parameters on linguistic variation in Ontarian French*

Factor groups	3pl. vs. 3sg. verb forms			sontaient vs. étaient (all communities)			sontaient vs. étaient (Cornwall)			Possessive à vs. de		
	3pl. (%)	Factor effects	Rank	sontaient (%)	Factor effects	Rank	sontaient (%)	Factor effects	Rank	à (%)	Factor effects	Rank
French-language use			3			NA			NA			NA
Unrestricted	98	.844		6	NA†		7	NA		19	NA	
Semi-restricted	86	.369		12	NA		39	NA		21	NA	
Restricted	81	.240		0	NA		0	NA		0	NA	
Locality of residence			2			NA			NA			NA
Hawkesbury	99	.658		0	NA		NA	NA		30	NA	
Cornwall	95	.671		22	NA		22	NA		8	NA	
North Bay	90	.490		0	NA		NA	NA		21	NA	
Pembroke	73	.210		0	NA		NA	NA		8	NA	
Social class			4			NA			NA			NA
Middle	91	.561		4	NA		–‡	NA		0	NA	
Lower-middle	90	.600		3	NA		12	NA		13	NA	
Working	84	.343		14	NA		35	NA		28	NA	
Sex			5			NA			NA			NA
Male	86	.389		9	NA		22	NA		12	NA	
Female	91	.611		4	NA		24	NA		21	NA	

Factor groups	vas vs. vais (V)			vas vs. vais and m'as (Aux)			vais vs. vas and m'as (Aux)			m'as vs. vas and vais (Aux)		
	vas (%)	Factor effects	Rank	vas (%)	Factor effects	Rank	vais (%)	Factor effects	Rank	m'as (%)	Factor effects	Rank
French-language use			not sig.			not sig.			not sig.			not sig.
Unrestricted	91	NA		64	NA		6	NA		30	NA	
Semi-restricted	84	NA		56	NA		17	NA		27	NA	
Restricted	86	NA		60	NA		13	NA		27	NA	
Locality of residence			not sig.			1			1			1
Hawkesbury	89	NA		78	.69		3	.19		19	.47	
Cornwall	94	NA		37	.27		7	.47		56	.79	
North Bay	84	NA		57	.46		36	.84		7	.19	
Pembroke	84	NA		70	.60		10	.59		20	.40	
Social class			2			not sig.			not sig.			not sig.
Middle	77	.29		59	NA		12	NA		29	NA	
Lower-middle	85	.41		61	NA		11	NA		29	NA	
Working	94	.71		60	NA		12	NA		28	NA	
Sex			1			not sig.			2			2
Male	93	.64		56	NA		8	.39		36	.57	
Female	80	.32		64	NA		16	.62		20	.43	

TABLE 12.1 (*cont.*)

Factor groups	chez vs. sur vs. à vs. à la maison (de)							chez vs. à la maison			à vs. sur + télévision, radio, etc.		
	chez (%)	sur (%)	à (%)	à la maison (%)	à la maison de (%)	Factor effects	Rank	chez (%)	Factor effects	Rank	sur (%)	Factor effects	Rank
French-language use							NA			not sig.			1
Unrestricted	77	2	0	20	1	NA		76	NA		26	.135	
Semi-restricted	54	6	3	34	3	NA		56	NA		82	.665	
Restricted	62	0	7	25	6	NA		61	NA		88	.763	
Locality of residence							NA			2			not sig.
Hawkesbury	83	2	0	15	0	NA		84	.745		0	KO§	
Cornwall	65	6	1	22	5	NA		69	.532		72	NA	
North Bay	52	3	4	37	3	NA		49	.342		73	NA	
Pembroke	61	0	6	30	3	NA		59	.366		78	NA	
Social class							NA			not sig.			not sig.
Middle	71	2	0	27	0	NA		67	NA		52	NA	
Lower-middle	59	1	2	33	5	NA		59	NA		82	NA	
Working	68	6	5	19	2	NA		72	NA		76	NA	
Sex							NA			not sig.			not sig.
Male	61	2	4	30	4	NA		60	NA		71	NA	
Female	67	4	2	24	2	NA		69	NA		82	NA	

Factor groups	so vs. ça fait que and alors			ça fait que vs. alors		
	so (%)	Factor effects	Rank	ça fait que (%)	Factor effects	Rank
French-language use			1			2
Unrestricted	8	.285		76	.649	
Semi-restricted	52	.763		38	.806	
Restricted	19	.437		5	.142	
Locality of residence			2			1
Hawkesbury	3	.160		99	.986	
Cornwall	62	.856		40	.308	
North Bay	28	.449		14	.044	
Pembroke	30	.521		41	.406	
Social class			3			4
Middle	14	.243		41	.322	
Lower-middle	29	.441		41	.596	
Working	48	.798		63	.588	
Sex			4			3
Male	38	.591		49	.678	
Female	27	.409		44	.322	

† NA = not applicable.
‡ Per cent not calculated (see Table 6.2 for explanation).
§ KO = knockout factor.

télévision, etc.) (Chapter 10), and lexical borrowing (the rise of *so* at the expense of *ça fait que* and *alors*) (Chapter 11).

The third type is what we called 'ambiguous' change, which can be defined as innovations which admit both an internal and an external explanation, and for which it is not possible to favour internal simplification over interference from the majority language, or vice-versa. Two examples of such change examined in the present volume (Chapter 9) are the emergence of the generic locative preposition *à* as an alternative to *chez* and the emergence of the transparent prepositional phrase *à la maison de* again as an alternative to *chez*.

The fourth type of change is sociolectal reduction, which can be defined as the loss of vernacular variants and concomitant rise of their standard alternatives. Three particularly telling instances of this type of change were examined: the loss of *sontaient* (Chapter 6), of possessive *à* (Chapter 7), and of *sur* meaning *chez* (Chapter 9), not to mention the quasi-extinction of *ça fait que* at the hands of the standard variant *alors* (Chapter 11).

Let us now review the effect of the extralinguistic parameters on these various types of change. We shall start by focusing on the effect of French-language-use restriction. This parameter will take up most of the discussion, as it is the one which is most central to the theme of the volume.

12.1. French-language-use restriction

As can be seen in Table 12.1, this parameter was selected four times and ranked number 3 (3pl. levelling), 1 (*à* vs. *sur*), 1 (*so* vs. *ça fait que* and *alors*), and 2 (*ça fait que* vs. *alors*) when VARBRUL analyses were performed. Furthermore, the analyses of variation which did not involve a factor analysis gathered additional evidence that this parameter plays a significant role in linguistic change, judging by the spread between the percentages associated with restricted, semi-restricted, and unrestricted speaker performance (see *sontaient* vs. *étaient*, possessive *à* vs. *de*, and *chez* vs. *sur* vs. *à* vs. *à la maison (de)* in Table 12.1). The above findings, then, indicate that minority-language-use restriction is a key predictor of linguistic change in a language-contact setting.

Another interesting finding to emerge from Table 12.1 is that the various types of change we have examined seem to be implicationally ordered according to level of French-language-use restriction (see Table 12.2, which involves some idealization). Interference-induced changes (i.e. the rise of *à la maison*, that of locative *sur*, and that of *so*) are the most pervasive in that they have been found in the speech of the three groups of subjects under investigation: the restricted speakers, the semi-restricted speakers, and the unrestricted speakers. Internal simplification (i.e. levelling of the 3pl. verb forms) and the ambiguous changes (i.e. substitution of *à* and *à la maison de* for *chez*) come in second place. They were found in the speech of the semi-restricted speakers

TABLE 12.2. *Thresholds of French-language use and associated types of linguistic change*

French-language use	Interference-induced change	Internal simplification and ambiguous change	Sociolectal reduction
Unrestricted (H)†	—	—	—
Unrestricted	+	—	—
Semi-restricted	+	+	—
Restricted	+	+	+

† H = Hawkesbury.

and in that of the restricted speakers, but not in the speech of the unrestricted speakers. Sociolectal reduction was found to occur only in the speech of the restricted speakers. Finally, none of the above-mentioned changes was found to occur in the conservative norm, i.e. Hawkesbury French.

12.1.1. Interference-induced change

The above findings suggest that bilingual speakers need not be dominant in the majority language (the reader will recall that none of the unrestricted users of French is dominant in English) or experience restriction in the use of the minority language for interference-induced change to manifest itself. These results thus provide an answer to the question formulated in Chapter 4 regarding the dominance threshold of interference-induced change.

The pervasiveness of the interference-induced changes which we have examined constitutes a confirmation of the experience of many bilinguals (even additive ones), namely that probably no speaker of two languages is immune to interference. This does not mean, though, that interference-induced change should be perceived negatively. Interference is, in a sense, the intersystemic equivalent of simplification. Like simplification, interference can offer 'solutions' to what the bilingual speaker perceives as non-optimal aspects of his/her languages, or to what any speaker (bilingual or not) perceives as non-optimal. We may mention, for example, the study of Canale, Mougeon, Bélanger, and Main (1977) of the borrowing of the English particle *back* by Franco-Ontarians, in which it was argued that *back* is a more optimal analytic alternative to the polysemous French prefix *re-*. Interference-induced changes, however, do not always constitute solutions to structural non-optimality. In the case of core as opposed to cultural lexical borrowing, for instance, one is often hard put to find structural motivation, although, as we have argued for *so*, there may well be good socio-psychological reasons for bilingual speakers to borrow from and into the core lexicon.

However startling or reprehensible they may appear to unilinguals or individuals only familiar with the unilingual norm, interference-induced innovations are not lacking in functional adequacy or in socio-psychological motivation and in time may come to constitute instances of new community norms (Haugen 1977). We would like to quote here from Romaine's (1989a: 281–2) recent book on bilingualism, since her views on the linguistic competence of bilinguals fit most adequately the present discussion, as well as more generally the findings of our research on the spoken French of bilingual adolescent Franco-Ontarians:

When speakers of different languages are in contact, the codes they use may not be stable. Because new and different norms develop in such situations, there are problems in talking about proficiency because competence may span several codes, which are unequally developed. It is possible for a bilingual to be fluent in both languages taken together without being able to function like a monolingual in either one on its own.

This means that the bilingual's system will be different in some respects from the monolingual's. I have shown how in some cases bilinguals have different norms for production. There is also experimental evidence that their perceptual norms operate differently.

The presence of a plus sign in the interference-induced-change column for the unrestricted speakers resident in Cornwall, North Bay, and Pembroke (see Table 12.2) should not be taken to mean that all types of interference-induced change will occur in their speech. The three cases of interference-induced change we have examined are in a sense surface phenomena, in that they do not affect the grammatical component of the minority language. As previously mentioned (see Chapter 4), Andersen (1982: 109) formulated the hypothesis that *morpho-syntactic* interference will be tied to dominance of the source language over the recipient one.

One such case of interference we have examined elsewhere (Mougeon, Heller, Beniak, and Canale 1984) confirms Andersen's hypothesis (or more conservatively, does not go against it). The change in question is the substitution of copula *être* for stative *avoir* to express the notion of being scared (e.g. *je suis peur* instead of *j'ai peur* 'I'm scared'), modelled on the English equivalent expressions 'to be scared', 'to be frightened', etc. The use of *avoir* to express a state is a basic feature of French which is used to express not only the notion of being scared but also those of being hot, hungry, cold, thirsty, X years old, etc. Because this interference-induced innovation occurs at the expense of a basic verbal construction and involves the rather odd use of the noun *peur* as an adjective, it is perhaps not surprising that it is confined to the speech of the restricted speakers whom, it will be recalled, are for the most part dominant in English. It is probable that the examination of other cases of morpho-syntactic interference will provide further support for Andersen's hypothesis. In any case, our findings suggest that specific instances of interference-induced change may also be ordered implicationally. In this connection, the relative infrequency of the change from *à* to *sur* in the speech of the unrestricted speakers, in contrast to the rise of *à la maison* (an innovation which seems to be equally widespread in the speech of the three groups of bilingual speakers), are additional bits of evidence to support the view that it would be naïve to expect interference-induced change always to pattern the same way on the implicational scale. Perhaps what matters more, in the end, is the central idea that individual instances of change attested in a contact setting—whether due to interference or not—are associated with specific thresholds of bilingualism and frequency of use of the minority language, and that it is possible, at least in theory, to account for such associations in a predictable and principled way.[1]

12.1.2. Internal simplification

Turning to internal simplification, we may want to attempt to explain why the case we examined was found only in the speech of the two groups of subjects that experience French-language-use restriction. One explanation is that, under 'normal' conditions of language use (i.e. absence of language contact and restriction), the distinctive 3pl. verb forms are simply non-problematic. While they may be rightly viewed as irregular from a paradigmatic perspective, their frequency of occurrence in discourse is high enough for them to be fully mastered by unrestricted-language users and thus to be impervious to simplification. In fact, Trudgill (1983: Chapter 5) goes as far as saying that, in a situation of 'normal' language use (as defined above), simplification of this particular type (involving levelling of morphology) is unlikely to manifest itself. He views such simplificatory change as 'non-natural' (p. 102):

Some forms of linguistic change may be relatively 'natural', in the sense that they are liable to occur in all linguistic systems, at all times, without external stimulus, because of the inherent nature of linguistic systems . . . Other types of linguistic change, on the other hand, may be relatively 'non-natural', in the sense that they take place mainly as a result of language contact. They are, that is, not due to the inherent nature of language systems, but to processes that take place in particular sociolinguistic situations.

The reason for the non-occurrence of such simplificatory change in non-contact settings is that in such situations we can expect that a language will be fully functionally adequate, either because many aspects of its structure are truly optimal (e.g. both regular and frequent) or because the irregular or marked aspects of its structure (from a paradigmatic viewpoint) have other

---

[1] According to Valdman (1979a: 10), contact varieties of French may exhibit internal restructurings that are peculiar to the speech of restricted speakers. Although we have not examined any in this volume—the cases of internal simplification and ambiguous change studied here extended to semi-restricted speaker performance too—, we did elsewhere in a corpus of Albertan French (Beniak, Carey, and Mougeon 1984). Dorian (1981) also observed internal restructurings of East Sutherland Gaelic which were the sole attribute of semi-speakers.

things going for them (e.g. frequency of occurrence) and hence do not need to be 'fixed', i.e. simplified. While we do not think it necessary to hold as strong a view as Trudgill's on the link between 'natural' linguistic change and absence of contact (if for no other reason than the commonly agreed fact that contact situations are by far the more frequent), it is true none the less that the non-occurrence of 3pl. levelling in the speech of the unrestricted speakers (i.e. those who use French in a situation close to Trudgill's idea of normalcy) provides support for his view that language contact and restriction can indeed trigger changes (i.e. simplifications) which have no counterpart in fully native speech. Which is not to say that fully native speech cannot undergo simplificatory changes. To deny this possibility would be tantamount to attributing *all* historical levelling to contact! In terms of implications for further research, it is only by engaging in more comparative studies of contact and non-contact varieties (preferably of a given language) that we can hope to understand better when contact is or is not required as an 'external stimulus' (to use Trudgill's words) for simplificatory changes.

Similar explanations can be offered for the absence of simpler alternatives to *chez* and *sur* in the speech of the unrestricted speakers. *Chez* and *sur* may be rightly viewed as non-transparent ways of expressing location at or motion to one's dwelling. However, in the absence of French-language restriction, they seem to occur frequently enough in discourse for them not to be replaced by transparent (i.e. *à la maison de*) or less specific (i.e. generic locative *à*) alternatives. In other words, we would like to argue that, when language restriction occurs, the frequency of occurrence of irregular, marked elements (like the ones we examined) falls below a critical threshold and makes it impossible for these elements to be fully mastered by the restricted speakers. This in turn brings about the emergence of alternative elements which the restricted speakers produce via a variety of means (internal simplification, intersystemic transfer, or a combination of both processes).

Finally, it should be pointed out again that, although individual instances of internal simplification may appear startling or deviant to unilinguals or to those who are only familiar with the unilingual norm, they are none the less perfectly functional linguistic alternatives. In fact, in many instances they represent an alternative which entails less effort for the encoder and which should pose no problem for the decoder.[2] Levelling of the marked 3pl. verb forms certainly fits this description, since it does nothing more than bring the minority of verbs displaying distinctive 3pl. forms in line with the majority of verbs, whose 3pl. forms are not morphologically marked. Furthermore, just like

---

[2] As far as decoding is concerned, it may be argued not only that ambiguous changes and/or internal simplifications are in most instances non-problematic, but also that their meaning is equally recoverable by community members and unilingual outsiders. The same cannot be said for transfer-induced innovations, which, in order to be understood, may require that the decoder be a member of the community or, if an outsider, that s/he be bilingual.

interference-induced changes, internal simplifications may become instances of new community norms.

12.1.3. Sociolectal reduction

As regards sociolectal reduction, the most interesting aspect of our findings is perhaps not so much that the restricted speakers exhibit it (their sociolinguistic profile leads us naturally to expect this), but that the semi-restricted speakers are immune to it (although it will be recalled that they are not immune to interference and simplification). Although it may be surmised that further examination of the phenomenon of sociolectal reduction may reveal cases that are also observable in the speech of the semi-restricted speakers (exceptions to the implicational scale), we believe that the evidence gathered so far under-scores the fact that, while the semi-restricted speakers experience the highest level of language contact, their restriction in the use of French is not pronounced enough to cut them off from the vernacular. Therefore these speakers can be rightly viewed as still belonging to the core of Ontario's French-speaking community.

Sociolectal reduction should not be confused with lexical reduction (also an outcome of language restriction). The latter phenomenon brings about a hole in the lexical stock (which, as Trudgill 1983: Chapter 6 has argued, is easily filled by compensatory borrowing from the majority language). If sociolectal reduction (when completed) entails a loss of social significance (*sontaient*, possessive *à*, *ça fait que*, *sur* meaning *chez* all have popular and informal connotations), it does not, however, involve a loss of notional meaning, since the speaker is left with at least one variant to express whatever notional meaning the formal and informal variants convey. Another way of describing sociolectal reduction would be to say that it entails a levelling of the indicators of sociolects and of the markers of registers through an elimination of non-standard variants. It is this latter aspect of sociolectal reduction which makes the speech of our restricted speakers sound like that of learners of French as a second language in an institutional setting. This similarity should not be over-stressed, however, as it is clear that the restricted speakers will on occasion use certain non-standard variants that they cannot have picked up but from the local vernacular, e.g. *m'as* (Chapter 8) or the verbal expression *avoir été*, a variant of *aller* 'to go' (Mougeon, Heller, Beniak, and Canale 1984), and hence are not fully equatable to classroom second-language learners of French.

12.1.4. The structural integrity of minority languages

We shall end this section on the effect of French-language-use restriction with an examination of an issue which was only partially tackled in Chapters 9 and 10, namely whether members of a linguistic minority who use the minority language roughly on a par with the majority language speak it in a form which suggests a loss of structural integrity (the latter being defined as departures from the conservative norm spoken by individuals who are dominant or unilingual in the minority language). The reader will recall that our examination of two cases of interference-induced change (one covert, the other overt) revealed that both types of change were found not only in the speech of the restricted speakers but also in that of the semi-restricted speakers, and even in that of the unrestricted speakers from the Franco-Ontarian minority communities. We pointed out that these findings stood in sharp contrast to those of Poplack (1982), who examined the speech of members of New York's Puerto Rican community and discovered through an analysis of plural marking and verb usage that their speech contained no evidence of influence from English.

Poplack's analysis, however, was not confined to a search for evidence of interference from the majority language. She also examined her data with a view to finding out whether the high levels of contact exhibited by her balanced-bilingual subjects had had an accelerating effect on internal linguistic change. Her search for such evidence turned out to be negative as well. As concerns plurality marking and verb usage, the speech of her balanced-bilingual subjects was found not to differ from that of her Spanish-dominant subjects in any way that might suggest an acceleration of linguistic change. Our own research on internal simplification contradicts Poplack's findings once again, since it will be recalled that 3pl. levelling (incidentally an aspect of French which involves both plural marking and verb usage) was almost as frequent in the speech of the semi-restricted speakers (the equivalent of Poplack's balanced bilinguals) as in that of the restricted speakers. The same can be said for our investigation of two instances of ambiguous change (i.e. substitution of *à* and *à la maison de* for *chez*), neither of which was confined to the speech of the restricted speakers (both were also observable in the speech of the semi-restricted speakers).

To sum up, we agree with Poplack (1982) that the study of linguistic change (whether internal or external) in minority languages needs to be based on an analysis of a corpus gathered according to the rules and principles of socio-linguistic methodology. Otherwise linguists will run the risk of making exaggerated or unwarranted claims about the purported loss of structural integrity shown by such languages. Our research, however, suggests that adhering to the principles of sociolinguistic research does not guarantee that the data thus gathered will necessarily support the view that balanced bilingualism and roughly equal language use have no negative effect on the structural integrity of the minority language under study. Obviously, more research needs to be conducted on this topic. Whatever its results turn out to be, it matters perhaps more that we change our perception of the types of change which arise in contact settings along the lines already suggested above (i.e. emphasize their functional adequacy), than strive to find the kind of evidence sought by Poplack (1982), which, although it certainly may be politically more palatable than ours, may prove more elusive than one thinks.

12.2. Locality of residence

As can be seen in Table 12.1, this parameter turned to be an important predictor of the different types of change under study. It was selected no fewer than seven times and consistently ranked first or second. In fact, it may be deemed to have been selected an eighth time, since, in our analysis of the change from *à* to *sur*, Hawkesbury turned out to have a 'knockout' effect. Furthermore, in the analyses of variation that were not based on the VARBRUL programme, we gathered supplementary evidence that locality of residence had an effect on variation (the hard-to-explain confinement of *sontaient* to Cornwall French).

As far as the effect of this parameter is concerned, a general pattern emerges from our research. It is characterized by a binary contrast between the Hawkesbury speakers on the one hand, and the speakers from the three minority communities on the other. More specifically, Hawkesbury French stands out as being virtually devoid of instances of the different types of internal and contact-induced change which we have attested, whereas the varieties of French spoken in Cornwall, North Bay, and Pembroke all feature these changes without there being much evidence that they do so to a signifi- cantly different degree (in only one instance, levelling of the distinctive 3pl. verb forms, did we find that the rate of change differed appreciably from one minority community to the other and in a way which was consistent with the differential degree of local francophone concentration).

In short, the investigation of the role of locality of residence has amply demonstrated that we were justified in positing that Hawkesbury French would provide us with an ideal intra-community bench-mark norm to assess the linguistic effects of language contact and restriction.

12.3. Social class

Turning to social class, we can see in Table 12.1 that this parameter was selected only four times (3pl. levelling, *vas* vs. *vais* as main verbs (V), *so* vs. *ça fait que* and *alors*, and *ça fait que* vs. *alors*) and ranked number 4, 2, 3, and 4 respect- ively. In the analyses of variation which did not rely on the VARBRUL programme, we gathered additional evidence of a social-class effect with respect to three other variables (*sontaient* vs. *étaient*, possessive *à* vs. *de*, and *sur* vs. *chez*). The relatively modest predictive power of social class may be surprising to sociolinguists who are accustomed to working in unilingual settings, where this parameter or some variant of it (e.g. position on the linguistic market) has almost always been shown to be a key predictor—and in many instances the best predictor—of variation (Guy 1988*b*; Kemp 1981).

One explanation for our own findings is that the phenomenon of sociolectal reduction (which amounts to a lessening of the social stratification of speech) may take away from the predictive power of social class. One supporting bit of evidence for this explanation is the fact that the best ranking for social class (i.e. second) was found precisely when sociolectal reduction was aborted (i.e. in the case of *vas* vs. *vais* as main verbs). A second explanation is that our investigation of the predictive power of social class was centred not only on cases of traditional variation (i.e. variation which dates back to earlier stages of the language and is observable in monolingual settings), but also on cases which are the direct outcome of language contact and restriction (hence which are new to the language and go unattested in monolingual settings). As concerns these latter cases of variation, six in all (3pl. vs. 3sg. verb forms, *à la maison de* vs. *chez*, *à* vs. *chez*, *à la maison* vs. *chez*, *à* vs. *sur*, and *so* vs. *ça fait que* and *alors*), it can be pointed out that social class was found to have either a secondary effect or no effect at all. What seems to be at stake in the case of innovations owing to language contact or restriction (unmarked 3pl. verb forms, *à la maison de* or *à* meaning *chez*, and *so*) is some measure of differential monitoring across social classes by the innovators, i.e. the restricted or semi-restricted speakers. Note that the rise of *so* seems to have had a disruptive effect on the social stratification of *ça fait que* vs. *alors* (a traditional case of variation), since *ça fait que* is losing its status of indicator of working-class speech. It is quite clear, however, that *so* has taken over that function in these speakers' variety of French. As for those innovations for which we found no effect of social class (*à* > *sur* and *chez* > *à la maison*), we note that they were both the product of interference (overt and covert respectively). Such innovations may be more difficult to monitor due to the fact that they involve the application of a more subtle type of language transfer than, say, lexical borrowing.

12.4. Sex

Let us finally briefly consider the effect of sex. This parameter was selected six times, its rank varying from 1 to 5 (3pl. levelling, *vas* vs. *vais* as main verbs, *vais* vs. *vas* and *m'as*, *m'as* vs. *vas* and *vais*, *so* vs. *ça fait que* and *alors*, and *ça fait que* vs. *alors*). Furthermore, when we did not perform a VARBRUL analysis, we found evidence that sex had an effect on variation in connection with an additional two cases (*sontaient*—all communities—and possessive *à*). In our research, then, sex has turned out to be a non-negligible predictor of variation. Labov (1972: 303) discovered that sex did not always pattern the same way: at times females were found to be leading in the use of the standard variant (the so-called 'classical' effect of sex on variation); at other times male speakers were found to do so. This led him to opine that the only thing that can be safely assumed is that sex differentiation often plays a role in linguistic change! The results of sociolinguistic research on Montreal French seem to support Labov's contention about the difficulty of predicting the behaviour of men and women in linguistic variation. Thus Kemp (1981) reports that older women conform more to the standard than older men, while the opposite is true for younger men and women. The findings of our own research are as follows: every time sex was selected by the VARBRUL programme, we found the classical effect, the non-standard variant showing a higher concentration in male speech; when we did not perform a VARBRUL analysis and there was evidence that sex had an effect on variation, we found the classical effect (*sontaient*—all communities) and the reverse or 'unclassical' effect, females leading in non-standard usage (possessive *à*). So, in the majority of cases where sex was found or suspected to play a role in variation (seven out of eight), the classical pattern of variation according to sex was found. Our findings, then, may be looked upon as a significant piece of supporting evidence for the view expressed by sociolinguists (e.g. Chambers and Trudgill 1980; Trudgill 1974) who believe that, in societies where women hold a subordinate position, they will tend to favour what they perceive as prestigious variants (usually standard variants).

It should be borne in mind, however, that our findings are consistent with a more general sociological trend which differentiates Franco-Ontarians from French Quebecers. The former have by and large retained the traditional ways and values of French-Canadian society to a greater extent than the latter. For instance, there is a significantly higher level of church attendance among Franco-Ontarians than among French Quebecers. Also, in the area of language, several features which are nowadays relegated to the speech of the older generations or to that of rural speakers in Quebec (e.g. aspirated *h*, dental *r*) are still present in the speech of the younger Franco-Ontarian generations (Thomas 1986). In other words, our findings concerning sex differentiation in Ontarian French may reflect the fact that Franco-Ontarian women are somewhat lagging behind Québécois women in the redefinition of their traditional roles. Should Franco-Ontarian women catch up to their Québécois counterparts, inconsistencies in the sexual patterning of variation similar to those observed by Kemp may show up in future sociolinguistic studies of Ontarian French.

References

ALLAIRE, YVAN, and TOULOUSE, JEAN-MARIE (1973), *Situation socioéconomique des Franco-Ontariens* (2 vols.; Ottawa: Association canadienne-française de l'Ontario).

AMASTAE, JON, and ELÍAS-OLIVARES, LUCÍA (eds.) (1982), *Spanish in the United States: Sociolinguistic Aspects* (Cambridge: Cambridge University Press).

ANDERSEN, ROGER W. (1982), 'Determining the Linguistic Attributes of Language Attrition', in Richard D. Lambert and Barbara F. Freed (eds.), *The Loss of Language Skills* (Rowley, Mass.: Newbury House Publishers), 83-118.

ANDERSON, JAMES M. (1973), *Structural Aspects of Language Change* (London: Longman).

APPEL, RENÉ and MUYSKEN, PIETER (1987), *Language Contact and Bilingualism* (London: Edward Arnold).

ARNOPOULOS, SHEILA McLEOD (1982), *Hors du Québec point de salut?* (Montreal: Éditions Libre Expression).

BAKER, PHILIP, and CORNE, CHRIS (1987), 'Histoire sociale et créolisation à la Réunion et à Maurice', *Revue québécoise de linguistique théorique et appliquée*, 6/2, 71-87.

BARBAUD, PHILIPPE (1984), *Le Choc des patois en Nouvelle-France: Essai sur l'histoire de la francisation au Canada* (Sillery, Quebec: Presses de l'Université du Québec).

BARBEAU, VICTOR (1970), *Le Français du Canada* (Quebec: Librairie Garneau).

BARON, NAOMI (1977), *Language Acquisition and Historical Change* (Amsterdam: North Holland).

BAUCHE, HENRI (1929), *Le Langage populaire* (3rd edn.; Paris: Payot).

BEAUCHEMIN, NORMAND, MARTEL, PIERRE, and THÉORET, MICHEL (1983), *Vocabulaire du québécois parlé en Estrie: Fréquence, dispersion, usage* (Recherches sociolinguistiques dans la région de Sherbrooke, Document de travail No 20; Sherbrooke: Université de Sherbrooke).

BEAUPRÉ, CHRISTIANE (1988), 'Entrevue avec le nouveau président de la Commission des services en français: La loi 8 est entre bonnes mains', *L'Express de Toronto*, 13/27, 1.

BEEBE, LESLIE M. (1988), 'Five Sociolinguistic Approaches to Second Language Acquisition', in Leslie M. Beebe (ed.), *Issues in Second Language Acquisition* (New York: Newbury House), 43-77.

BÉLISLE, LOUIS-ALEXANDRE (1974), *Dictionnaire général de la langue française au Canada* (Montreal: Librairie Beauchemin Ltée).

BENIAK, ÉDOUARD, CAREY, STEPHEN, and MOUGEON, RAYMOND (1984), 'A Sociolinguistic and Ethnographic Approach to Albertan French and its Implications for French-as-a-first-language Pedagogy', *The Canadian Modern Language Review*, 41/2, 308-14.

—— and MOUGEON, RAYMOND (1989), 'Recherches sociolinguistiques sur la variabilité en français ontarien', in Raymond Mougeon and Édouard Beniak (eds.), 69-104.

—— —— and CÔTÉ, NORMAND (1980), 'Acquisition of French Pronominal Verbs by Groups of Young Monolingual and Bilingual Canadian Students', in William C.

McCormack and Herbert J. Izzo (eds.), *The Sixth LACUS Forum* (Columbia, Sth. Ca.: Hornbeam Press, Inc.), 355-68.

BERRENDONNER, ALAIN, LE GUERN, MICHEL, and PUECH, GILBERT (1983), *Principes de grammaire polylectale* (Lyons: Presses Universitaires de Lyon).

BICKERTON, DEREK (1981), *Roots of Language* (Ann Arbor, Mi.: Karoma).

—— (1984*a*), 'The Language Bioprogram Hypothesis and Second Language Acquisition', in William E. Rutherford (ed.), *Language Universals and Second Language Acquisition* (Amsterdam/Philadelphia: John Benjamins), 141-61.

—— (1984*b*), 'The Language Bioprogram Hypothesis', *The Behavioral and Brain Sciences*, 7, 173-221.

BLOCH, OSCAR (1917), *Les Parlers des Vosges méridionales* (Paris: Librairie Ancienne M. Champion).

—— and WARTBURG, WALTHER VON (1950), *Dictionnaire étymologique de la langue française* (Paris: Presses Universitaires de France).

BOURDIEU, PIERRE (1982), *Ce que parler veut dire* (Paris: Fayard).

BOURHIS, RICHARD Y. (ed.) (1984), *Conflict and Language Planning in Quebec* (Clevedon, England: Multilingual Matters).

BRONCKART, JEAN-PIERRE (1976), *Genèse et organisation des formes verbales chez l'enfant* (Brussels: Dessart et Mardaga).

BROUSSARD, JAMES FRANCIS (1942), *Louisiana Creole Dialect* (Romance Language Series, 5; Baton Rouge: Louisiana State University).

BRUNOT, FERDINAND (1909), *Histoire de la langue française des origines à 1900*, iii. *La formation de la langue classique (1600–1660)* (Paris: Librairie Armand Colin).

—— and BRUNEAU, CHARLES (1969), *Grammaire historique de la langue française* (Paris: Masson et Cie).

CANALE, MICHAEL, MOUGEON, RAYMOND, and BÉLANGER, MONIQUE (1978), 'Analogical Leveling of the Auxiliary *être* in Ontarian French', in Margarita Suñer (ed.), *Contemporary Studies in Romance Linguistics* (Washington, DC: Georgetown University Press), 41–61.

—— —— —— and MAIN, CHRISTINE (1977), 'Recherches en dialectologie franco-ontarienne', *Working Papers on Bilingualism*, 14, 1-20.

—— —— and BENIAK, ÉDOUARD (1978), 'Acquisition of Some Grammatical Elements in English and French by Monolingual and Bilingual Canadian Students', *The Canadian Modern Language Review*, 34/3, 505-24.

—— —— HELLER, MONICA, and BÉLANGER, MONIQUE (1987), *Programmes dans les écoles élémentaires de langue française pour les élèves de compétence inégale en français* (Report submitted to the Ontario Ministry of Education, Toronto).

CASSANO, PAUL (1977), 'Le Français de Windsor', *Bulletin du Centre de recherche en civilisation canadienne-française de l'Université d'Ottawa*, 14, 27-30.

CASTONGUAY, CHARLES (1979), 'Exogamie et anglicisation chez les minorités canadiennes-françaises', *Canadian Journal of Sociology and Anthropology*, 16, 21-31.

—— (1981), *Exogamie et anglicisation dans les régions de Montréal, Hull, Ottawa et Sudbury* (Quebec: International Center for Research on Bilingualism).

—— (1984), 'Le Dilemme démolinguistique du Québec', in Pierre Vadeboncœur (ed.), *Douze essais sur l'avenir du français au Québec* (Documentation du Conseil de la langue française, 14; Quebec: Éditeur officiel du Québec), 13-36.

CAZABON, BENOÎT and FRENETTE, NORMAND (1982), *Le Français parlé en situation minoritaire*, ii (Quebec: International Center for Research on Bilingualism).

CHAMBERS, JACK K., and TRUDGILL, PETER (1980), *Dialectology* (Cambridge: Cambridge University Press).

CHAPERON-LOR, DIANE (1974), *Une minorité s'explique* (Toronto: OISE Press).

CHAUDENSON, ROBERT (1973), 'Pour une étude comparée des créoles et parlers français d'outre-mer: Survivance et innovation', *Revue de linguistique romane*, 37, 342-71.

—— (1974), *Le Lexique du parler créole de la Réunion* (2 vols.; Paris: Librairie Honoré Champion).

—— (1979), *Les Créoles français* (Paris, Nathan).

—— (1982), 'Review article' (Bickerton, Derek (1981), *Roots of Language* (Ann Arbor, Mi.: Karoma)), *Studies in Second Language Acquisition*, 5/1, 82-102.

—— (1989a), 'Préface', in Raymond Mougeon and Édouard Beniak (eds.), pp. vii-ix.

—— (1989b), *Créoles et enseignement du français* (Paris: L'Harmattan).

—— VÉRONIQUE, DANIEL, and VALLI, ANDRÉ (1986), 'The Dynamics of Linguistic Systems and the Acquisition of French as a Second Language', *Studies in Second Language Acquisition*, 8/13, 277-92.

CHESHIRE, JENNY (1982), *Variation in an English Dialect: A Sociolinguistic Study* (Cambridge: Cambridge University Press).

CHOQUETTE, ROBERT (1980), *L'Ontario français* (Montreal: Études Vivantes).

CHURCHILL, STACY (1976), 'National Linguistic Minorities: The Franco-Ontarian Educational Renaissance', *Prospects*, 5, 439-49.

—— QUAZI, SAEED, and FRENETTE, NORMAND (1985), *Éducation et besoins des Franco-ontariens: Le diagnostic d'un système d'éducation* (2 vols.; Toronto: Le Conseil de l'éducation franco-ontarienne).

CLARK, EVE (1985), 'The Acquisition of Romance, with Special Reference to French', in Dan I. Slobin (ed.), 687-782.

CLIFT, DOMINIQUE, and ARNOPOULOS, SHEILA McLEOD (1979), *Le Fait anglais au Québec* (Montreal: Éditions Libre Expression).

COHEN, MARCEL (1967), *Histoire d'une langue: Le français* (3rd edn.; Paris: Éditions Sociales).

COLE, ROGER L. (1975), 'Divergent and Convergent Attitudes toward the Alsatian Dialect', *Anthropological Linguistics*, 17, 293-304.

COLPRON, GILLES (1973), *Les Anglicismes au Québec* (Montreal: Librairie Beauchemin Ltée).

CONWELL, MARILYN J., and JUILLAND, ALPHONSE (1963), *Louisiana French Grammar* (The Hague: Mouton).

CORBEIL, JEAN-CLAUDE (1976), 'Origine historique de la situation linguistique québécoise', *Langue française*, 31, 6-19.

CRESTOR, RICHARD (1987), *Annou palé kréyòl* (Martinique: Richard Crestor Éditions).

D'COSTA, RONALD B. (1972), *L'Accessibilité aux études post-secondaires pour la population francophone de l'Ontario* (Ottawa: The Queen's Printer).

DE BOISREGARD, NICOLAS ANDRY (1972), *Réflexions sur l'usage présent de la langue françoise* (Geneva: Slatkine Reprints; repr. of the original Paris/Geneva edns. of 1689 and 1693).

DEBRIE, RENÉ (1982), 'D'une tournure originale et mal expliquée pour traduire "je vais" en picard', *Éklitra*, 16, 7-11.

—— (1988), 'Note de phonétique', *Éklitra*, 22, 15.

DE LA CHAUSSÉE, FRANÇOIS (1977), *Initiation à la morphologie historique de l'ancien français* (Paris: Klincksieck).

DESHAIES, DENISE, MARTIN, CLAIRE, and NOËL, DANY (1981), 'Régularisation et analogie dans le système verbal en français parlé dans la ville de Québec', in David Sankoff and Henrietta Cedergren (eds.), 411-18.

DESJARLAIS, LIONEL, and CARRIER, MAURICE (1975), *Étude de l'enseignement de l'anglais langue seconde dans les écoles franco-ontariennes* (Toronto: Ontario Ministry of Education).

—— CYR, HERVÉ, BRÛLÉ, GÉRALD, and GAUTHIER, VINCENT (1980), *L'Élève parlant peu ou pas français dans les écoles de langue française* (Toronto: Ontario Ministry of Education).

DESSUREAULT-DOBER, DIANE (1975), '*Ça fait que*: Opérateur logique et marqueur d'interaction' (unpublished MA thesis; Montreal: Département de linguistique, Université du Québec à Montréal).

DIONNE, NARCISSE-E. (1974), *Le Parler populaire des Canadiens français* (Quebec: Les Presses de l'Université Laval).

DORIAN, NANCY C. (1978), 'The Fate of Morphological Complexity in Language Death: Evidence from East Sutherland Gaelic', *Language*, 54/3, 590-609.

—— (1981), *Language Death: The Life Cycle of a Scottish Gaelic Dialect* (Philadelphia: University of Pennsylvania Press).

—— (1982), 'Defining the Speech Community to Include its Working Margins', in Suzanne Romaine (ed.), 25-33.

—— (1985), 'Radical Asymmetries in the Skills of Speakers of Obsolescent Languages' (invited paper presented at the Centre for Franco-Ontarian Studies, The Ontario Institute for Studies in Education, Toronto, 1 May).

—— (1986), 'Gathering Language Data in Terminal Speech Communities', in Joshua A. Fishman, Andrée Tabouret-Keller, *et al.* (eds.), *The Fergusonian Impact*, ii. *Sociolinguistics and the Sociology of Language* (Berlin: Mouton de Gruyter), 555-75.

—— (1987), 'The Value of Language-maintenance Efforts that are Unlikely to Succeed', *International Journal of the Sociology of Language*, 68, 57-67.

—— (ed.) (1989), *Investigating Obsolescence: Studies in Language Contraction and Death* (Cambridge: Cambridge University Press).

DRAPEAU, LYNN (1982), 'Les Paradigmes *sontaient*-tu régularisés?', in Claire Lefebvre (ed.), *La Syntaxe comparée du français standard et populaire: Approches formelle et fonctionnelle*, ii (Quebec: Office de la langue française), 127-47.

DRESSLER, WOLFGANG, and WODAK-LEODOLTER, RUTH (1977), 'Language Preservation and Language Death in Brittany', *International Journal of the Sociology of Language*, 12, 33-44.

DUMAS, DENIS (1974), 'La Fusion vocalique en français québécois', *Montreal Working Papers in Linguistics*, 2, 23-51.

—— (1977), 'Phonologie des réductions vocaliques en français québécois' (unpublished Ph.D. thesis; Montreal: Département de linguistique, Université de Montréal).

FASOLD, RALPH (1984), *The Sociolinguistics of Society* (Oxford: Basil Blackwell).

Fédération des francophones hors Québec (1978), *Deux poids deux mesures. Les francophones hors Québec et les anglophones au Québec: Un dossier comparatif* (Ottawa: Fédération des francophones hors Québec).

FISHMAN, JOSHUA A. (1987), 'Language Spread and Language Policy for Endangered Languages', in Peter H. Lowenberg (ed.), *Language Spread and Language Policy:*

Issues, Implications, and Case Studies (Washington, DC: Georgetown University Press), 1-15.

FISHMAN, JOSHUA A., GERTNER, MICHAEL H., LOWY, ESTHER G., and MILAN, WILLIAM G. (eds.) (1985), *The Rise and Fall of the Ethnic Revival: Perspectives of Language and Ethnicity* (Berlin: Mouton Publishers).

FLIKEID, KARIN (1989), 'Recherches sociolinguistiques sur les parlers acadiens du Nouveau-Brunswick et de la Nouvelle-Écosse', in Raymond Mougeon and Édouard Beniak (eds.), 183-99.

FOUCHÉ, PIERRE (1967), *Le Verbe français: Étude morphologique* (Paris: Éditions Klincksieck).

FOULET, LUCIEN (1977), *Petite syntaxe de l'ancien français* (rev. 3rd edn.; Paris: Librairie Honoré Champion).

FOURNIER, ROBERT (1987), 'Le Bioprogramme et les français créoles: Vérification d'une hypothèse' (unpublished Ph.D. thesis; Sherbrooke: Département d'études françaises, Université de Sherbrooke).

FREI, HENRI (1971), *La Grammaire des fautes* (Geneva: Slatkine Reprints; repr. of the original 1929 edn., Paris/Geneva: Geuthner-Kundis).

GAFFIOT, FÉLIX (1934), *Dictionnaire illustré latin français* (Paris: Librairie Hachette).

GAGNÉ, GILLES (1980), *Pédagogie de la langue ou pédagogie de la parole?* (Montreal: PPMF primaire, Université de Montréal).

—— and BARBAUD, PHILIPPE (1981), 'Remarques sur la langue parlée d'enfants de six–sept ans', in Gilles Gagné, Michel Pagé, *et al.* (eds.), *Études sur la langue parlée des enfants québécois (1969–1980)* (Montreal: Les Presses de l'Université de Montréal), 49-69.

GAL, SUSAN (1984), 'Phonological Style in Bilingualism: The Interaction of Structure and Use', in Deborah Schiffrin (ed.), *Meaning, Form, and Use in Context: Linguistic Applications* (Washington, DC: Georgetown University Press), 290-302.

GESNER, B. EDWARD (1979), *Étude morphosyntaxique du parler acadien de la Baie Sainte-Marie, Nouvelle-Écosse, Canada* (Quebec: International Center for Research on Bilingualism).

GIACALONE RAMAT, ANNA (1979), 'Language Function and Language Change in Minority Languages', *Journal of Italian Linguistics*, 4, 141-62.

GOODMAN, MORRIS (1964), *A Comparative Study of Creole French Dialects* (The Hague: Mouton).

GOUGENHEIM, GEORGES (1929), *La Langue populaire dans le premier quart du XIXe siècle d'après le Petit Dictionnaire du Peuple de J. C. L. P. Desgranges (1821)* (Paris: Société d'édition «Les Belles Lettres»).

—— (1951), *Grammaire de la langue française du seizième siècle* (Lyons: IAC).

—— (1971), *Étude sur les périphrases verbales de la langue française* (Paris: Librairie A.-G. Nizet).

GOVERNMENT OF CANADA (1969), *Report of the Royal Commission on Bilingualism and Biculturalism* (Ottawa: The Queen's Printer).

GOVERNMENT OF ONTARIO (1984), *Ontario Universities: Options and Futures* (Toronto: Queen's Printer for Ontario).

—— (1985), *Education Act* (Toronto: Queen's Printer for Ontario).

—— (1986), *French Language Services Act* (Toronto: Queen's Printer for Ontario).

GRÉGOIRE, ANTOINE (1968), *L'Apprentissage du langage*, ii (Paris: Société d'édition «Les Belles Lettres»; repr. of the original 1947 edn., Paris: Droz).

GREIMAS, ALGIRDAS J. (1968), *Dictionnaire de l'ancien français* (Paris: Larousse).

GREVISSE, MAURICE (1975), *Le Bon Usage* (rev. 10th edn.; Paris/Gembloux: Éditions Duculot).

—— (1986), *Le Bon Usage* (rev. 12th edn.; Paris/Gembloux: Éditions Duculot).

GUIRAUD, PIERRE (1973), *Le Français populaire* (3rd edn.; Paris: Presses Universitaires de France).

GUMPERZ, JOHN J., and HERNÁNDEZ-CHAVEZ, ÉDUARDO (1972), 'Bilingualism, Bidialectalism, and Classroom Interaction', in Courtney B. Cazden, Vera P. John, and Dell Hymes (eds.), *Functions of Language in the Classroom* (New York: Teachers College Press), 84-108.

—— and WILSON, ROBERT (1971), 'Convergence and Creolization: A Case from the Indo-Aryan/Dravidian Border', in Dell Hymes (ed.), *Pidginization and Creolization of Languages* (Cambridge: Cambridge University Press), 151-67.

GUY, GREGORY (1988a), 'Variation and the Hearer: The Role of Perception in the Creation of "Functional" Constraints' (paper presented at NWAV-XVII, Université de Montréal, 28-30 Oct.).

—— (1988b), 'Language and Social Class', in Frederick J. Newmeyer (ed.), *Linguistics: The Cambridge Survey*, iv. *Language: The Socio-cultural Context* (Cambridge: Cambridge University Press), 37-63.

HAADSMA, R. A., and NUCHELMANS, J. (1966), *Précis de latin vulgaire* (2nd edn.; Groningen: J. B. Wolters).

HAASE, A. (1969), *Syntaxe française du XVIIe siècle* (Paris: Librairie Delagrave).

HARLEY, BIRGIT (1984), 'How Good Is their French?', *Language and Society*, 12, 55-60.

—— (1986), *Age in Second Language Acquisition* (Clevedon, England: Multilingual Matters).

—— and SWAIN, MERRILL (1978), 'An Analysis of the Verb System Used by Young Learners of French', *Interlanguage Studies Bulletin*, 3, 35-79.

HARRIS, MARTIN (1978), *The Evolution of French Syntax: A Comparative Approach* (London: Longman).

HAUGEN, EINAR (1969), *The Norwegian Language in America: A Study in Bilingual Behavior* (Bloomington: Indiana University Press; repr. of the original 1953 edn., Philadelphia: University of Pennsylvania Press).

—— (1977), 'Norm and Deviation in Bilingual Communities', in Peter A. Hornby (ed.), *Bilingualism: Psychological, Social, and Educational Implications* (New York: Academic Press), 91-102.

—— McCLURE, J. DERRICK, and THOMSON, DERICK (eds.) (1981), *Minority Languages Today* (Edinburgh: Edinburgh University Press).

HÉBRARD, PIERRE, and MOUGEON, RAYMOND (1975), 'La Langue parlée entre les parents et les enfants: Un facteur crucial dans l'acquisition linguistique de l'enfant dans un milieu bilingue', *Working Papers on Bilingualism*, 7, 52-70.

HELLER, MONICA (1982), 'Language, Ethnicity and Politics in Quebec' (unpublished Ph.D. thesis; Berkeley: Department of Linguistics, University of California).

—— (1984), 'Language and Ethnicity in a Toronto French-language School', *Canadian Ethnic Studies*, 16, 1-14.

—— (1988), 'Strategic Ambiguity: Code-switching in the Management of Conflict', in Monica Heller (ed.), *Codeswitching: Anthropological and Sociolinguistic Perspectives* (Berlin: Mouton de Gruyter), 77-97.

—— (1989), 'Variation dans l'emploi du français et de l'anglais par les élèves des écoles de langue française de Toronto', in Raymond Mougeon and Édouard Beniak (eds.), 153-68.

HELLER, MONICA, and SWAIN, MERRILL (1985), *Le Rôle de l'école de langue française dans la formation de l'identité française à Toronto* (report submitted to the Multiculturalism Directorate, Secretary of State, Government of Canada, Ottawa).

HERMAN, JOSEPH (1967), *Le Latin vulgaire* (Paris: Presses Universitaires de France).

HIGHFIELD, ARNOLD R. (1979), *The French dialect of Saint Thomas, U.S. Virgin Islands* (Ann Arbor, Mi.: Karoma).

HILL, JANE, and HILL, KENNETH (1977), 'Language Death and Relexification', *International Journal of the Sociology of Language*, 12, 55-69.

HOOPER, JOAN B. (1976), 'Word Frequency in Lexical Diffusion and the Source of Morphophonological Change', in William M. Christie, Jr. (ed.), *Current Progress in Historical Linguistics* (Amsterdam: North Holland), 95-105.

—— (1980), 'Child Morphology and Morphophonemic Change', in Jacek Fisiak (ed.), *Historical Morphology* (The Hague: Mouton), 157-87.

HUDSON, RICHARD A. (1980), *Sociolinguistics* (Cambridge: Cambridge University Press).

HUGUET, EDMOND (1925), *Dictionnaire de la langue française du seizième siècle*, i (Paris: Librairie Ancienne E. Champion).

—— (1967), *Dictionnaire de la langue française du seizième siècle*, vii (Paris: Didier).

HULL, ALEXANDER (1956), 'The Franco-Canadian Dialect of Windsor, Ontario: A Preliminary Study', *Orbis*, 5, 35-60.

—— (1979), 'Affinités entre les variétés du français', in Albert Valdman, Robert Chaudenson, and Gabriel Manessy (eds.), 165-80.

JUILLAND, ALPHONSE, BRODIN, DOROTHY, and DAVIDOVITCH, CATHERINE (1970), *Frequency Dictionary of French Words* (The Hague: Mouton).

JUNEAU, MARCEL (1972), *Contribution à l'histoire de la prononciation française au Québec* (Quebec: Les Presses de l'Université Laval).

—— (1976), *La Jument qui crotte de l'argent* (Quebec: Les Presses de l'Université Laval).

KARTTUNEN, FRANCES (1977), 'Finnish in America: A Case Study in Monogenerational Language Change', in Ben G. Blount and Mary Sanches (eds.), *Sociocultural Dimensions of Language Change* (New York: Academic Press), 173-84.

KEMP, WILLIAM (1981), 'Major Sociolinguistic Patterns in Montreal French', in David Sankoff and Henrietta Cedergren (eds.), 3-16.

KENEMER, VIRGINIA LYNN (1982), *Le 'Français populaire' and French as a Second Language: A Comparative Study of Language Simplification* (Quebec: International Center for Research on Bilingualism).

KING, RUTH (1985), 'Linguistic Variation and Language Contact: A Study of French Spoken in Four Newfoundland Communities', in Henry J. Warkentyne (ed.), 211-31.

KIPARSKY, PAUL (1980), 'Concluding Statement', in Elizabeth C. Traugott, Rebecca Labrum, and Susan Shepherd (eds.), *Papers from the 4th International Conference on Historical Linguistics* (Amsterdam: John Benjamins), 409-17.

KLEIN-ANDREU, FLORA (1980), 'A Quantitative Study of Syntactic and Pragmatic Indications of Change in the Spanish of Bilinguals in the U.S.', in William Labov (ed.), 69-82.

—— (1985), 'La cuestión del anglicismo: Apriorismos y métodos', *Thesaurus* (Boletín del Instituto Caro y Cuervo, Bogotá), 40, 1-16.

LABOV, WILLIAM (1964), 'Stages in the Acquisition of Standard English', in Roger W.

Shuy (ed.), *Social Dialects and Language Learning* (Champaign, Ill.: National Council of Teachers of English), 473-99.

—— (1972), *Sociolinguistic Patterns* (Philadelphia: University of Pennsylvania Press).

—— (1980a), 'The Social Origins of Sound Change', in William Labov (ed.), 251-65.

—— (ed.) (1980b), *Locating Language in Time and Space* (New York: Academic Press).

—— (1981), 'What Can Be Learned about Change in Progress from Synchronic Description?', in David Sankoff and Henrietta Cedergren (eds.), 177-99.

LA FOLLETTE, JAMES (1969), *Étude linguistique de quatre contes folkloriques du Canada français* (Quebec: Les Presses de l'Université Laval).

LAMY, PAUL (1977), 'Education and Survival: French Language Education and Linguistic Assimilation' (paper presented at the annual meeting of the Western Association of Sociology and Anthropology, Calgary, Alberta, December).

LAPOINTE, JEAN, POULIN, R., and THÉRIAULT, J. YVON (1987), 'La Minorité francophone de Welland et ses rapports avec les institutions' (report submitted to the Office of the Commissioner of Official Languages, Ottawa).

LAROUSSE, PIERRE (1966), *Dictionnaire du français contemporain* (Paris: Librairie Larousse).

La Société du parler français au Canada (1968), *Glossaire du parler français au Canada* (Quebec: Les Presses de l'Université Laval).

LASS, ROGER (1980), *On Explaining Language Change* (Cambridge: Cambridge University Press).

LÉARD, JEAN-MARIE (1983), 'Le Statut de *fak* en québécois: Un simple équivalent de *alors?*', *Travaux de linguistique québécoise*, 4, 59-100.

LE BLANC, JEAN-CLAUDE (1988), 'Debunking a Myth', *Language and Society*, 22, 24-5.

LEFEBVRE, CLAIRE (1980), 'Variation in Plural Marking: The Case of Cuzco Quechua' (unpublished manuscript; Montreal: Département de linguistique, Université du Québec à Montréal).

Le Nouveau Bescherelle (1980) (Montreal: Hurtubise HMH).

LIEBERSON, STANLEY (1972), 'Bilingualism in Montreal: A Demographic Analysis', in Joshua A. Fishman (ed.), *Advances in the Sociology of Language: Selected Studies and Applications*, ii (The Hague: Mouton), 231-55.

LITTRÉ, ÉMILE (1967), *Dictionnaire de la langue française*, iv (Paris: Gallimard/Hachette).

—— (1968a), *Dictionnaire de la langue française*, ii (Paris: Gallimard/Hachette).

—— (1968b), *Dictionnaire de la langue française*, vii (Paris: Gallimard/Hachette).

MACKEY, WILLIAM F. (1970), 'Interference, Integration and the Synchronic Fallacy', in James E. Alatis (ed.), *Bilingualism and Language Contact* (Washington, DC: Georgetown University Press), 195-227.

MANESSY, GABRIEL, and WALD, PAUL (1984), *Le Français en Afrique noire tel qu'on le parle, tel qu'on l'écrit* (Paris: L'Harmattan).

MARTINET, ANDRÉ (1969), *Le Français sans fard* (Paris: Presses Universitaires de France).

MAXWELL, THOMAS R. (1977), *The Invisible French: The French in Metropolitan Toronto* (Waterloo, Ont.: Wilfrid Laurier University Press).

MÉNAGE, GILLES (1972), *Observations sur la langue française* (Geneva: Slatkine Reprints; repr. of the original 1675-6 edn., Paris: C. Barbin).

MERTZ, ELIZABETH (1989), 'Sociolinguistic Creativity: Cape Breton Gaelic's Linguistic "Tip"', in Nancy C. Dorian (ed.), 103-16.

MILROY, JAMES, and MILROY, LESLEY (1985), 'Linguistic Change, Social Network and Speaker Innovation', *Journal of Linguistics*, 21, 339-84.

MORIN, YVES-CHARLES (1981), 'Où sont passés les *s* finals de l'ancien français?', in David Sankoff and Henrietta Cedergren (eds.), 35-48.

—— (1983), 'Lettre du professeur Yves-Charles Morin', *Éklitra*, 17, 17.

—— (1985), 'On the Two Subjectless Verbs *voici* and *voilà*', *Language*, 61/4, 777-820.

MOUGEON, RAYMOND (1977), 'French Language Replacement and Mixed Marriages: The Case of the Francophone Minority of Welland, Ontario', *Anthropological Linguistics*, 19/8, 368-77.

—— (1982), 'Paramètres extralinguistiques de la variabilité morphologique en français ontarien', in Norbert Dittmar and Brigitte Schlieben-Lange (eds.), *Die Sociolinguistik in romanischprachigen Ländern* (Tübigen: Gunter Narr), 113-20.

—— (1984), 'Retention of French among Young Franco-Ontarians', *Language and Society*, 13, 17-21.

—— (1985), *J'ai à cœur le français* (2 vols.; Montreal: Guérin).

—— (1986), *J'ai à cœur le français: Guide du maître* (Montreal: Guérin).

—— BÉLANGER, MONIQUE, and CANALE, MICHAEL (1978), 'Le Rôle de l'interférence dans l'emploi des prépositions en français et en anglais par des jeunes Franco-ontariens bilingues', in Michel Paradis (ed.), *The Fourth LACUS Forum* (Columbia, Sth. Ca.: Hornbeam Press, Inc.), 550-9.

—— —— —— and ITUEN, STEVE (1977), 'L'Usage de la préposition "sur" en franco-ontarien', *The Canadian Journal of Linguistics*, 22/2, 95-124.

—— —— HELLER, MONICA, and CANALE, MICHAEL (1984), 'Programmes dans les écoles de langue française pour les élèves qui parlent peu ou pas français en dehors du milieu scolaire', in Armand E. Gervais and Benoît Cazabon (eds.), *L'Expression de soi: Actes du 3e congrès de l'AOPF* (Sudbury: Institut Franco-Ontarien), 25-36.

—— and BENIAK, ÉDOUARD (1979), 'Recherches linguistiques appliquées à l'enseignement du français langue maternelle en Ontario', *Revue des sciences de l'éducation*, 5/1, 87-105.

—— —— (1989*a*), 'Language Contraction and Linguistic Change: The Case of Welland French', in Nancy C. Dorian (ed.), 287-312.

—— —— (eds.) (1989*b*), *Le Français canadien parlé hors Québec: Aperçu sociolinguistique* (Quebec: Les Presses de l'Université Laval).

—— —— and BÉLANGER, MONIQUE (1982), 'Morphologie et évolution des pronoms déterminatifs dans le français parlé à Welland (Ontario)', *The Canadian Journal of Linguistics*, 27/1, 1-22.

—— —— and CÔTÉ, NORMAND (1981), 'Variation géographique en français ontarien: Rôle du maintien de la langue maternelle', *Journal of the Atlantic Provinces Linguistics Association*, 3, 64-82.

—— —— and VALLI, ANDRÉ (1988), '*Vais, vas, m'as* in Canadian French: A Sociohistorical Study', in Kathleen Ferrara, Becky Brown, Keith Walters, and John Baugh (eds.), *Linguistic Change and Contact* (Texas Linguistics Forum, 30; Austin: Department of Linguistics, The University of Texas at Austin), 250-62.

—— —— and VALOIS, DANIEL (1985*a*), 'Issues in the Study of Language Contact: Evidence from Ontarian French' (unpublished manuscript, Toronto: Centre for Franco-Ontarian Studies, The Ontario Institute for Studies in Education).

—— —— —— (1985*b*), 'Répertoire classifié des emprunts lexicaux à l'anglais dans le français parlé de Welland (Ontario)' (unpublished manuscript; Toronto: Centre for Franco-Ontarian Studies, The Ontario Institute for Studies in Education).

—— Brent-Palmer, Cora, Bélanger, Monique, and Cichocki, Wladyslaw (1982), *Le Français parlé en situation minoritaire*, i (Quebec: International Center for Research on Bilingualism).

—— and Canale, Michael (1979), 'Maintenance of French in Ontario: Is Education in French enough?', *Interchange*, 9/4, 30-9.

—— —— (1982), 'Apprentissage et enseignement du français dans les écoles de langue française de l'Ontario: Français langue première ou langue seconde?', in Pierre R. Léon (ed.), *Options nouvelles en didactique du français langue étrangère* (Paris: Didier), 75-85.

—— —— and Carroll, Susanne (1979), 'Acquisition of English Prepositions by Monolingual and Bilingual (French/English) Ontarian Students', in Fred R. Eckman and Ashley J. Hastings (eds.), *Studies in First and Second Language Acquisition* (Rowley, Mass.: Newbury House), 194-256.

—— and Carroll, Susanne (1976a), 'Certains problèmes linguistiques des jeunes Franco-ontariens. Première partie', *Working Papers on Bilingualism*, 9, 91-111.

—— —— (1976b), 'Certains problèmes linguistiques des jeunes Franco-ontariens. Deuxième partie', *Working Papers on Bilingualism*, 10, 76-99.

—— and Hébrard, Pierre (1975), 'Aspects de l'assimilation linguistique dans une communauté francophone de l'Ontario', *Working Papers on Bilingualism*, 5, 1-38.

—— —— and Sugunasiri, Suwanda (1979), 'The Acquisition of English by French-Canadian Students in Welland, Ontario', in Jacob Ornstein and Robert St Clair (eds.), *Bilingualism and Bilingual Education: New Readings and Insights* (San Antonio, Texas: Trinity University Press), 97-144.

—— and Heller, Monica (1986), 'The Social and Historical Context of Minority French Language Education in Ontario', *Journal of Multilingual and Multicultural Development*, 7/2 & 3, 199-227.

—— —— Beniak, Édouard, and Canale, Michael (1984), 'Acquisition et enseignement du français en situation minoritaire: Le cas des Franco-ontariens', *The Canadian Modern Language Review*, 41/2, 315-35.

Muysken, Pieter (1984), 'Linguistic Dimensions of Language Contact: The State of the Art in Interlinguistics', *Revue québécoise de linguistique*, 14/1, 49-76.

Naro, Anthony J. (1981), 'The Social and Structural Dimensions of a Syntactic Change', *Language*, 57/1, 63-98.

—— and Lemle, Miriam (1976), 'Syntactic Diffusion', in S. B. Steever, C. Walker, and S. S. Mufwene (eds.), *Papers from the Parasession on Diachronic Syntax* (Chicago: CLS), 221-39; repr. in *Ciência e cultura*, 29, 259-68.

Nuffield Foundation (1966 and 1968), *Enquête sur le langage de l'enfant français* (Nuffield Foreign Languages Teaching Materials Project, Reports and Occasional Papers 20 and 39; Paris: CREDIF).

Nyrop, Kristoffer (1899), *Grammaire historique de la langue française*, i (Copenhagen: Det Nordiske Forlag).

—— (1925), *Grammaire historique de la langue française*, v (Copenhagen: Gyldendalske Boghandel, Nordisk Forlag).

—— (1930), *Grammaire historique de la langue française*, vi (Copenhagen: Gyldendalske Boghandel, Nordisk Forlag).

Orkin, Mark M. (1971), *Speaking Canadian French* (Toronto: General Publishing Co. Ltd.).

PAPEN, ROBERT A. (1984), 'Quelques remarques sur un parler français méconnu de l'Ouest canadien: Le métis', *Revue québécoise de linguistique*, 14/1, 114-39.

PHILLIPS, HOSEA (1979), 'Le Français parlé de la Louisiane', in Albert Valdman, Robert Chaudenson, and Gabriel Manessy (eds.), 93-110.

PIAT, L. (1970), *Dictionnaire français-occitanien* (Aix-en-Provence: Pierre Rollet).

POIRIER, CLAUDE (1979), 'Créoles à base française, français régionaux et français québécois: Éclairages réciproques', *Revue de linguistique romane*, 43, 400-25.

POPLACK, SHANA (1980a), 'Deletion and Disambiguation in Puerto Rican Spanish', *Language*, 56/2, 371-85.

—— (1980b), *Variable Concord in Sentential Plural Marking* (Working Paper No. 6; New York: Centre for Puerto Rican Studies, CUNY).

—— (1982), 'Bilingualism and the Vernacular', in Albert Valdman and B. Hartford (eds.), *Issues in International Bilingual Education: The Role of the Vernacular* (New York: Plenum Publishing Co.), 1-24.

—— (1983), 'Bilingual Competence: Linguistic Interference or Grammatical Integrity?', in Lucía Elías-Olivares (ed.), *Spanish in the U.S. Setting: Beyond the Southwest* (Washington, DC: National Clearinghouse for Bilingual Education), 108-29.

—— (1984), 'Intergenerational Variation in Language Use and Structure in a Bilingual Context', in Charlene Rivera (ed.), *An Ethnographic/Sociolinguistic Approach to Language Proficiency Assessment* (Clevedon, England: Multilingual Matters Ltd.), 42-70.

—— (1985), 'Contrasting Patterns of Code-Switching in Two Communities', in Henry J. Warkentyne (ed.), 363-87.

—— (1989), 'Statut de langue et accommodation langagière le long d'une frontière linguistique', in Raymond Mougeon and Édouard Beniak (eds.), 126-51.

—— and SANKOFF, DAVID (1984), 'Borrowing: The Synchrony of Integration', *Linguistics*, 22, 99-135.

—— —— and MILLER, CHRISTOPHER (1988), 'The Social Correlates and Linguistic Processes of Lexical Borrowing and Assimilation', *Linguistics*, 26, 47-104.

REY, ALAIN (ed.) (1986), *Le grand Robert de la langue française* (Paris: Le Robert).

ROBERT, PAUL (1972), *Dictionnaire alphabétique et analogique de la langue française* (Paris: Société du Nouveau Littré).

ROBERTSON, BARBARA (1980), 'The Socio-cultural Determiners of French Language Maintenance: The Case of Niagara Falls, Ontario' (unpublished Ph.D. thesis; Buffalo: Department of Linguistics, SUNY).

ROMAINE, SUZANNE (1982a), 'What is a speech community?', in Suzanne Romaine (ed.), 13-24.

—— (1982b), *Socio-historical Linguistics: Its Status and Methodology* (Cambridge: Cambridge University Press).

—— (ed.) (1982c), *Sociolinguistic Variation in Speech Communities* (London: Edward Arnold).

—— (1988a), 'Typological Contrasts between Pidgin and Creole Languages in Relation to their European Language Superstrates' (paper prepared for the European Science Foundation Workshop on Typology of Languages in Europe, Rome, 7-9 January).

—— (1988b), *Pidgin and Creole Languages* (London: Longman).

—— (1989a), *Bilingualism* (Oxford: Basil Blackwell).

—— (1989b), 'Pidgins, Creoles, Immigrant and Dying Languages', in Nancy C. Dorian (ed.), 369-83.

Rousseau, Pascale (1983), *A Versatile Program for the Analysis of Sociolinguistic Data* (Montreal: Centre de recherche de mathématiques appliquées, Université de Montréal).

—— and Sankoff, David (1978), 'Advances in Variable Rule Methodology', in David Sankoff (ed.), 57-69.

Roy, Marie-Marthe (1979), 'Les Conjonctions anglaises *but* et *so* dans le français parlé de Moncton' (unpublished MA thesis; Montreal: Département de linguistique, Université du Québec à Montréal).

Rūke-Dravina, Velta (1959), 'On the Emergence of Inflection in Child Language', in Charles Ferguson and Dan I. Slobin (eds.), *Studies in Child Language Development* (New York: Holt, Rinehart, and Winston), 252-67.

Sankoff, David (ed.) (1978), *Linguistic Variation: Models and Methods* (New York: Academic Press).

—— (1979), varbrul 2s, Appendix B, in Shana Poplack, 'Function and Process in a Variable Phonology' (unpublished Ph.D. thesis; Philadelphia: Department of Linguistics, University of Pennsylvania).

—— (1988), 'Variable Rules', in Ulrich Ammon, Norbert Dittmar, and Klauss J. Mattheier (eds.), *Sociolinguistics: An International Handbook of the Science of Language and Society*, ii (Berlin: Walter de Gruyter), 984-97.

—— and Cedergren, Henrietta (eds.) (1981), *Variation Omnibus* (Edmonton: Linguistic Research, Inc.).

—— and Laberge, Suzanne (1978), 'The Linguistic Market and the Statistical Explanation of Variability', in David Sankoff (ed.), 239-50.

—— and Labov, William (1979), 'On the Uses of Variable Rules', *Language in Society*, 8, 189-222.

—— and Rousseau, Pascale (1989), 'Statistical Evidence for Rule Ordering', *Language Variation and Change*, 1/1, 1-18.

—— Sankoff, Gillian, Laberge, Suzanne, and Topham, Marjorie (1976), 'Méthodes d'échantillonnage et utilisation de l'ordinateur dans l'étude de la variation grammaticale', *Cahiers de linguistique de l'Université du Québec*, 6, 85-126.

Sankoff, Gillian (1980), *The Social Life of Language* (Philadelphia: University of Pennsylvania Press).

Saussure, Ferdinand de (1974), *Cours de linguistique générale* (Paris: Payot).

Scotton, Carol Myers, and Okeju, John (1973), 'Neighbors and Lexical Borrowings', *Language*, 49/4, 871-89.

Seutin, Émile (1975), *Description grammaticale du parler de l'Île-aux-Coudres* (Montreal: Les Presses de l'Université de Montréal).

Silva-Corvalán, Carmen (1983), 'Convergent and Autonomous Adaptations in the Spanish of Mexican-American Bilinguals' (paper presented at El español en los Estados Unidos IV, Hunter College, CUNY, 7-8 Oct.).

—— (1986a), 'Bilingualism and Language Change: The Extension of *estar* in Los Angeles Spanish', *Language*, 62/3, 587-608.

—— (1986b), 'Tense-mood-aspect across the Spanish-English Bilingual Continuum' (unpublished manuscript; Los Angeles: Department of Spanish and Portuguese, University of Southern California).

—— (1987), 'Tense-mood-aspect across the Spanish-English Bilingual Continuum', in Keith M. Denning, Sharon Inkelas, Faye C. McNair-Knox, and John R. Rickford (eds.), *Variation in Language: NWAV-XV at Stanford* (Stanford: Department of Linguistics, Stanford University), 395-410.

Simões, Maria C. P., and Stoel-Gammon, Carol (1978), 'The Acquisition of Inflections in Portuguese: A Study of the Development of Person Markers on Verbs', *Journal of Child Language*, 6, 53-67.

Slobin, Dan I. (ed.) (1985), *The Crosslinguistic Study of Language Acquisition* (2 vols.; Hillsdale, NJ: Lawrence Erlbaum Associates).

Spilka, Irène (1976), 'Assessment of Second-language Performance in Immersion Programs', *The Canadian Modern Language Review*, 32, 543-61.

Steinmeyer, Georg (1979), *Historische aspekte des français avancé* (Geneva: Droz).

Straka, Georges (1965), 'Contribution à l'histoire de la consonne R en français', *Neuphilologische Mitteilungen*, 66, 572-606.

Swain, Merrill, and Lapkin, Sharon (1982), *Evaluating Bilingual Education: A Canadian Case Study* (Clevedon, England: Multilingual Matters).

—— —— (in press), 'Aspects of the Sociolinguistic Performance of Early and Late French Immersion Students', in Robin C. Scarcella, Elaine S. Andersen, and Stephen D. Krashen (eds.), *Developing Communicative Competence in a Second Language* (New York: Newbury House).

Thibault, Pierrette (ed.) (1979), *Le Français parlé: Études sociolinguistiques* (Edmonton: Linguistic Research, Inc.).

—— (1983), 'Équivalence et grammaticalisation' (unpublished Ph.D. thesis; Montreal: Département d'anthropologie, Université de Montréal).

Thogmartin, Clyde (1979), 'Old Mines, Missouri et la survivance du français dans la haute vallée du Mississippi', in Albert Valdman, Robert Chaudenson, and Gabriel Manessy (eds.), 111-18.

Thomas, Alain (1986) *La Variation phonétique: Cas du franco-ontarien* (Studia Phonetica, 21; Montreal: Didier).

Thomason, Sarah Grey (1985), 'Contact-induced Language Change: Possibilities and Probabilities', in Norbert Boretzky, Werner Enninger, and Thomas Stolz (eds.), *Akten des 2. Essener Kolloquiums über 'Kreolsprachen und Sprachkontakten'* (Bochum: Studienverlag Dr. N. Brockmeier), 261-84.

—— (1986), 'On Establishing External Causes of Language Change', in Soonja Choi *et al.* (eds.), *Proceedings of the Second Eastern States Conference on Linguistics* (Columbus: Department of Linguistics, Ohio State University), 243-51.

—— and Kaufman, Terrence (1988), *Language Contact, Creolization, and Genetic Linguistics* (Berkeley: University of California Press).

Toblers, Adolf, and Lommatzsch, Erhard (1925), *Altfranzösiches Wörterbuch* i (Berlin: Weidmannsche Buchhandlung).

—— —— (1954), *Altfranzösiches Wörterbuch*, iii (Wiesbaden: Franz Steiner Verlag GMBH).

Trudgill, Peter (1974), *Sociolinguistics: An Introduction* (Middlesex: Penguin Books).

—— (1976/7), 'Creolization in Reverse: Reduction and Simplification in the Albanian Dialects of Greece', *Transactions of the Philological Society*, 32-50.

—— (1983), *On Dialect* (Oxford: Basil Blackwell).

—— (1986), *Dialects in Contact* (Oxford: Basil Blackwell).

Väänänen, Veikko (1956), 'La Préposition latine *de* et le génitif: Une mise au point', *Revue de linguistique romane*, 20, 1-20.

— (1963), *Introduction au latin vulgaire* (Paris: Klincksieck).

VADÉ, JEAN-JOSEPH (1875), *Œuvres* (Paris: Garnier).

VALDMAN, ALBERT (1979*a*), 'Avant-propos', in Albert Valdman, Robert Chaudenson, and Gabriel Manessy (eds.), 5-18.

— (1979*b*), 'Créolisation, français populaire et le parler des isolats francophones d'Amérique du Nord', in Albert Valdman, Robert Chaudenson, and Gabriel Manessy (eds.), 181-97.

— (1980), 'L'Acadie dans la francophonie nord-américaine', *Journal of the Atlantic Provinces Linguistic Association*, 2, 3-18.

— CHAUDENSON, ROBERT, and MANESSY, GABRIEL (eds.) (1979), *Le Français hors de France* (Paris: Éditions Honoré Champion).

VALLI, ANDRÉ (n.d.), 'Le Traitement de la variation dans l'étude de l'acquisition des langues secondes' (unpublished manuscript; Aix-en-Provence: Département de linguistique, Université de Provence).

VALLIÈRES, GAÉTAN (1980), *L'Ontario français par les documents* (Montreal: Études Vivantes).

VAUGELAS, CLAUDE FAVRE DE (1981), *Remarques sur la langue française* (Paris: Éditions Champ Libre; repr. of the original edn. of 1647).

WADE, MASON (1968), *The French Canadians 1760-1967* (London: Macmillan).

WARKENTYNE, HENRY J. (ed.) (1985), *Methods V: Papers from the 5th International Conference on Methods in Dialectology* (Victoria, BC: Department of Linguistics, University of Victoria).

WARTBURG, WALTHER VON (1940), *Französisches etymologisches Wörterbuch*, ii (Leipzig: B. G. Teubner).

— (1962), *Évolution et structure de la langue française* (6th edn.; Berne: Éditions A. Francke).

— (1966), *Französisches etymologisches Wörterbuch*, xii (Basel: Zbinden Druck und Verlag AG).

— (1969), *Französisches etymologisches Wörterbuch*, vi (Basel: Zbinden Druck und Verlag AG).

WEINREICH, URIEL (1968), *Languages in Contact* (The Hague: Mouton; repr. of the original 1953 edn., New York: Linguistic Circle of New York).

— LABOV, WILLIAM, and HERZOG, MARVIN I. (1968), 'Empirical Foundations for a Theory of Language Change', in Winfred P. Lehman and Yakov Malkiel (eds.), *Directions for Historical Linguistics* (Austin: University of Texas Press), 95-195.

WELCH, DAVID (1988), 'The Social Construction of Franco-Ontarian Interests towards French Language Schooling' (unpublished Ph.D. thesis; Toronto: Department of Education, University of Toronto).

WILLIAMS, GLYN (1987), 'Bilingualism, Class Dialect, and Social Reproduction', *International Journal of the Sociology of Language*, 66, 85-98.

WILLIAMSON, ROBERT C., and VAN EERDE, JOHN A. (1980), 'Subcultural Factors in the Survival of Secondary Languages: A Cross-national Sample', *International Journal of the Sociology of Language*, 25, 59-83.

WITTMANN, HENRI, and FOURNIER, ROBERT (1983), 'Le Créole, c'est du français, coudon!', *Revue de l'Association québécoise de linguistique*, 3/2, 187-202.

Index